THE LEADERSHIP JOURNEY

★ HOW FOUR KIDS BECAME PRESIDENT ★

DORIS KEARNS GOODWIN

THE LEADERSHIP JOURNEY
★ ★ ★ HOW FOUR KIDS BECAME PRESIDENT ★ ★ ★

Adapted by Ruby Shamir

Illustrations by Amy June Bates

SIMON & SCHUSTER BOOKS FOR YOUNG READERS
NEW YORK LONDON TORONTO SYDNEY NEW DELHI

SIMON & SCHUSTER BOOKS FOR YOUNG READERS
An imprint of Simon & Schuster Children's Publishing Division
1230 Avenue of the Americas, New York, New York 10020

This book adapts material from several books by Doris Kearns Goodwin, including *Leadership: In Turbulent Times* (Simon & Schuster, 2018), *The Bully Pulpit* (Simon & Schuster, 2013), *Team of Rivals* (Simon & Schuster, 2005), *Wait Till Next Year* (Simon & Schuster, 1997), *No Ordinary Time* (Simon & Schuster, 1994), and *Lyndon Johnson and the American Dream* (Harper & Row, 1976).

Jacket illustration and interior illustration © 2024 by Amy June Bates
Jacket photographs of Abraham Lincoln and Theodore Roosevelt courtesy of the Library of Congress; jacket photograph of Franklin Roosevelt courtesy of the Franklin D. Roosevelt Presidential Library and Museum; jacket photograph of Lyndon Johnson by Yoichi Okamoto
Jacket and interior design by Laurent Linn
Interior photographs and images on pages 20, 44, 59, 66, 87, and 135 courtesy of the Library of Congress; photograph on page 95 courtesy of the US Office of Federal Management (now the US Office of Personnel Management); photographs on pages 104 and 123 courtesy of Harvard Library; photograph on page 144 by Bettmann via Getty Images; photographs and images on pages 170, 177, 185, 205, 214, 225, 236, and 247 courtesy of the Franklin D. Roosevelt Presidential Library and Museum; photographs and images on pages 262, 266, 278, 309, and 329 courtesy of the Lyndon B. Johnson Presidential Library and Museum; photograph on page 291 by Vernon Lewis Gallery/Stocktrek Images/Alamy

Simon & Schuster: Celebrating 100 Years of Publishing in 2024
For information about special discounts for bulk purchases, please contact Simon & Schuster Special Sales at 1-866-506-1949 or business@simonandschuster.com.
The Simon & Schuster Speakers Bureau can bring authors to your live event. For more information or to book an event, contact the Simon & Schuster Speakers Bureau at 1-866-248-3049 or visit our website at www.simonspeakers.com.
The text for this book was set in Nyte Book.
The illustrations for this book were rendered in ink and brush.
Manufactured in the United States of America
0724 WOR
First Edition
2 4 6 8 10 9 7 5 3 1

CIP data for this book is available from the Library of Congress.
ISBN 9781665925723
ISBN 9781665925747 (ebook)

*For Beth Laski, my truest friend, my cabinet of one,
to whom I lovingly dedicate this book*

—DKG

CONTENTS

$\star\ \ \star\ \ \star\ \ \star\ \ \star$

PREFACE

$\star\ \ \star\ \ \star\ \ \star\ \ \star$

I HAVE LOVED HISTORY FOR AS LONG AS I CAN REMEMBER. That love began when I was six years old and my father gave me a bright red scorebook that opened my heart to the game of baseball. He taught me how to keep score while listening to baseball games on the radio so that while he was at work in New York City during the day, I could record for him the history of that afternoon's Brooklyn Dodgers game. After dinner on long summer nights, Dad would sit beside me in our small, enclosed porch to look at my scorebook filled with the odd collection of symbols, numbers, and letters and to hear my play-by-play account of every inning of every game.

Little did I know that these nightly sessions with my father would also open the door to my future career, for I am convinced I learned the art of storytelling then. At first I would blurt out "the Dodgers won" or "the Dodgers lost," which took away much of the excitement of the story I was just about to tell. So I learned how to build a dramatic narrative from beginning to middle to end. These first lessons in storytelling about facts, figures, and real-life events turned out to be the basis of my work as a historian, which I became two decades later. That's what history is: the telling of stories about people who lived before us in the hope that we can learn from their struggles and their triumphs.

My father never told me then that the whole game would be recounted in the sports pages of the newspapers the next day. So I thought without me he would never know what even happened to our beloved Brooklyn Dodgers. And therein lies the magic of history—if only four hours old—to keep my father's attention all that time!

I also loved listening to stories about what things were like before I was born. My mother was ill with a heart ailment for much of my childhood, and I would beg her to share memories from her past with me, to give me a glimpse into the life she'd led before she was weakened by her condition. I liked to hear about the days when she could jump rope, play hopscotch, and ride her bike so I could imagine her young and healthy. I would constantly ask her, "Mom, tell me a story about you when you were my age," not realizing how unusual this request was until I had my own three sons, who never once asked me to tell stories of what I was like when I was their age!

In college I read an essay by my heroine, Barbara Tuchman, the Pulitzer Prize–winning historian, who explained that even if you're writing about a war as a narrative historian, you have to imagine to yourself that you do not know how that war ended so you can carry your reader with you every step along the way from beginning to middle to end. Later, as a graduate student, I worked with President Lyndon Johnson in the White House in the last year of his presidency and thereafter with him on his memoirs. He was a mesmerizing story-teller, by turns serious, funny, vulnerable, wise, insistent, frustrated, and sad—recounting stories that I did not then realize would help ignite my career as a historian as I went on to study the presidents of our past.

It may seem an odd career to spend days and nights with dead presidents, but I wouldn't change it for anything in the world. My only fear is that in the afterlife there will be a panel of all the presidents I've studied, and Lyndon Johnson will be the first to protest: *How come that darn book on the Roosevelts is twice as long as the book about me?* But he'd have a point, because I believe the privilege of working with him fired within me the drive to understand the inner person behind the public figure, to look empathetically at my subjects—really imagine walking in their shoes—as I have tried to do ever since.

So after studying and writing lengthy biographies on Abraham Lincoln, Theodore Roosevelt, Franklin Roosevelt, and Lyndon Johnson, waking with them in the morning and thinking about them each night as I drifted off to sleep, I thought I knew "my guys," as I like to call them, pretty well before I embarked on a study of their specific leadership styles. But this project taught me much more as I sought to understand not just the plotlines of historic transformation that each person was part of, but especially the role leadership played in those changes.

The idea for the structure of this book came to me one evening when I was lecturing about Lincoln and Franklin Roosevelt on a college campus. A student asked me how he could ever become like these presidents, these larger-than-life figures—they were on Mount Rushmore, on currency, and in movies. It seemed too hard to become them. So I decided for this study of leadership to start when they were young, to look at the lives of these presidents when they stood before the public for the first time, when their paths were still anything but certain. Their early stories are full of confusion, hope, failure, and fear. We follow mistakes they made along the way—from inexperience, carelessness, misjudgments, and arrogance—and see the efforts they made to acknowledge, conceal, or overcome these mistakes. Their struggles are not so different from our own.

By immersing myself in their personal letters and those of their friends, families, and colleagues, their diaries, oral histories, memoirs, newspaper archives, and periodicals, I searched for revealing details that, taken together, would provide an intimate understanding of them as young people and later as leaders, their inner circles, and the times in which they lived.

As you'll see, no single route carried my guys to the height of political leadership.

Theodore Roosevelt and Franklin Roosevelt were born to extraordinary privilege and wealth. Abraham Lincoln endured relentless poverty. Lyndon Johnson experienced occasional hard times. They differed widely in temperament, appearance, and physical ability. They had a wide range of qualities often recognized in leadership—intelligence, energy, empathy, verbal and written gifts, and skills in dealing with people. They were united by a fierce ambition, an unusual drive to succeed. With perseverance and very hard work, they all essentially made themselves leaders by enhancing talents they were born with.

All four were recognized as leaders long before they reached the presidency. Dramatic events that shattered the private and public lives of all four men are part of each of their stories. They were at different life stages when forced to deal with events that ruptured their sense of self and threatened to limit their prospects. More important than what happened to them was how they responded to these reversals, how they managed in various ways to put themselves back together, how these watershed experiences at first blocked, then deepened, and finally and decisively molded their leadership. The four leaders presented in this book all took office at moments of uncertainty and turmoil, and each left the presidency, and the country, greatly improved for generations to come.

But you might be wondering, how does presidential leadership apply to my life today? Well, just as you learn from your parents, grandparents, and caregivers, you're going to learn from these people who came before you, people who went on to become president. Leadership in general is the ability to use your talent, skills, and emotional intelligence to mobilize people to a common purpose. And hopefully that common purpose is to make a positive difference in the lives of others. Some of the most important qualities you may have been born with or you can develop are humility, empathy, resilience, self-awareness, self-reflection, the ability to communicate, and the willingness to take a risk because the ambition for the greater good has become more important for you than the ambition for yourself. These are at their essence character traits that are needed for leaders but also apply to our everyday lives. The four people profiled in this book excelled in these areas and were able to create change, but there is still so much work left to do, and you can play an important part in it.

In the United States, our Constitution established a democratic form of government, which means we the people choose our leaders, and they in turn serve us, with the hope that leadership itself is kept responsive and innovative. The decisions that leaders make in Washington, DC, in the statehouse, or in the mayor's office might seem remote, like they don't have an impact on your life. Or it might seem like you don't have a say in them, but you do. Even before you can vote at age eighteen, you can become an activist for issues you care about in your family, your school, and your community—whether protecting the planet from climate change, feeding the hungry, combatting injustice, or anything else that needs getting done. One day in the not-too-distant future you will be the decision-makers—and some of you may even rise to be president of the United States.

But even if you choose not to lead in a formal way, embodying the qualities of a good leader is important to the way you live now and in the future. Because we elect our leaders, at all levels of government—from the local city council and school board all the way up to the White House—what I hope you will ask yourself after reading this book is *What do we want from our leaders today? What do we deserve? What will we no longer tolerate? What does progress look like, and how can we help get there? Most important, what is our role, individually and collectively?* My guys changed the history and direction of the United States, but they didn't operate in a vacuum; they were motivated by activists—individuals and groups who were often outside elected positions—who pressed them on the moral stakes of their policies and urged them to live up to our highest principles. Each president was accountable to the citizens, who determined if his vision was worth the continued investment of their votes.

These leaders set a standard and a bar for all of us, but they were far from perfect. They were limited by the context of their times. But they learned from one another, and we can learn from them, both from the ways they pushed America toward progress built on our founding ideals and in the ways their actions reflected some of the most troubling aspects of the times in which they lived. From them we can gain a better perspective on the divisions of our own times and on what it takes to bring about change. Progress is not inevitable, nor is it a straight line. The future is not settled. By debating, challenging, talking, listening, and working with one another, we set the direction of our schools and neighborhoods, our cities, our states, our country, and the world. For leadership is a two-way street. I hope this book inspires you to imagine and think big about where *your* leadership will take us.

When I was in graduate school, my friends and I would stay up late debating what you might think are nerdy subjects: Are leaders born or made? Where does ambition come from? How does hardship affect the growth of leadership? Do the times make the leader, or does the leader shape the times? How can a leader fill people's lives with a sense of purpose and meaning? What is the difference between power, title, and leadership? Is leadership truly successful without a purpose larger than personal ambition?

This book is not a full accounting of the historical moments of all the people who made an impact on our country—it isn't even really about my guys' terms in the White House. It's a snapshot of four boys—Abraham, Teddy, Franklin, and Lyndon—growing into men at specific eras in history, and what we can learn about what made them the leaders they became.

There are four sections in this book, one for each president, and the first chapter in each section opens in childhood. You will learn about the very different families and circumstances and times in which they spent their boyhoods. The next few chapters will track the journey they each took to emerge as a leader. Each of them had major successes and failures, good luck and bad, helpers and rivals, as they figured out who they were and what drove them to lead. The stories of all four should hearten anyone who falls and fails, for each experienced loss, failure, and disappointment. Yet not one of them gave up in pursuit of a dream to serve other people. The final chapter in each section offers a brief glimpse into their presidencies, so you can get an idea of how they brought their gifts and lessons to the White House. There are other books you can read that detail the administrations and policies of each president; the purpose here is for us to see how the character traits and skills developed in youth helped shape the leaders they became. Lincoln's hero was George Washington, Teddy Roosevelt looked up to Lincoln as his guide, FDR admired and modeled himself after his distant cousin Teddy Roosevelt, and LBJ revered FDR and referred to him as his political daddy.

As you read this book, I hope you will be inspired by each president's journey and ask yourself: *Who is my hero?*

A Note on Language in the Book

EVERY GENERATION IN AMERICAN HISTORY following the civil rights era has strived to become more kind, more inclusive, more respectful, and more accurate in its descriptions of the different ways people identify—whether according to ethnicity, race, gender, ability, or other factors. Some of the language from earlier eras quoted in the following pages might seem out of touch, even jarring or disturbing. That's because, based on what we know today, it is! I have tried to provide context so that you can understand why certain language was used during different periods in our history. In the time of Lincoln, enslaved people were referred to as slaves, as if that were the sole defining aspect of their humanity. Wealthy white plantation owners held Black men, women, and children in bondage. Powerful white men debated their fate over the course of decades. In Theodore Roosevelt's time, white Christian men of wealth and high social status were assumed to have special license to lead, and in some cases this fed unfortunate forms of discrimination. In Franklin Roosevelt's time, disabled survivors of polio and other people with disabilities were misunderstood and often mocked by able-bodied people for what their bodies could not do, despite their triumphs in overcoming tremendous challenges to get along in a world that was often unkind and closed to them. In Lyndon

Johnson's time, Black people were called, and often referred to themselves as, Negroes and colored people. Men in power denied women the right to vote during the terms of the first two presidents in this book, and women did not have equal rights and opportunities during any of these presidencies; they faced deep chauvinism and discrimination. In all of these eras, people of color, women, immigrants, the poor, the disabled, Indigenous people, LGBTQ+ people, and any other marginalized individuals, including those who held more than one of these identities, were often seen and described as less than by the people in power, who were usually male, white, Christian, and well-off. In my telling of the stories of these leaders I wanted to remain true to the facts, to situate you with accuracy and precision in the times our leaders lived through, even if that meant sometimes using language that might offend today. I hope this account will give you an understanding of what was bold and unprecedented in their leadership, and also what social conventions held them back.

Abraham Lincoln

Chapter One

"I'll study and get ready, and then the chance will come."

AS A CHILD, ABRAHAM LINCOLN DREAMED HEROIC DREAMS. Through stories and books he imagined a different world from his life on the harsh, isolated frontier where he was born in 1809. His family's small, simple cabin had no electricity, no running water, and no heat, and offered little protection against the elements and the wild animals that prowled around their rough farm.

When asked later to shed light on his beginnings, Lincoln claimed his background could be "condensed into a single sentence . . . : 'The short and simple annals of the poor.'" His father, Thomas, had never learned to read and, according to his son, could barely sign his own name. Trapped in poverty, Thomas cleared enough land only for survival and moved the family from one dirt farm to another in Kentucky, Indiana, and Illinois. While details about Lincoln's mother, Nancy Hanks, are few, those who knew her agreed she was intelligent, perceptive, and kind, and credited her with sparking young Abraham's interest in reading.

When Abraham was nine, his mother died from what was known as milk sickness, a disease transmitted by way of cows that had eaten poisonous plants. "I am going away from you, Abraham," she reportedly told her young son shortly before she died, "and I shall not return." After her burial, Thomas abandoned his young son and his twelve-year-old daughter, Sarah, for seven months while he returned to Kentucky to find a new wife. The children were left on their own in a floorless cabin that lacked even a door in what Lincoln described as "a wild region," a night-marish place where "the panther's scream filled the night with fear and bears preyed on the swine." Inside the cabin, there were few furnishings, no beds, and barely any bedding. Abraham's sister did her best to take care of them both. Sarah Lincoln was much like her brother, smart, with a good sense of humor that could put anyone at ease. But the lonely months of living without adult supervision or care were harrowing.

When Abraham's new stepmother, Sarah Bush Johnston, arrived with Thomas, she found the children ragged and dirty. Sarah brought with her what was needed to create a cozy and welcoming home. A floor was laid and a door and windows hung, the children received clothing, and most important for Abraham, she brought books.

Even as a young boy in this bleak setting, it was clear that Abraham was gifted with an exceptionally intelligent, clear, and curious mind; "a Boy of uncommon natural Talents" was how his stepmother described him, and she did all she could to encourage him to learn, read, and grow. Schoolmates at the ABC school in rural Kentucky, "a low-ceilinged, flea-infested cabin," recalled that he was able to learn more swiftly and understand more deeply than others. Though he could only attend school occasionally, when his father didn't require his labor on their hardscrabble farm, he stood at the top of every class. "He was the learned boy among us unlearned folks," one classmate recalled. "He carried away from his brief schooling," biographer David Herbert Donald wrote, "the self-confidence of a man who has never met his intellectual equal." A dream that he might someday make the most of his talents began to take hold.

From his earliest days in school, Lincoln's friends remarked upon his phenomenal memory. His mind seemed "a wonder," one friend told him. Lincoln told his friend he was mistaken. What appeared a gift, he argued, was, in his case, a developed talent. "I am slow to learn," he explained, "and slow to forget what I have learned. My mind is like a piece of steel—very hard to scratch anything on it, and almost impossible after you get it there to rub it out." His stepmother, who came to love him as if he were her own son, observed the process by which he engraved things into his memory. "When he came upon a passage that Struck him, he would write it down on boards if he had no paper & keep it there until he did get paper," she recalled, "and then he would rewrite it" and keep it in a scrapbook so that he could preserve it.

Young Lincoln also possessed remarkable powers of reasoning and comprehension, a thirst for knowledge, and a fierce, almost irresistible, drive to understand the meaning of what he heard, read, or was taught. "When a mere child," Lincoln later said, "I used to get irritated when anybody talked to me in a way I could not understand. I do not think I ever got angry at anything else in my life." And when he "got on a hunt for an idea" he could not sleep until he "caught it."

Early on, Abraham revealed the motivation and willpower to develop his every talent to the fullest. "The ambition of the man soared above us," his childhood friend Nathaniel Grigsby recalled. "He read and thoroughly read his books whilst we played." When he first learned how to print the letters of the alphabet, he was so excited that he formed "letters, words and sentences wherever he found suitable material. He scrawled them in charcoal, he scored them in the dust, in the sand, in the snow—anywhere and everywhere that lines could be drawn." He soon became "the best penman in the neighborhood."

Sharing his knowledge with his schoolmates at every turn, he was their leader. A friend recalled the effort he took to explain to her how the heavenly bodies moved, patiently telling her that the moon was not really sinking during the night, as she had thought; it was the earth that was moving, not the moon; "we do the sinking as you call it," he told her. "The moon as to us is Comparatively still." His skeptical friend responded, "Abe—what a fool you are!" But that same friend said later, "I know now that I was the fool, not Lincoln. I am now thoroughly satisfied that Abe knew the general laws of astronomy and the movements of the heavenly bodies. He was better read then than the world knows, or is likely to know exactly."

Abraham understood early on that stories, examples, and patience were the best tools for teaching. He had developed his talent for storytelling, in part, from watching his father. Though Thomas Lincoln was unable to read or write, he had an uncanny memory for exceptional stories and a flair for telling them. Night after night, Thomas would exchange tales with farmers, carpenters, neighbors, and peddlers, while young Lincoln listened intently. After hearing the adults chatter through the evening, Abraham would spend "no small part of the night walking up and down, trying to make out the exact meaning" of what the men had said so he could entertain his friends the next day with a simplified translation of the mysterious adult world.

Wherever he was, another childhood friend recalled, "the boys would gather & cluster around him to hear him talk." He would climb onto a tree stump or log that served as an impromptu stage and mesmerize his own circle of young listeners. He had built a collection of stories and great storytelling skills and was thrilled by his friends' reaction. At the age of ten, a relative recalled, Abraham learned to mimic the voice and style of the Baptist preachers who traveled through the region. To the delight of his friends, he could reproduce their rip-roaring sermons almost word for word, complete with full-body gestures to emphasize emotion. As he got older, he found additional material for his storytelling by walking fifteen miles to the nearest courthouse, where he soaked up the accounts of trials and then retold the sometimes gruesome cases in vivid detail.

At a time when radio, television, movies, computers, phones, and

social media were unimaginable, storytelling was the most common form of entertainment, and those who could master it held a lot of influence. Abraham's stories often had a point—a moral along the lines of one of his favorite books, *Aesop's Fables*—but sometimes they were simply funny tales that he had heard and would retell with liveliness. When he began to speak, his face, which had a sorrowful appearance, would light up with a transforming smile. And when he reached the end of his story, he would laugh with such heartiness that soon everyone was laughing with him.

If he was the center of his young circle's entertainment, Abraham was also willing to face their disapproval rather than abandon what he knew was right. The boys in the neighborhood, one schoolmate recollected, liked to play a game of catching turtles and putting hot coals on their backs to see them wriggle. Abraham not only told them "it was wrong," he wrote a short essay in school against "cruelty to animals." Nor did Lincoln like to hunt, an activity common throughout the frontier for survival and for sport. After killing a wild turkey with his father's rifle when he was eight years old, he never again "pulled a trigger on any larger game."

The young boy possessed a profound sense of empathy—the ability to put himself in the place of others, to imagine their situations and identify with their feelings—and he acted on it. When playmates tormented his friend Nathaniel's brother James Grigsby, who had a severe stutter, Lincoln stepped in. "Abe took me in charge," Grigsby recalled, when "rough boys teased me and made fun of me for stuttering. Abe soon showed them how wrong it was and most of them quit." His empathy extended even to strangers. One winter night, a friend remembered, he and Abraham were walking home when they saw a man lying in a mudhole, drunk and almost frozen. Abraham picked him up and carried him all the way to his cousin's house, where he built a fire to warm him up. On another occasion, when Lincoln was walking with a group of friends, he passed a pig caught in a stretch of boggy ground. The group had continued on for half a mile when Lincoln suddenly stopped. He insisted on turning back to rescue the pig. He couldn't bear the pain he felt when he thought of the animal.

Lincoln's size and strength boosted his authority and popularity with friends. From an early age, Abraham was more athletic than most of the boys in the neighborhood, "ready to out-run, out-jump and out-wrestle or out-lift anybody." As a young man, one friend reported, he "could carry what 3 ordinary men would grunt & sweat at." He was not only strong but healthy, too. Relatives recalled that he was never sick. But Lincoln's physical dominance proved a double-edged sword. He was expected, from the age of eight to the age of twenty-one, to accompany his father into the fields, carrying an axe, chopping down trees, digging up stumps, plowing, planting, and splitting open thick logs to create rails for fencing. While Lincoln was good at physical labor, he would much rather have been in school. His father, however, considered spending time in school as "doubly wasted," for in rural areas, schools cost money, and the classroom pulled him away from farmwork. Thomas also hired out Abraham to work off any money the family owed, which put the prospects of attending school even further out of reach. That is why, when Lincoln reached the age of nine or ten, after less than a year total of schooling, his own formal education was cut short.

From then on, Abraham had to educate himself. He had to take the initiative, assume responsibility for finding books, decide what to study, and become his own teacher. Gaining access to reading material proved nearly impossible; books were considered a "luxury" to poor farming families on the frontier. Relatives and neighbors recalled that Lincoln scoured the countryside to borrow books and read every volume "he could lay his hands on." When he took hold of one, "his eyes

Young Abraham reading by the fire, in a portrait painted by Eastman Johnson after Lincoln's death.

sparkled, and that day he could not eat, and that night he could not sleep." A book was his constant companion. Every break from the daily physical tasks was a time to read a page or two from *The Pilgrim's Progress* or *Aesop's Fables*, pausing while resting his horse at the end of a long row of planting.

When his father found his son in the field reading a book or, worse still, distracting fellow workers with tales or passages from one of his books, he would angrily put an end to the recess so work could continue. On occasion, he would go so far as to destroy Abraham's books and whip him for neglecting his labors. While Lincoln's adoring stepmother took "particular Care not to disturb him—would let him read on and on," to Thomas, Abraham's constant reading was a mark of laziness and irresponsibility. He thought his son was deceiving himself with his quest for education. "I tried to stop it, but he has got that fool idea into his head, and it can't be got out," Thomas told a friend.

At times, when the tensions with his father seemed unbearable, when the gap between his ambitions and the reality of his circumstances seemed too great to bridge, Lincoln felt overwhelmed by sadness. It was in this period, during his teenage years, that he suffered another shattering loss when his older sister, Sarah, died while giving birth at the age of nineteen. A relative recalled that when Lincoln was told of her death, he "sat down on a log and hid his face in his hands while the tears rolled down through his long bony fingers. Those present turned away in pity and left him to his grief." He had lost the two women he had loved. "From then on," a neighbor said, "he was alone in the world you might say." Years later, his junior law partner, William Herndon, noted, "His melancholy dript from him as he walked," an observation echoed by dozens of others. Yet, if sadness was part of his nature, so, too, was his sense of humor that allowed him to see what was funny or absurd in life, lightening his despair and strengthening his will. Both Lincoln's storytelling and his humor, friends believed, were "necessary to his very existence"; they were intended "to whistle off sadness."

Ultimately, the unending strain with his father enhanced young Lincoln's ambition. Year after year, as he persevered in defiance of his father's wishes, managing his negative emotions and exercising his will to slowly master one subject after another, he developed an increasing belief in his own strengths and powers. He came to trust that he could rise from his humble beginnings, slowly creating what one leadership scholar calls "a vision of an alternative future." He told a neighbor he did not intend to lead the same life as his father. "I'll study and get ready, and then the chance will come."

Chapter Two

"Your own resolution to succeed, is more important than any other one thing."

OPPORTUNITY ARRIVED THE MOMENT LINCOLN REACHED ADULTHOOD at twenty-one, when he was no longer required by law to hand over all of his wages to his father. He was finally free to build a life of his own. Bundling his few possessions on his shoulders, he headed west, walking more than one hundred miles to reach New Salem, Illinois, where he had been promised a job as a clerk and bookkeeper in a general store.

A bustling small town, recently sprung up along the Sangamon River, New Salem consisted of a few hundred people, fifteen log cabins, a tavern, a church, a blacksmith, a schoolmaster, a preacher, and a general store. It was considerably bigger than the rural outpost Lincoln had come from. To the villagers of New Salem, the six-foot-four-inch-tall, young stranger struck them as awkward with his arms and legs too long for his pants and coat. Shortly after arriving, Abraham was greeted by the Clary's Grove Boys, a local gang "of rude, roystering, good-natured fellows, who lived in and around 'Clary's Grove,' a settlement near New Salem," who took it upon themselves to test the strength and will of every newcomer. Seeing how tall and strong Lincoln was, they sent their leader and champion fighter, Jack Armstrong, "strong as an ox, and who was believed by his partisans to be able to whip any man on the Sangamon River." The two men would fight to determine who was "the better man," although Lincoln "tried to avoid such contests." But the men began to wrestle "for some time, without any decided advantage of either side." According to one account, Armstrong "resorted to some foul play," which made Lincoln angry. So Lincoln fought a little harder, even while Armstrong's friends looked like they would gang up on Lincoln. But Lincoln's "cool courage" inspired Armstrong to instead shake Lincoln's hand declaring, "Boys! Abe Lincoln is the best fellow that ever broke into this settlement. He shall be one of us." And from this unsteady start, Lincoln proved himself to the townspeople using more than his fists.

Lincoln had a warm, good nature; as one local man explained, "Everybody loved him." He would help travelers whose carriages were stuck in mud; he volunteered to chop wood for widows; he was ever ready to lend a hand. Almost anyone who had contact with him in the little community spoke of his kindness, generosity, intelligence, humor, and humility, and his striking, original character.

Working as a clerk in New Salem's general store provided Lincoln with an ideal foundation upon which to build his political career. The general store filled a special place on the frontier. Beyond the sale of groceries, hardware, cloth, and bonnets, the village store provided "a kind of intellectual and social center," a place where villagers gathered to read the newspaper, discuss the local sporting contests, and, mainly, argue about politics in an era when politics was a consuming, almost universal concern. For the farmers, who might ride fifty miles to grind grain into flour at the village gristmill, the store offered a common meeting place to unwind, exchange opinions, and share stories.

Within weeks of Lincoln's arrival, a fellow clerk recalled, his outgoing nature and funny stories had made him "a Center of attraction." The townspeople regarded him as one of the best clerks they had ever seen. "He was attentive to his business," one villager remembered, "was kind and considerate to his customers & friends and always treated them with great tenderness." At the same time, his "eagerness to learn" deeply impressed the people of New Salem. He always kept a volume of poetry or book of prose behind the counter so he could read during a lull in the general store's business. Lincoln kept himself informed on politics and the issues of the day. His love of learning continued, and his reflective, gentle temperament inspired local families to help him succeed. They lent him books, and the village barrel maker even kept a fire at night so that Lincoln would have a place to read in the evenings.

"When he was ignorant on any subject," one friend recalled, "no matter how simple it might make him appear, he was always willing to acknowledge it." When Lincoln told his schoolmaster friend William Mentor Graham that he had never studied grammar and wanted to because he was interested in public speaking, Graham agreed this was something he should learn. While no one in New Salem had a proper grammar text, Graham said he knew of a volume in a house six miles away. Lincoln rose from the table and started walking. Returning with a treasured copy of Samuel Kirkham's *English Grammar in Familiar Lectures,* he began at once to sort through the complicated rules governing the structure of sentences and the use of adverbs and adjectives. He worked hard to develop a simple, compact style of speaking and writing, using short, clear sentences that could be understood by all. Even this early on, he had a democratic instinct and desire to appeal to all the people.

For many ambitious young men in the 1800s, politics was the chosen arena for advancement; young women were not afforded the same opportunities. Abraham Lincoln was only twenty-three years old on March 9, 1832, when he declared his intention to run for a seat in the

Illinois state legislature just eight months after he arrived in New Salem. "Every man is said to have his peculiar ambition," Lincoln wrote in a pamphlet announcing his candidacy, as he sought to earn the respect and votes of his neighbors. "I have no other so great as that of being truly esteemed of my fellow men, by rendering myself worthy of their esteem. How far I shall succeed in gratifying this ambition is yet to be developed. I am young and unknown to many of you."

Lincoln's ambition was not simply for himself; it was also for the people he hoped to lead. His desire was to distinguish himself in their eyes and accomplish deeds that would gain the people's lasting respect. He asked for the opportunity to prove himself worthy on his own merits: "I was born and have ever remained in the most humble walks of life. I have no wealthy or popular relations to recommend me."

Lincoln ran for the assembly as a member of the Whig Party in Sangamon County, where most voters were members of the Democratic Party. He called for government funds to be spent on public education and for infrastructure projects that would improve roads, rivers, harbors, and railways, not simply because those policies were part of the Whig Party platform, but mainly because they were what his community needed. New Salem's lifeline was the Sangamon River, which allowed settlers to send their produce to market and receive necessary

---

What is the state legislature?

The government in the United States is divided into federal, state, and local entities. Every state has a governor, the chief executive of the state, just as the president of the United States is the chief executive of the federal government. State legislatures are the lawmaking bodies for the state government; they write, vote on, and pass bills that the governor signs into law—a state-level version of the United States Congress, which is made up of elected representatives from every state in the country. Each state legislature is made up of elected representatives from around the state. Most state legislatures include both an assembly, which is like the US House of Representatives, and a senate. Someone who runs for a seat in their state assembly or state senate is seeking to represent citizens in a section, or district, of that state.

goods. Unless it was cleared of obstacles, channels dug and drifting logs removed, New Salem would never grow. The previous year Lincoln had piloted a flatboat on the river, gaining firsthand knowledge of the obstacles and challenges. This experience allowed him to speak confidently about a subject closely tied to his own ambitions. If rivers and roads could be improved, if the government could aid in economic growth and development, New Salem and hundreds of other small towns would thrive. "If elected," Lincoln pledged, any law providing dependable roads and accessible waterways for "the poorest and most thinly populated" communities "shall receive my support."

On the topic of education, he declared, "I can only say that I view it as the most important subject which we as a people can be engaged in." He wanted every citizen to treasure books and, most important, to read the history of the country, "to appreciate the value of our free institutions," which emerged as a result of a democratic system that empowers Americans to choose their leaders and govern themselves. He spoke with the passion of a young man who had made ferocious efforts to educate himself in the hope of building a bridge between "the humble walks of life" of his upbringing and his dreams of an expansive future. The education he continued to seek for himself was one he wanted available for everyone.

What were the political parties in Lincoln's day?

At the time Lincoln ran for office, there were two major political parties—the Whigs and the Democrats—but they were different from the parties of today. The Whig Party was formed in the 1830s in opposition to the policies of then president Andrew Jackson, a proslavery Democrat. The Whigs supported the creation of a national bank and using government funds for improvements to infrastructure, including roads, harbors, rivers, and bridges on both the federal and state level. Many Whigs opposed slavery, but the party did not take an official position on the issue. The Democratic Party was formed in 1828 and supported the narrowest possible role for the federal and state government, believing that government spending on public works would benefit only the wealthy. Many Democrats, especially those from the South, supported slavery. By the time of Lincoln's campaign for president in 1860, slavery was the most divisive, unresolvable issue in the country, and the Whig Party crumbled after antislavery advocates formed the new Republican Party just a few years prior.

In this first attempt at politics, Lincoln also pledged that if he was wrong, he would admit it, revealing early on a quality that would characterize his leadership for the rest of his life—a willingness to acknowledge errors and learn from his mistakes.

While uncertain about his prospects in this first election, Lincoln made it clear that failure did not intimidate him. Should he lose, he had said when declaring his intention to run, he would take the loss in stride, for he was already "too familiar with disappointments." And yet, he fore-warned, only after being defeated "some 5 or 6 times" would he deem it "a disgrace" and be certain "never to try it again." So, along with the uncertainty of whether his ambition would be realized was the promise of resilience.

Traveling by horseback across a large county that was sparsely popu-lated, Lincoln campaigned at country stores and small village squares. On Saturdays, he joined his fellow candidates in the largest towns, where farmers gathered to sell fruits and vegetables, "buy supplies, see their neighbors and get the news." The speeches would start in mid-morning and last until sunset. Each candidate was given a turn. Lincoln, one con-tender recalled, set himself apart by the open and honest way in which he approached every question and by his habit of illustrating his argu-ments with stories based on observations from daily life. At times his language was clumsy, as were his gestures, but few who heard him speak ever forgot him.

When the votes were counted, Lincoln found he had lost the election, but that news "did not dampen his hopes nor sour his ambi-tion," a friend recalled. On the contrary, he gained confidence from the knowledge that in his own town of New Salem, he had received an overwhelming total of 277 of the 300 votes cast. Those who knew him best had voted for him in huge numbers. So if he were to run again, he would have to reach out to people in neighboring communities. After teaching himself the principles of geometry and trigonometry involved in determining boundaries of plots of land, he took a job as deputy surveyor for Sangamon County, a position that allowed him to travel from one village to another, marking property lines and borders between neighbors and meeting more people. So swiftly did his reputation for storytelling spread, a friend of Lincoln's recalled, that no sooner had he arrived in a village than "men and boys gathered from far and near, ready to carry chains, drive stakes, and blaze trees, if they could hear Lincoln's odd stories and jokes."

In 1834, now twenty-five, he ran for the state legislature once again, making good on his joke that he would keep trying a half dozen times before giving up. Once again he crisscrossed the district on horseback, delivering speeches, shaking hands, introducing himself, joining in local activities. Seeing thirty men in the field during a harvest, he offered to help, thereby winning every vote in the crowd. One group of young men made him a wager. "'See here Lincoln, if you can throw this Cannon ball further than we Can, We'll vote for you.' Lincoln picked up the large Cannon ball—felt it—swung it around—and around and said, 'Well, boys if that's all I have to do I'll get your votes.'" He then proceeded to throw the cannonball "four or Six feet further than any one Could throw it."

Having expanded his contacts throughout the county, this time Lincoln easily won. As he prepared to leave for the capital to take up his assembly seat in the legislature, his friends chipped in to help him buy "suitable clothing" that would allow him "to maintain his new dignity." They recognized a leader in their midst just as surely as he had begun to feel the makings of a leader within himself.

The rookie assemblyman remained quiet at first, patiently educating himself about how the assembly operated, how bills were written and introduced, how laws were passed. He carefully monitored debates and the divisions between his fellow Whigs and the opposition Democrats. Lincoln was neither bashful nor timid. He was simply paying close attention, absorbing, readying to act as soon as he had gained enough knowledge to do so.

Between legislative sessions, Lincoln began to read law, knowing that a legal education would nourish his political career. He "studied with nobody," he later said, poring over historical legal cases deep into the night after working long days as surveyor and postal clerk. He borrowed law books, one at a time, from the set of John Stuart, a fellow legislator who had a law practice in Springfield. After finishing each book, he would hike the twenty miles from New Salem to Springfield to secure another loaner. "Get the books, and read and study them," he told a law student seeking advice two decades later. It did not matter whether the reading was done in a small town or a large city, by oneself or in the company of others, in a university library or in a modest cabin. "The books, and your capacity for understanding them, are just the same in all places," Lincoln said. "Always bear in mind that your own resolution to succeed, is more important than any other one thing."

At the start of the second session two years later, Lincoln had so thoroughly mastered both the law and rules of the assembly that his colleagues called on him to write bills and amendments. The clear handwriting he had perfected as a child proved useful, since, at that time, government documents were still written by hand. More important, when he finally rose to speak on the assembly floor, his colleagues witnessed what the citizens of New Salem had already seen—a young man with remarkable speech-making gifts. "They say I tell a great many stories," Lincoln told a friend. "I reckon I do; but I have learned from long experience that plain people, take them as they run, are more easily influenced through the medium of a broad and humorous illustration than any other way." As people read his speeches in the newspapers or heard about his lively metaphors and analogies through word of mouth, awareness of Lincoln's unique ability to communicate spread throughout the state.

Lincoln, the second youngest member of the assembly, was selected by his fellow Whig assemblymen as their leader for his political intuition and his ability to grasp the feelings and intentions of his fellow Whigs and the opposing Democrats, as well. It was "his thorough knowledge of human nature," one fellow legislator observed, that propelled him ahead of "any man that I have ever known."

In Lincoln's time, politics were as popular as sports are today. Debates between Whigs and Democrats regularly attracted the devoted attention of hundreds of people. Opponents attacked each other with fiery, harsh words, much to the delight of boisterous audiences, provoking an atmosphere that could escalate into fistfights, and even, on occasion, to guns being drawn. While Lincoln could be as thin-skinned and prickly as most politicians, his responses were generally full of such good humor that members of both parties could not help but laugh and relax in the pleasure of his company.

On certain occasions, however, Lincoln's humor could be mean-spirited. After Democrat Jesse Thomas had "indulged in some fun" at Lincoln's expense, Lincoln "imitated Thomas in gesture and voice, at times caricaturing his walk and the very motion of his body" and viciously mocking the "ludicrous" way Thomas spoke. Seated in the audience, Thomas broke down in tears, and soon the "skinning of Thomas" became "the talk of the town." Realizing he had badly overstepped, Lincoln went to Thomas and wholeheartedly apologized. For years afterward, the memory of that misstep filled Lincoln with deep regret.

Early on in Lincoln's political journey, he exhibited a moral courage that outweighed his ferocious ambition. At the age of twenty-six, he made a public statement against slavery that threatened to drastically diminish his support in a state that had been settled largely by white Southerners who came from proslavery states. Tensions over slavery were erupting around the country. Antislavery Northeasterners were calling for the abolition of slavery, to outlaw it throughout the United States. In acts of resistance against the Fugitive Slave Act, some Northern states refused to return enslaved people who had escaped to freedom from the South.

In response, proslavery lawmakers in both Southern and Northern states passed resolutions confirming the constitutional right of white citizens to hold Black Americans in enslavement.

The general assembly in Illinois did so too. By a lopsided vote of seventy-seven to six, the assembly opposed "the formation of abolition societies" and held "sacred" the "right of property in slaves." Lincoln was among the six who voted no, proclaiming that "the institution of slavery is founded on both injustice and bad policy." He had always believed, he later said, that "if slavery is not wrong, nothing is wrong."

While his statement and vote were bold compared to the proslavery attitudes surrounding him, Lincoln believed that the only way to abolish slavery once and for all throughout the land was to change the US Constitution. This was a more moderate position than that of fierce abolitionists who urgently demanded the immediate and full end to slavery by the federal government; every day of debate was another day that

How did slavery become part of American history?

In 1619, white English sailors kidnapped twenty to thirty captive Africans from a Spanish slave ship and brought them to an English colony in Virginia to trade them for supplies, treating people as property. By that time, free and enslaved Africans had already been in the Americas for at least a century since Portuguese merchants sailing down the West African coast to trade gold and spices had found an even more valuable commodity: human beings. Ultimately, white Europeans and Americans would force 12.5 million Africans to sail to the American colonies in North and South America in chains. Even though the US Constitution establishes the rights of "we the people" to "secure the blessings of liberty," it also extended the transatlantic slave trade for twenty years after it was signed. When those twenty years were up, white Americans continued to trade the descendants of the original captive slaves for money and goods.

men, women, and children were in chains. The Constitution does not explicitly include the word "slavery," but it did provide protections to slaveholders. Lincoln felt that until such time as the Constitution was amended to allow Congress to outlaw slavery nationwide, it was impossible to end slavery in states where it was already established and supported by local voters, as it had long been throughout the South. Fearing chaos above all, he believed that the law must be followed until it could be lawfully changed.

Lincoln cautioned of such potential chaos in a major speech to the Young Men's Lyceum of Springfield. He opened his address with a warning that "something of ill-omen" was developing among the people—a tendency to substitute violence, murder, and lynching for the rule of law, the courts, and the Constitution. Two months earlier, the North had been rocked when a proslavery mob in Alton, Illinois, killed the white abolitionist editor Elijah Lovejoy. Separately, in Mississippi, a white mob hanged a group of Black men and their white co-conspirators after accusing them of provoking rebellion. If this mob-like spirit continued to spread, Lincoln signaled, good people would lose faith in a government too weak to protect them. In the chaos of mob violence, the country would be vulnerable to the rise of dictators, men of "towering" egos whose ambition was disconnected from the people's best interests.

To prevent the rise of a dictatorship, Lincoln called upon his fellow citizens to renew the values of America's founders and to embrace the Constitution and its laws. The rule of law—not of armed mobs or of

Enslavers denied freedom to those they enslaved, and bought and sold them without regard for their humanity, brutally separating parents from their children and husbands and wives from each other. America built its economy on their forced labor. The lawmakers of many Northern states outlawed slavery around the time of the American Revolution, but Northerners still benefitted from slavery, because, throughout the country, white entrepreneurs had created entire industries around trading, shipping, and insuring enslaved people and on commodities, like cotton, rice, and tobacco, that enslaved people labored to produce on Southern plantations. By the time of Lincoln's speech against slavery in 1835, slavery had been outlawed for two years in England, but in the United States its hold was stronger than ever.

kings—means that ultimately the power lies with the people. "Let reverence for the laws, be breathed by every American mother," taught in every school, preached in every pulpit. The great shield against a potential dictator is an educated and informed people "attached to the government and laws." This is why Lincoln always believed education was the foundation of democracy. He argued that learning about the American Revolution and the crafting of the Constitution was all the more urgent as the spirit of common purpose and compromise that the drove the founding of the Union—the United States of America—had begun to fade from the collective memory of the country. Indeed, Lincoln declared that the story of America's birth should "be read of, and recounted, so long as the bible shall be read." The founders' grand experiment—their ambition to show the world that ordinary people could govern themselves—had succeeded, and now, Lincoln concluded, it was up to his generation to preserve this "proud fabric of freedom."

Though all this was going on, the heart of Lincoln's work in the assembly in these early years of his political career was remaining true to his original promise to secure government funds for infrastructure improvements. He used the power of his leading position in the assembly to mobilize support for a series of bills to spend millions of dollars for a

---

What was the abolition movement?

The fight to abolish slavery in the United States is as old as the country itself, and throughout our history Black men and women have been at the forefront of that struggle. The first woman to denounce slavery before a "promiscuous" audience (composed of men *and* women) was Maria W. Stewart, a Black woman from Boston. A forerunner to abolitionists Sojourner Truth, Harriet Tubman, and Frederick Douglass, Stewart forcefully opposed slavery, boldly pressed for women's rights, and called out prejudice: "Give the man of color an equal opportunity with the white from the cradle to manhood, and from manhood to the grave, and you would discover the dignified statesman, the man of science, and the philosopher. But there is no such opportunity for the sons of Africa. . . . Had we as a people received one-half the early advantages the whites have received, I would defy the Government of these United States to deprive us any longer of our rights," she said publicly in 1833, just a few years before Lincoln's famous Lyceum address.

spectacular range of projects to widen rivers, build railroads, dig canals, and create roads. Lincoln hoped that these projects would expand job opportunities, encourage new settlers to come, create bustling towns, and help people live more prosperous and comfortable lives. Like Lincoln, those born into poverty could rise as far as their talents and hard work might take them, and the promise of the American dream would be realized.

In April 1837, Lincoln decided to move to the capital, Springfield, Illinois, to expand his prospects and practice law while he served in the legislature. With nowhere to live and virtually no money, Lincoln wandered into a general store looking for a place to stay, and it was there he met Joshua Speed, who would

> Stewart called out the hypocrisy of white Americans who relied on enslaved Black people for everything they valued and then denied them opportunities to live freely: "The unfriendly whites first drove the native American from his much loved home. Then they stole our fathers from their peaceful and quiet dwellings, and brought them hither, and made bondmen and bond-women of them and their little ones; they have obliged our brethren to labor, kept them in utter ignorance, nourished them in vice, and raised them in degradation; and now that we have enriched their soil, and filled their coffers, they say that we are not capable of becoming like white men, and that we never can rise to respectability in this country."

become his closest friend. When Lincoln realized he couldn't afford the cost of a bed, and probably couldn't even pay back a loan for it, Speed "never saw a sadder face." Without hesitation, Speed offered a solution: "I have a large room with a double bed upstairs, which you are very welcome to share with me." Lincoln reacted quickly to Speed's unexpected offer. He raced upstairs to drop off his bags in the loft, then came clattering down again, his face entirely transformed. "Beaming with pleasure he exclaimed, 'Well, Speed, I am moved!'" In an era when private quarters were a rare luxury, it was common practice for men to share beds with one another in academies, boardinghouses, and overcrowded hotels. The room above Speed's store functioned as a sort of dormitory, with two other young men living there part of the time as well.

Lincoln and Speed became the best of friends, traveling together to political events, dances, and parties. And Speed's general store was the hub of Springfield's political and social life. While Lincoln worked during the day to build his law practice, evenings would find him with friends and colleagues, gathered around a fire in Speed's store to read newspapers, gossip, and engage in philosophical debates. "They came there," Speed recalled, "because they were sure to find Lincoln," who never failed to entertain with his remarkable stories.

Soon thereafter, Lincoln met Mary Todd, who came from a prominent Kentucky family and had moved to Springfield to live with her sister Elizabeth, the wife of Ninian Wirt Edwards, son of a former governor of Illinois. Lincoln was thirty-one, Mary was twenty-one, and they came from very different backgrounds—she was sophisticated and educated, and she spoke fluent French. One night at a party, Lincoln, captivated by Mary's lively manner, intelligent face, clear blue eyes, and dimpled smile, reportedly told her, "I want to dance with you in the worst way." And, Mary laughingly told her cousin later that night, "he certainly did." The two fell in love and within a short time became engaged to marry.

In less than half a dozen years, Lincoln had risen to become a respected leader in the state legislature, among Springfield's powerful elite, a central figure in the fight for infrastructure improvements, and a practicing lawyer with a vibrant new fiancée. The life Lincoln was building had steadily lifted him to heights he could only have conjured in his wildest childhood imaginings, a dream come true. But dreams tend to follow their own logic, and even the best dreams have a way of shifting in an instant.

Chapter Three

*"How hard it is to die and leave one's country
no better than if one had never lived...."*

GOOD FORTUNE CAN CHANGE QUICKLY. An economic panic that was
sweeping the country hit especially hard in Illinois in 1840, when the legislature had to stop work on half-finished railroads, canals, bridges, and
roads. The state was drowning in unpaid bills from the projects Lincoln
had championed, and new pioneers stopped settling in the Prairie State.
Thousands of people lost their homes because they couldn't make their
mortgage payments, and banks were failing. As one of the chief architects and advocates of the state's big dreams, Lincoln received most of
the blame.

This impacted Lincoln greatly, because he considered his promises
to improve the land and citizens' lives binding upon his honor, reputation, and character. His pledge could not be fulfilled. His belief in
himself shaken, he announced his retirement from the state legislature
at the end of the current term.

Adding to his woes, that very winter, Joshua Speed was preparing
to leave Springfield to return to his family's plantation in Kentucky.
Speed's father had died, and he felt a responsibility to care for his widowed mother. His upcoming departure represented the loss of Lincoln's
closest friend at a time when he needed companionship the most. "I shall

be verry [sic] lonesome without you," Lincoln told Speed. "How miserably things seem to be arranged in this world. If we have no friends, we have no pleasure; and if we have them, we are sure to lose them, and be doubly pained by the loss."

During these trying months, Lincoln also decided to break off his engagement to Mary Todd. The couple had initially been drawn together by their shared love of poetry, politics, and humor. Lincoln's idol, Whig Party leader Henry Clay, had been a frequent guest at the Todd family home. Mary considered herself a passionate Whig; she took pride in her "unladylike" enthusiasm for politics. Her faith in Lincoln's destiny spurred his ambitions and drew them together. As the courtship moved toward marriage, however, Lincoln began to question the strength of his love for the hot-tempered young woman who could be affectionate and generous one day and depressed and irritable the next. Friends and relatives considered Mary "the exact reverse" of Lincoln. While Mary possessed an open, passionate, and impulsive nature, "her face an index to every passing emotion," Lincoln was, Mary admitted, a self-controlled man. What "he felt most deeply," she observed, "he expressed, the least." Speed recalled that "in the winter of 40 & 41, Lincoln was very unhappy about

What was the role of women in American society in Mary's time?

Imagine: you can't play organized sports, wear pants, or choose if you want to get married, because you were born a girl. For most of American history, women had few rights of citizenship and very narrow roles they were expected to fill. In 1840, laws made by men dictated that women did not have the right to vote; very few women could attend college or hold jobs of any kind, and instead were expected to devote their lives to marrying men and the hard work of keeping house and raising children. Marriage stripped women of legal, political, and economic independence. Under the legal doctrine of coverture, a wife's identity was absorbed into that of her husband, symbolized by her taking of his name. An unmarried woman was usually a dependent of the men in her family, unless in rare cases she had financial means of her own. At the time, it was unthinkable for most men and women to break the social custom that expected them to marry an opposite-gender partner and have children with them, regardless of what they wanted.

Also in 1840, six American women, including white abolitionists Lucretia Mott and his engagement to Mary—Not being entirely satisfied that his heart was going with his hand—How much he suffered on that account none Know so well as myself."

Beyond Lincoln's uncertainty about his feelings for Mary, he was also anxious about his personal finances and his ability to support a wife and family. His work in the legislature and campaigning had kept him from growing his legal practice. "I am so poor, and make so little headway in the world," Lincoln acknowledged. He had no model of a successful career or family life, no foundation on which to construct his own life and family. He had seen glimpses of traditional family life—people sitting together at meals, fathers serving as providers—but had never experienced it. Riddled with self-doubt, Lincoln broke the engagement on the "fatal first of January," 1841.

This "breach of honor" soon became known throughout the small town of Springfield, magnifying Mary's humiliation. Feeling Mary's sorrows as intensely as his own, Lincoln could not bear the idea that he was responsible for her unhappiness. He wrote and spoke freely to his close friends of the despair that possessed him, and of his sense of dishonor. It "kills my soul," he said. Most damaging of all, he confessed to Speed, was that he had lost confidence in his ability to keep

Elizabeth Cady Stanton, traveled to a world antislavery convention in London, where the male organizers of the event excluded them from participating or even entering because they were women. Outraged, Mott and Stanton vowed to fight for women's equal rights. In 1848, they gathered a group of white women (and a few men, including Frederick Douglass) in Seneca Falls, New York, to demand equal rights. The group created the Declaration of Sentiments, based on the Declaration of Independence, and it stated that "all men *and women* are created equal," although some argue they prioritized the concerns of middle-class, white women over others.

Despite the activism of this group and others that followed, American lawmakers continued to prevent women from voting until nearly eighty years later with the passage of the Nineteenth Amendment in 1920, made possible by generations of women leading the charge. Only after the 1960s did lawmakers—under pressure from activists—begin to make significant changes to the laws that impacted women's rights in other areas, including the ability to get their own credit cards and bank loans, to not be harassed at their jobs, to play sports, and more.

his promises, his "resolves when they are made. In that ability you know, I once prided myself as the only or at least, the chief gem of my character; that gem I lost," and until it is recovered, "I cannot trust myself in any matter of much importance."

These private and public defeats plunged Lincoln into what became a devastating depression. Lincoln had suffered from episodes of melancholy before, most publicly when his first love, Ann Rutledge, died of typhoid fever at the age of twenty-two. But this breakdown, when he was thirty-two, was the most serious of his lifetime. "I am now the most miserable man living," Lincoln wrote to his then law partner. "If what I feel were equally distributed to the whole human family, there would not be one cheerful face on the earth. Whether I shall ever be better I can not tell; I awfully forebode I shall not. To remain as I am is impossible; I must die or be better, it appears to me." The letter ended abruptly with the simple statement "I can write no more."

For days he remained in bed, unable to eat or sleep. His friends feared he might kill himself. They took away all knives, razors, and scissors from his room. He no longer looked "like the same person," one friend remarked. He was skin and bones, another friend observed, "and seems scarcely to possess strength enough to speak above a whisper. His case at present is truly deplorable."

Speed postponed his departure and remained with Lincoln throughout this

---

How was mental health treated in this era?

In Lincoln's time, understanding, diagnosing, and treating mental health issues was unheard of—very different from today. Lincoln's combination of symptoms—mood swings, feelings of hopelessness and sluggishness, depression, and thoughts of death—was then called hypochondriasis ("the hypo") or "the vapours." Its source was thought to be in the hypochondria, the section of the abdomen that was then considered the seat of emotions, containing the liver, gallbladder, and spleen. For Lincoln, doctors recommended treatment of the liver and digestive system as a cure. So he began taking blue mass, a drug commonly prescribed to treat "hypochondriasis." It contained high doses of mercury, believed to benefit the liver by countering the buildup of "black bile," but which may have had negative side effects.

distressing time. The conversations that passed between them stayed with both men for the rest of their lives. When Speed warned Lincoln that he must somehow revive his spirits or he would certainly die, Lincoln replied that he was more than willing to die, but that he had "done nothing to make any human being remember that he had lived." His greatest desire, he confessed to Speed, was "to link his name with something" that would be meaningful to "his fellow man."

Lincoln's depression may be attributed to the string of losses he suffered in his life and his fear of not following through on his promises. He was just nine years old when his mother suddenly died. By the time he was twenty, his aunt, uncle, sister, and a newborn brother had also died. He did not have a good relationship with his father, which was followed by the broken relationship with Mary and the citizens who he had disappointed. But fueled by his resilience, conviction, strength of will, desire to accomplish something by which to be remembered, and with the support of those who cared deeply about him, Lincoln gradually overcame his depression.

Having left the legislature, he formed a new partnership with Stephen Logan, a leading lawyer in the frontier region. Logan knew that Lincoln had little formal training in law—at the time law schools did not exist as we know them today, and passing the bar to practice law in his state was an informal process—but he had seen Lincoln's speaking skills before juries and believed the younger man would be a hard worker. The partnership turned out well for both men. Lincoln found in Logan a mentor who guided his general reading in the law and became, Lincoln said, "almost a father to me." Logan taught Lincoln "how to prepare his cases" and, most important, boosted the confidence of the self-made lawyer when he occasionally despaired of ever catching up to his college-educated colleagues. "It does not depend on the start a man gets," Logan told him, "it depends on how he keeps up his labors and efforts until middle life." Working together, the two men built a reliable practice, and finally, Lincoln began to make a decent paycheck.

As his doubts about his ability to support a wife began to fade and he was still "unreconciled to his separation" from Mary, Lincoln resumed his courtship with her, and they married November 4, 1842. By committing himself once again to the relationship he had broken, he began to restore his sense of honor; he had proved to himself that he could, indeed, keep his "resolves"—"the chief gem" of his character. While his marriage to Mary proved challenging at times, Lincoln made great efforts to be a good husband and a kindly, playful father, forging a relationship with his children he had never experienced with his own father. First came Robert, born nine months after the wedding, followed by Edward, who would die from tuberculosis just before his fourth birthday, then William and Tad. The boys experienced love, affection, and encouragement from their father. "It is my pleasure that my children are free— happy and unrestrained by paternal tyranny," Lincoln noted. "Love is the chain whereby to lock a child to its parent." The life he was leading may have seemed commonplace, but to him it was no small thing to have built, for the first time, a stable home and financial security, without which little else would have been possible.

As the Illinois economy began to revive, so, too, did Lincoln's political ambitions. He ran for a two-year term to the House of Representatives in 1846 when he was thirty-seven years old, and the campaign was rough. During the race, he faced criticism for not being an active churchgoer. Though Lincoln grew up in a Baptist household, he was not baptized, and in his early twenties he was outspoken about his religious skepticism. He was not a member of any church's congregation, although he rented pews for his family at First Presbyterian Church in Springfield, Illinois. "That I am not a member of any Christian Church, is true," he responded to critics in an 1846 flyer after he had secured the Whig nomination for the House seat, "but I have never denied the truth of the Scriptures; and I have never spoken with intentional disrespect of religion in general, or of any denomination of Christians in particular." Lincoln won the race, but his term started out rocky too. Hardly two weeks after Lincoln's arrival in Washington, he harshly criticized President James K. Polk's recent "victory" in the Mexican-American War. This was a far cry from the careful, step-by-step analysis that Lincoln

The earliest known photograph of Lincoln, taken by Nicholas H. Shepherd when Lincoln was thirty-seven and a newly minted member of Congress.

would later be known for. His impatient need for attention had managed only to anger Democrats, annoy fellow Whigs, and lose him support in Illinois, where the victorious war was popular.

During the 1848 presidential race Lincoln distinguished himself among his colleagues with his unique charisma and storytelling gifts as he spoke on the House floor on behalf of the Whigs' presidential candidate, war hero General Zachary Taylor. From fellow Whigs and reporters alike, Lincoln won high praise for his thoughtful yet humorous speech. A Baltimore newspaper observed that "Lincoln's manner was so good-natured and his style so peculiar that he kept the House in a continuous roar of merriment." He strolled up and down the aisles as he spoke, gesturing in a fashion so electrifying and entertaining that he became known as "the best story teller in the House." Whig Party officials were so taken by his speech that they invited Lincoln to campaign for Taylor that fall in New England.

It was on the campaign trail that Lincoln gained greater conscious-ness, sensitivity, and emotional understanding about the issue of slavery. In Massachusetts, unlike in Illinois, heated discussions about slavery dominated public forums. This experience would quicken Lincoln's evolving views on the issue that would tear the country apart in the decade ahead. At Tremont Temple in Boston, he heard a passionate speech by William Henry Seward, the former governor of and future senator from New York. Seward argued that the issue of slavery was urgent, that "the time had come for sharp definition of opinion and boldness of utterance." Lincoln and Seward shared a room the following night and stayed up long past midnight discussing slavery. "I reckon you are right," Lincoln told Seward in the early morning hours. "We have got to deal with this slavery question, and got to give much more attention to it hereafter than we have been doing."

While Lincoln had served the Whig Party well during his only term in Congress, overall historians consider his term a failure, and Lincoln would likely agree. His ambition was higher than party and wider than the narrow geographic section of his state that he represented in Washington, DC. After Taylor won the presidential election in November 1848, Lincoln expected that his energetic campaigning would gain him an important job in the new administration. In the end, though, the post was given to another Whig politician who had not spoken out impul-sively against the popular Mexican-American War.

When he learned that he had not been selected for the job, Lincoln "despaired of ever rising in the world," his law partner Herndon remem-bered. Lincoln's own words reflected his mood over those years: "How hard—Oh how hard it is to die and leave one's country no better than if one had never lived." Years later, after he had become president, the emotions of this moment remained so intense, Lincoln remembered, that "I hardly ever felt so bad about any failure in my life."

Chapter Four

"A house divided against itself cannot stand."

LINCOLN SAID HE "WAS LOSING INTEREST IN POLITICS" during the years that followed his brief and unhappy term in Congress. While this sounds unconvincing coming from an extraordinarily ambitious man who would one day become president, he did use this break from elected office to work once again as a lawyer. During this period, he gazed in the mirror and honestly examined himself, willing to confront his weaknesses, reflect on his failures, and consider the kind of leader he wanted to be. With matter-of-fact honesty, Lincoln noted: "I am not an accomplished lawyer," so he set out to change that. William Herndon observed that "no man had greater power of application. Once fixing his mind on any subject, nothing could interfere with or disturb him."

In Lincoln's day, the judges, lawyers, and other court officials traveled together on "the circuit" for eight weeks every spring and fall. Covering some 150 miles, the traveling court of law, like a theater troupe, moved from one county to another, holding court and trying cases in dozens of small villages and towns. Just as young Abraham had watched court proceedings when he was a child collecting stories to share with his friends, villagers came from miles around to witness the courtroom drama unfold as hundreds of cases were tried, including murder, assault, robbery, and other disputes. When the circuit arrived, the county bustled with excitement and anticipation, much like a fair coming to town. When the lawyers settled into the overcrowded local taverns for the night, they were always forced to share rooms and often beds and stayed up late preparing for the next day's proceedings.

Lincoln enjoyed this social setting, but more important, it was on the circuit that he managed to create the time and space needed to conduct his intensive, self-directed course of study in philosophy, astronomy, science, political economy, history, literature, poetry, and drama.

Lincoln "would read and study for hours," Herndon recalled, long after everyone else had gone to sleep, "placing a candle on a chair at the head of his bed," often remaining in this position until two a.m. How he could maintain his focus while the snores of his roommates rumbled the air was a puzzle "none of us could ever solve," marveled Herndon. Not only did Lincoln stay up later than his colleagues, but "he was in the habit of rising earlier." Lincoln would "sit by the fire, having uncovered the coals," and think aloud, one colleague recalled. A stranger entering the room and hearing Lincoln "muttering to himself" might have imagined "he had suddenly gone insane." But his fellow circuit riders only "listened and laughed." This was how Lincoln figured things out—a form of mental wrestling. Then, once the breakfast bell rang, he hurriedly dressed, joined his colleagues at breakfast, and readied himself for the cases he would try over the course of the day. So successful was Lincoln in defending his clients and speaking before juries that he soon developed "the largest trial practice of all his peers in central Illinois."

The key to Lincoln's success as a lawyer was his ability to break down the most complex case or issue "into its simplest elements." He never lost a jury by fumbling with or reading from a prepared argument, relying instead "on his well-trained memory." His thoughtful, logical, "easy to follow" arguments were designed as intimate conversations with the jurors, so it would seem he was conversing with friends. An

Illinois judge captured the essence of Lincoln's unique appeal and abilities: he had a talent for "making the jury believe they—and not he—were trying the case."

When the courtroom closed, the lawyers, who were opponents during the day, would come together as friends in the tavern at night, eating supper at the same communal table with Judge David Davis presiding. Once the meal was done, they would gather before a blazing fire to drink, smoke tobacco, and engage in conversation. Neither a smoker nor a drinker, Lincoln nevertheless commanded respect and attention with his never-ending stream of stories, whether the crowd was ten, fifty, or several hundred. "His little gray eyes sparkled," and when he reached the point of a funny story or joke, "no one's laugh was heartier than his."

Lincoln's stories provided more than just laughs. Drawn from his own experiences, they frequently included sayings or proverbs that usually connected to the lives of his audience. He possessed a talent to convey practical wisdom and humor that could be remembered and repeated.

Lincoln's popularity, ambition, and self-education did not change who he was. He treated everyone, no matter their job or social status, with the same tenderhearted patience, the same generous and helpful kindliness and empathy that had made him so beloved from his days in New Salem. "No lawyer on the circuit was more unassuming than was Mr. Lincoln," a colleague recalled. The seating arrangements at the tavern table reflected the hierarchy of the court, with Judge Davis at the head, surrounded by the lawyers. On one occasion, when Lincoln had settled himself at the foot of the table among the common customers, the landlord told him, "You're in the wrong place, Mr. Lincoln, come up here." Lincoln's response: "Have you anything better to eat up there, Joe? If not, I'll stay here."

As Lincoln became a leader in the legal profession, he assumed responsibility for mentoring the next generation. "He was remarkably gentle with young lawyers," a colleague noted. One young lawyer recalled he was deeply touched by how "kindly and cordially" Lincoln treated him. If a new clerk appeared in court, "Lincoln was the first—sometimes the only one—to shake hands with him and congratulate him."

The art of communication, Lincoln advised newcomers, "is the lawyer's avenue to the public." Yet, Lincoln warned, the lawyer must not rely on persuasiveness alone. What is well-spoken must be tied to what is well-thought. And such thought is the product of a lot of work, "the drudgery of the law." Without that labor, the most eloquent words are meaningless. Indeed, "the leading rule for the lawyer, as for the man of every other calling, is diligence. Leave nothing for tomorrow that can be done to-day." The key to success, he insisted, is "work, work, work."

Lincoln's mind was his "workshop," a fellow lawyer recalled. "He needed no office, no pen, ink and paper." During this period, he was not simply enlarging his understanding of law and his growing practice, nor was he generally educating himself to fulfill his curiosity. For although he avoided politics and continued to claim no great interest in it, his pursuit of knowledge was anything but random. It was directed toward understanding the role and the purpose of leadership. He would soon apply this self-guided education to the divisions that were hardening within the country over the toughest, most consuming issue of the day: slavery.

While the slavery issue had divided North and South from the beginning of the nation, every expansion of territory to create new states reignited the flames. When the white citizens of Missouri, part of the vast territory the US acquired from France by the 1803 Louisiana Purchase, sought admission to the Union as a state that would allow slavery, it created an angry struggle between North and South. The

Missouri Compromise of 1820, constructed under the leadership of Senator Henry Clay, who Lincoln admired as "the man for a crisis," brought an end to the rising tensions, though it did not ease the suffering of enslaved people. The legislation admitted Missouri as a slave state and Maine as a non-slave state at the same time. An imaginary line was drawn across the country—territories north of that line would enter the Union as free states, and those below would be slave states. For the next three decades, the Missouri Compromise kept that peace until Congress was called upon to decide the fate of the territories the US had acquired in the Mexican-American War.

While slavery was protected by the Constitution in states where it already existed, that protection did not apply to the newly acquired territories, and it was there that conflict erupted anew. Speaking for many white Southerners and proslavery Democrats, Robert Toombs of Georgia warned: "If by your legislation you seek to drive us from the territories of California and New Mexico, purchased by the common blood and treasure of the whole people, I am for disunion." The seeds of a civil war were planted.

Once again, the nation turned to Henry Clay, and once again, the now seventy-three-year-old senator constructed a compromise designed to keep the Union intact. The Compromise of 1850 admitted California as a free state but brought Utah and New Mexico into the Union with no restrictions on slavery; it called for an end to the slave trade in the District of Columbia, but asked Congress to strengthen the old Fugitive Slave Act, to empower federal officials to recruit citizens to hunt down escapees in free states. While the Compromise of 1850 seemed to end the crisis, the new, more strenuous and cruel terms in the Fugitive Slave Act sparked the fury of antislavery activists in the North. Violent disturbances erupted when slaveholders tried to recapture enslaved people who had run away to Boston and New York.

The issue of slavery began to dominate discussion on the circuit, as the lawyers argued over the various journals they were reading—the anti-slavery papers in the North and the proslavery papers in the South. Both sides were hunkering down with deep hostility. The grounds for compromise were crumbling. This is to say nothing of the enslaved people who were still held captive by enslavers, powerless to publicly register their opposition to their enslavement. "The time is coming," a fellow lawyer told Lincoln, "when we shall have to be all either Abolitionists or Democrats." The Compromise of 1850 lasted only four years.

Lincoln was on the circuit in 1854 when he heard the news that Congress, after prolonged debate, had passed the controversial Kansas-Nebraska Act. Designed by Senator Stephen Douglas of Illinois, the popular leader of the Democratic Party (presently in his second term in the US Senate and a likely candidate for president), the bill would allow white settlers in the new territories of Kansas and Nebraska, both of which stood above the dividing line created by the 1820 Missouri Compromise, to decide for themselves whether they wanted to enter the Union as slave or free states.

In one stroke, the three-decades-old Missouri Compromise had been obliterated; with this decision, Douglas and his supporters in power were allowing slavery to spread aggressively beyond the South. Lincoln grasped at once the significance of the new law. No longer was slavery on the path to ultimate extinction, as he had hoped and believed. The situation of enslaved people was now "fixed, and hopeless of change for the better."

The country was growing more deeply divided and on edge as violence erupted with greater frequency and brutality all over the country. Kansas became the ultimate battleground under the "popular sovereignty" provision of the Kansas-Nebraska Act, which empowered voters to determine the status of Kansas as a free or slave state. There, a guerrilla war broke out between Northerners who moved to Kansas to make it a free state and so-called border ruffians, who crossed the river from Missouri and cast illegal votes to make Kansas a slave state. As the violence spiraled, "Bleeding Kansas" became a new rallying cry for the antislavery forces. Kansas was not merely a contest between settlers but a war between North and South.

Violence even spilled into the halls of the United States Senate. In May 1856, the outspoken and fiercely abolitionist senator Charles Sumner of Massachusetts gave a fiery speech attacking slavery and calling out several senators specifically for their support of it. Two days later, South Carolina congressman Preston Brooks entered the Senate chamber armed with a heavy cane. Walking up to Sumner, who was writing at his desk, Brooks brought the cane down upon his head, beating him repeatedly as Sumner tried to escape. Covered with blood, Sumner fell unconscious and was carried from the floor. News of the brutal assault, which left Sumner with severe injuries to his brain and spinal cord and kept him out of the Senate for three years, fired up antislavery sentiment in the North. Sumner became a hero in the North, but Brooks was equally celebrated in the South, where the press almost universally applauded the assault, and the South Carolina governor presented him with a silver cane in honor of his attack on Sumner.

The uproar caused by the Kansas-Nebraska bill and the Sumner attack destroyed what was left of the Whig Party, as antislavery activists moved to form the explicitly antislavery Republican Party and call for the repeal of the bill. For decades, America's political battles had been fought between the Democrats and the Whigs. By the early 1850s, however, the issue of slavery had split the Whigs into warring factions and divided Democrats between North and South.

With emotions running high and chaos the order of the day, a pro-South Democrat, James Buchanan, was elected to the presidency. Two days after his inauguration in March 1857, the Supreme Court ruled on a case brought by Dred Scott, an enslaved man who was suing for his freedom. The shameful and dire 7–2 decision ruled that Black people "are not included, and were not intended to be included, under the word 'citizens' in the Constitution." Therefore, Scott had no standing in federal court. This should have decided the case, but Chief Justice Roger Taney widened the scope of the decision in writing the court's majority opinion, declaring that neither the Declaration of Independence nor the Constitution had been intended to apply to Black people. Black people were "so far inferior that they had no rights which the white man was bound to respect." Beyond that, Taney went on to say that Congress had no right to outlaw slavery in the newly acquired territories by such legislation as the Missouri Compromise, for slaves were private property protected by the Constitution. In other words, the Missouri Compromise was unconstitutional.

The formerly enslaved abolitionist Frederick Douglass fought back to "lift up our hearts and voices in earnest denunciation of the vile and shocking abomination" of the Scott decision. Douglass had declared himself "free" in 1838 after taking a perilous train trip from Baltimore to New York City disguised as a sailor and carrying papers purchased for him by a young free Black woman named Anna Murray, who he later married. In a celebrated speech before the American Anti-Slavery Society in New York, he condemned the Supreme Court decision. "Judge Taney can do many things, but he cannot perform impossibilities. . . . He cannot change the essential nature of things—making evil good, and good evil."

Lincoln also denounced the Scott decision, and while Frederick Douglass did so with the deep moral force of his convictions, background, and experience, Lincoln's approach was to rely on his legal mind and skills by painstakingly picking apart the logic of the proslavery side.

Who was Frederick Douglass?

The abolitionist leader Frederick Douglass had been born into slavery and went on to become the most celebrated Black man of his era. Separated at birth from his mother, he never knew his father. Not permitted to attend school, and in defiance of state law that made educating enslaved people illegal, he was taught the alphabet as a young boy by Sophia Auld, the wife of Baltimore slaveholder Hugh Auld. His lessons ended abruptly one day when he heard Auld reprimand his wife, telling her that if a slave learned how to read and write, he would no longer be suited to be a slave. From that moment on, Frederick knew that education would be his ticket to freedom.

At the age of twenty, he met a young free Black woman, Anna Murray, who agreed to help him escape and would later become his wife. He disguised himself as a sailor and boarded a northbound train, using money from Anna to pay for his ticket. In less than twenty-four hours, Frederick arrived in New York City and declared himself free. "A new world has opened upon me. Anguish and grief, like darkness and rain, may be depicted, but gladness and joy, like the rainbow, defy the skill of pen or pencil," he wrote in one of his three autobiographies.

To develop his arguments, Lincoln withdrew to the State Library, where he investigated the slavery issue and the debates at the time the framers created the Constitution, searching and researching step-by-step until, as Herndon once remarked, he knew his subject "inside and outside, upside and downside." As a boy, when Lincoln was on "such a hunt for an idea," he could not sleep until he had "caught it." He was on a hunt now and would not sleep until he caught what he was after—a way of dismantling the excuses for slavery to set America on a different path, while addressing the crisis of the moment.

Lincoln's notes from this time reveal his attempt to boil down the slavery argument into its most basic elements, which he dramatized through a person A and person B scenario, building a logical case against slavery. "If A. can prove, however conclusively, that he may, of right, enslave B," Lincoln began, "why may not B. snatch the same argument, and prove equally, that he may enslave A? You say A. is white, and B. is black. It is color, then; the lighter, having the right to enslave the darker? Take care. By this rule, you are to be slave to the first man you meet, with a fairer skin than your own. You do not mean color exactly? You mean the whites are intellectually the superiors of the blacks, and therefore have the right to enslave them? Take care again. By this rule, you are to be slave to the first man you meet, with an intellect superior to your own."

It would not be long before Lincoln's deep thinking on the issue of slavery would dramatically unfold as full-blown arguments with Stephen Douglas, the author of the Kansas-Nebraska Act. The controversial act inspired Lincoln to reenter politics as a Republican and to challenge Douglas in a race for the Senate in 1858. Lincoln and Douglas had met two decades earlier during nightly sessions around the fire in Joshua Speed's general store. Douglas had even courted Mary. "We were both young then," Lincoln later wrote. "Even then, we were both ambitious; I, perhaps, quite as much so as he. With me the race of ambition has been a failure—a flat failure; with him it has been one of splendid success. His name fills the nation."

The Senate race became a vote on slavery and the battle over its extension into new territories, as well as the fortunes of the new Republican Party. Lincoln opened his Senate campaign stating "A house divided against itself cannot stand," painting an easily approachable image of the Union as a house in danger of collapse under the pressure of slavery advocates who, by repealing the Missouri Compromise, had threatened the stability of the entire structure. Despite the gloomy metaphor of a collapsing house, the tone of Lincoln's speech was positive, calling on Republicans to restore the laws that prevented the extension of slavery beyond where it was already established. If slavery was once more on a course to eventual extinction, as the framers of the Constitution had

> Douglass dedicated his life to abolishing slavery and advocating for women's rights and racial equity. As an activist, writer, and public speaker, through his words and deeds, he would provide inspiration and hope for millions and profoundly influence President Lincoln, who he met three times in the White House, making Douglass the most prominent Black caller to the White House in its first century.

intended, people in all sections could live peaceably in the revered house their forefathers had imagined.

And so began the historic Lincoln-Douglas debates, seven spirited face-to-face encounters in different towns throughout Illinois that attracted tens of thousands of people and held the attention of tens of millions more who read the full transcripts of the debates in leading papers across the country. With marching bands, parades, fireworks, banners, flags, and picnics, the public devoured news of the debates with "all the devoted attention," one historian has noted, "that many later Americans would reserve for athletic contests." Douglas, the short, stocky "little giant," as Mary called him, "traveled in what was called in those days 'great style,' with a secretary and servants and numerous loud companions, moving from place to place by special train with cars specially decorated for the occasion, all of which contrasted strongly with Lincoln's extreme modest simplicity."

Once on-site, each fiery debate followed the same rules. The first candidate spoke for an hour, followed by a one-and-a-half-hour response, after which the man who had gone first would deliver a half-hour rebuttal. The huge crowds were riveted for the full three hours, often interjecting comments, cheering for their champion, grumbling at the jabs of his opponent. In this setting, Lincoln's sense of humor was on full display. At one debate, when someone in the audience attacked him as two-faced, Lincoln responded, "If I had two faces, do you think I'd be wearing this face?" Hearty laughter from the audience followed!

While the spectacle was entertaining, it was the substance of the debates that most captivated the people who traveled from near and far. Throughout the debates, from August to October, Lincoln carried with him a small notebook that contained clippings relevant to the questions of the day sent to him by his law partner, William Herndon, along with the opening lines of his own "House Divided" speech and the paragraph

What did the Declaration of Independence say about freedom?

When American colonists gathered in Philadelphia in 1776 to sign the Declaration of Independence, it was a cry of freedom, an act of cutting the thirteen colonies' ties to the British Crown. Its goals were to announce the founding of a new nation—a declaration of its independence—made up of thirteen states instead of colonies, and a call to defend liberty at home and abroad. The Declaration states that "all men are created equal, that they are endowed by their Creator with certain unalienable Rights, that among these are Life, Liberty and the pursuit of Happiness."

Yet the founders did not extend those ideals to enslaved people, Native Americans, women, or poor people. The paradox of the stirring words of the Declaration is that they were written by Thomas Jefferson, a lifelong slaveholder. He and other of the country's founders who opposed slavery did not insist on abolishing it. It still took eighty-seven years—and the Civil War, the Emancipation Proclamation, and the Thirteenth Amendment—to end slavery in America.

Still, these inspiring words of the Declaration of Independence would light the path for every fight for freedom in this country and become a beacon for the world for centuries to come.

of the Declaration of Independence proclaiming that "all men are created equal, that they are endowed by their Creator with certain unalienable Rights, that among these are Life, Liberty and the pursuit of Happiness." It was upon the meaning of the Declaration and the future of the Union that battle lines with Douglas were drawn.

Although unfulfilled in the present, Lincoln argued, the Declaration's promise of equality was "a beacon to guide" not only "the whole race of man then living" but "their children and their children's children, and the countless myriads who should inhabit the earth in other ages." For Douglas, the heart of the controversy was the right of self-government, the principle that the people in each territory and each state should decide for themselves whether to introduce or exclude slavery; the term he used to describe it was "popular sovereignty." Lincoln agreed that "the doctrine of self government is right—absolutely and eternally right," but argued that "it has no just application" to the cruel and oppressive power of slavery. Using "self-government" to justify slavery was a distortion of the meaning of self-government. "When the white man governs himself," Lincoln asserted, "that is self-government; but when he governs himself, and also governs another man, that is more

A political cartoon by Louis Maurer depicting the 1860 presidential election as a baseball game, with candidates John Bell, Stephen Douglas, and John C. Breckinridge being bested by Lincoln.

than self-government—that is despotism." If all men are created equal, Lincoln said, "there can be no moral right in connection with one man's making a slave of another."

While Lincoln quoted Douglas as saying he didn't care "whether slavery is voted up or voted down," for Lincoln there was no question. "The difference between the Republican and the Democratic parties on the leading issue of this contest," declared Lincoln, "is, that the former consider slavery a moral, social and political wrong, while the latter do not."

And while it was Douglas, the better known politician, who drew the public and national journalists to the debates, it was Lincoln, then barely known outside his state, who made the everlasting impression on the people. "Who is this man that is replying to Douglas in your State?" an Eastern political figure asked an Illinois journalist. "Do you realize that no greater speeches have been made on public questions in the history of our country; that his knowledge of the subject is profound, his logic unanswerable, his style inimitable?"

When voters went to the polls that November, it was not a direct election. No one in November 1858 cast a vote for Lincoln or for Douglas. The US Constitution mandated that members of the US Senate were to be chosen by elected members of the state legislatures. In this contest, Lincoln and other Republicans won 53 percent of the popular vote statewide. But the congressional districts represented in the Illinois legislature were divided up in a way that favored the Democrats, who thus retained control, and the state legislature promptly reelected Douglas to the US Senate. It would be another half century before the Constitution was amended in 1912 to enable voters to directly elect US senators.

Once more, Lincoln's personal aspirations were dashed, but again he accepted the loss with dignity and grace, and his impressive and eloquent debate performances began to establish him as an important national figure. Days later, while "the emotions of defeat" were still "fresh" upon him, he wrote dozens of consoling letters to his supporters. Characteristically, it was he who comforted them rather than the other way around. "I expect the result of the election went hard with you," Lincoln wrote to a lifelong friend. "I have an abiding faith that we shall beat them in the long run. . . . I write merely to let you know that I am neither dead nor dying. Please give my respects to your good family, and all inquiring friends." The calm Lincoln exhibited was not simply to uplift his followers. Lincoln trusted that this was a temporary loss. In the antislavery struggle, he had found the great purpose that had thrust him back into public life, and that purpose, larger by far than his own sizable personal ambition, would hold him fast until he died. The antislavery fight not only would continue; it must continue until it was won.

Chapter Five

"We must settle this question now, whether in a free government the minority have the right to break up the government whenever they choose."

NEWS OF LINCOLN'S REPUTATION WAS RAPIDLY SPREADING across the country and drew the attention of Republican Party leaders in New York and New England. When a friend suggested that he might well be considered a strong presidential candidate in 1860, however, Lincoln resisted, noting that William Henry Seward, Salmon Chase, and other antislavery Republicans were more accomplished and "much better known." They were the men who had "carried this movement forward to its present status." Seward had been New York's youngest governor before his election to the Senate, where his impassioned speeches won an enthusiastic and loyal following among Northern liberals and marked him as the nation's most celebrated antislavery politician. Chase, now the first Republican governor of Ohio, had been the Senate leader in the fight against the passage of the Kansas-Nebraska Act and was one of the founders of the new Republican Party. Judge Edward Bates, a widely respected native Virginian who had moved to Missouri and joined the antislavery cause, had support from conservatives throughout the North and several Midwestern states.

Lincoln, having served just one term in Congress, losing two Senate contests, with only little formal education and no cache of national political contacts, knew his chances of winning the Republican presidential nomination were low. But still, he was persuaded by a small group of Republican politicians to throw his hat in the ring. "I admit the force of much of what you say, and admit that I am ambitious, and would like to be President," Lincoln told his longtime friend and supporter Jesse Fell.

From the start, Lincoln understood that the path to his nomination against three famous opponents required a lesser-known candidate as himself to have a combination of relentless determination, persuasiveness, and humility. He gained the goodwill of tens of thousands of fellow Republicans by speaking solely on behalf of the antislavery party and the Republican position of condemning slavery "as an immoral institution, a relic of barbarism." He positioned himself in the center, as a moderate, not as radical as Seward or Chase and not as conservative as Bates. Most Republicans of the time "thought that by confining slavery within its present boundaries, the institution would be placed on the road to eventual extinction . . . but most rejected a more radical stand that would associate them with abolitionism."

In dozens of rousing speeches, delivered in cities and towns throughout the

North, from Kansas, Missouri, and Ohio to New York, Connecticut, and Rhode Island, Lincoln never attacked his rivals, and he asked Republicans to put their differences aside and unite behind the movement that was their new party. Aware that beyond his home state he was not the first choice of any of the delegates, he said to his campaign managers, "Just tell everybody if they can't get their first love, I'm there. I'll be the second love."

As Lincoln's national reputation continued to swell, so his belief in his own chances improved. In all likelihood, he had been dreaming about being president long before he made his candidacy known. "No man knows," Lincoln said years later, "when the presidential grub gets to gnawing at him, just how deeply it will get until he has tried it." As the possibility of success became more likely, Lincoln intensified his efforts, working harder than all his opponents combined. Seward, confident that the nomination was his, traveled through Europe for eight months prior to the presidential nominating convention in Chicago. All the while, Lincoln worked daily, continuing to research and sharpen his speeches and delivery, keeping the ideas fresh with notes he had made and saved on stray pieces of paper.

As he crafted each speech, he would withdraw into a cocoon, finding a corner in the State Library or a back room or small chamber wherever he was speaking. There, he could be alone to focus his thoughts and feelings. At times, he used his closest friends as sounding boards, but the more he traveled the country, the more he relied upon his own perceptions of what he should say and exactly what it would take to win the nomination.

> where the nominee was chosen by the votes of the delegates in the room, and there was a lot of dealmaking in the convention hall to win over delegates. Today, conventions are largely ceremonial events, as delegates are set following each primary contest, and the winner of the nomination is usually determined before the convention. Once each party selects its nominee, the general election race begins between the nominees of the major parties; voting for the president occurs on Election Day in November, on the first Tuesday following the first Monday of the month.

At the invitation of the Young Men's Central Republican Union, Lincoln spoke at the Cooper Union school in New York, taking the position that the Republican Party's platform on the westward expansion of slavery was not revolutionary, but instead was consistent with the wishes of America's founders. "Let us have faith that right makes might, and in that faith, let us, to the end, dare to do our duty as we understand it," Lincoln said in what was the most carefully prepared and important speech of his career to date, and which helped his candidacy grow even stronger.

But even so, Lincoln himself took nothing for granted. Realizing that a successful bid would require the unanimous support of the Illinois delegation, he worked to bridge the divisions within the state party, openly asking for help from delegates representing different factions in the party. "I am not in a position where it would hurt much for me not to be nominated on the national ticket; but I am where it would hurt some for me to not get the Illinois delegates," he wrote to a politician in the northern part of the state. "Can you not help me in this matter, in your end of the vineyard?" When Illinois Republicans met ten days ahead of the national convention, they passed a resolution instructing the delegates to "vote as a unit" for Abraham Lincoln. By contrast, Salmon Chase did not lift a finger to ensure a united Ohio delegation, having mistakenly assumed that every delegate would automatically vote for him, given all he had done for the party and the state.

In the middle of May 1860, forty thousand visitors descended upon Chicago, drawn by the festive excitement surrounding the Republican National Convention, where Republican delegates from each state would cast ballots to nominate the man who would face the Democratic Party's nominee in November's general election. No team there worked harder than Lincoln's to round up votes. While some in Lincoln's circle had political ambitions of their own, "most of them," his ally Henry Whitney observed, worked "chiefly from love of the man, his lofty moral tone, his pure political morality."

When the delegates began voting, Seward was widely considered the front-runner, followed by Chase and Bates. There were other candidates too—a total of eight—and given the number, several rounds of balloting needed to take place to determine the victor. By the third round, the race had narrowed to Lincoln versus Seward. Tensions in the convention hall mounted as the balloting began. When Lincoln was just one and a half votes away from winning, a delegate from Ohio stood up and announced a switch of four votes to Lincoln. For a moment "a profound stillness" filled the hall, until Lincoln's supporters "rose to their feet applauding wildly, the ladies waving their handkerchiefs, the men waving and throwing up their hats by thousands, cheering again and again." To the surprise of many, Abraham Lincoln had emerged as the Republican nominee for president.

Over the years, people have debated the factors that led to Lincoln's victory in the Republican primary. Some say it was his moderate stance, not restricting slavery in states where it was already present, but promising to stop expansion in the Western territories. Others say luck played a role, because the convention was held in his home state of Illinois. In the end, however, his leadership skills should be credited for his success—his shrewd understanding of the politics, growing confidence in his own judgment and intuition, unmatched work ethic, his writing and eloquence in speaking, calm nature, and elevated ambition. He never allowed his personal motivations to overtake his kindheartedness or to change his commitment to the antislavery cause. While the delegates may not have recognized the true measure of Lincoln's leadership strengths, events would soon prove that they had chosen the best candidate to lead their new party to the White House in November against Lincoln's repeated rival, Democrat Stephen Douglas.

As Lincoln began his campaign to become president of the United States, he understood that his first task as the Republican nominee was to unite

A lithograph of Lincoln as a presidential candidate in 1860, by Leopold Grozelier and Thomas Hicks.

the candidates he had defeated into a single Republican movement. To that end, he wrote a personal letter to Chase humbly asking for his "especial assistance" in the campaign; he dispatched a close friend to St. Louis to ask Judge Bates to write a public letter on his behalf; and most important, he secured Seward's willingness to act as his chief supporter on the campaign trail. As was the campaign tradition of the time, Lincoln remained at home in Springfield throughout the campaign, meeting with supporters, politicians, and reporters there or at an office at the state capitol. Aware that anything he said or wrote would be taken out of context to inflame his opposition, he simply pointed to the Republican Party platform and his many published speeches when asked about an issue; these carefully crafted documents fully represented his positions on the central issues of the day.

By the fall of 1860, the slavery issue had smashed the Democratic Party much as it had shattered the Whigs, weakening Senator Douglas's chances of winning the presidency in November. Nonetheless, Lincoln understood that nothing must be left to chance. So Lincoln agreed, after much hesitation, to write and have published a short autobiography. While he refused to romanticize the extreme hardships of his frontier childhood, he supplied memories of building his log cabin and splitting

logs for the rail fence that surrounded its ten acres. Soon rails suppos-
edly split by young Lincoln began surfacing at public gatherings. The
image caught fire: rails appeared on campaign medals, in newspaper
cartoons, in campaign slogans and jingles. While Lincoln never claimed
he had split a particular rail presented to him with great fanfare, he
acknowledged that he had indeed been "a hired laborer, mauling rails, at
work on a flat boat, just what might happen to any man's son!" The story
of his life and his strenuous efforts to educate himself made Lincoln
into "a man of the people," the American dream personified.

On Election Day, Lincoln was understandably restless. Struggle had
been his birthright, hardship his expectation. By nine o'clock that night,
as vote tallies were relayed from distant states, Lincoln and a few friends
and advisers gathered at the telegraph office in Springfield's statehouse for immediate access to the returns. While Lincoln reclined on a
sofa, the telegraph tapped out good news all around. New England, the
Northwest, Indiana, and Pennsylvania had all come into the Republican
camp. When ten o'clock arrived, however, with no word from New York,
Lincoln grew fretful; he needed support from that state to win the presidency. "The news would come quick enough if it was good," he told his
cohorts, but if the news was bad, he was not anxious to receive it.

Soon after midnight, the returns from New York came in; Lincoln
had won the state! Celebrations began in earnest, for Lincoln's victory was now assured. Church bells rang. Cheers for "Old Abe" echoed
through the streets. Lincoln was jubilant, admitting that he was "a very
happy man . . . who could help being so under such circumstances?" He
raced home to tell Mary, who had been waiting anxiously all day. "Mary,
Mary," he cried out, "we are elected!"

Rising to the rare rank of president-elect was the culmination of an
evolving ambition that saw Lincoln grow from a twenty-three-year-old

who craved the opportunity to accomplish important deeds that would benefit his fellows to a fifty-two-year-old who now had the opportunity to do so. Yet he was keenly aware that the country was in a perilous time. Chaos was loose in the land, no longer limited to isolated acts of aggression or to one single state like Kansas. Chaos was engulfing the nation. Lincoln had found his mature voice at just the moment when the country was most desperately in need of the leadership that had been incubating in him.

On the night he won the election, he could not sleep. He made the decision that would define his presidency. To meet the terrible burden he faced, Lincoln would piece together the most unusual cabinet in American history, representing every faction of the new Republican Party—former Whigs, antislavery Democrats, and others, a combination of conservatives, moderates, and radicals, of hard-liners and conciliators. "I began at once to feel that I needed support," he later noted, "others to share with me the burden." Where his predecessor, President James Buchanan, had deliberately chosen like-minded men who would not question his authority, Lincoln created a team of independent, strong-minded men, all of whom were more experienced in public life, better educated, and more celebrated than he. In the top three positions, at the State Department, the Treasury, and the Justice Department, he placed his three chief rivals from the race for the Republican nomination—William Seward, Salmon Chase, and Edward Bates—who each thought he himself should have been president instead of the prairie lawyer from Illinois.

When asked why he was doing this, Lincoln's answer was simple: The country was in grave danger. These were the strongest and most able men in the country. He needed them by his side. Furthermore, Lincoln had developed over time a deep confidence in his leadership skills and felt that he would be able to join together this quarrelsome, personally ambitious, gifted, yet potentially dysfunctional group into an administrative family whose loyalty to the Union was unquestionable.

But by the time Lincoln was to take office on March 4, 1861, the house was not merely divided; the house was on fire. In the four months between his election and inauguration, seven Southern states—South Carolina, Mississippi, Florida, Alabama, Georgia, Louisiana, and Texas—had passed resolutions to secede from the Union to form the breakaway Confederate States of America. At a meeting in Montgomery, Alabama, representatives from these seven states formed a new government with a new constitution, selecting former Mississippi senator Jefferson Davis as provisional president of the Confederacy. Meanwhile, a growing hostility threatened to tear apart the Republican Party. On one side stood conciliators convinced that with the right compromises, the remaining slaveholding states could be kept in the Union; on the other, hard-liners who believed compromise would further inflame the unruly South.

From the start, Lincoln correctly identified the full weight of the challenge that secession posed to the continued existence of his country's communal life, its shared experiences, its memories, its role as a beacon of hope to the world at large. "We must settle this question now, whether in a free government the minority have the right to break up the government whenever they choose," Lincoln said. "If we fail it will go far to prove the incapability of the people to govern themselves." This was not merely a hypothetical question—there was truly no way to know if the Union would hold. The threat of civil war hung in the air.

On February 11, 1861, as Lincoln began his train journey from Illinois to New York to Philadelphia to the nation's capital for his inauguration, he bid farewell to friends gathered at the train station to see him off. "No one, not in my situation, can appreciate my feeling of sadness at this parting," he said. He had just returned from a difficult and emotional visit to Farmington, where he said goodbye to his beloved stepmother, Sarah, and visited his father's grave. "I now leave," he said to his friends, "not knowing when or whether ever, I may return."

Lincoln could not have imagined how true that statement might have been if private detective Allan Pinkerton, hired to guard Lincoln for the trip, hadn't stumbled upon a plot to kill the president-elect during his train journey. Pinkerton learned the attack was planned to occur during Lincoln's scheduled Maryland stop in Baltimore, a city full of Southern sympathizers. So he advised Lincoln to leave Philadelphia at once and pass through Baltimore on a night train ahead of schedule to confuse the conspirators. But Ward Lamon, who accompanied Lincoln on the trip, said Lincoln "flatly refused," because he had planned to meet with citizens and "raise a flag over Independence Hall in the morning, and to exhibit himself at Harrisburg in the afternoon."

Eventually Lincoln agreed to leave Philadelphia for Washington on the night train as soon as his event in Harrisburg was completed. Pinkerton insisted, against Mary's judgment, that she and their sons should remain behind and travel to Washington in the afternoon as scheduled.

Wearing a soft felt hat in place of his familiar stovepipe hat and hunching down to disguise his height, Lincoln secretly boarded a special car on the night train, accompanied by Lamon and Detective Pinkerton and his associate Kate Warne, known as America's first female detective. All other trains were to be "side-tracked" until Lincoln's had passed. All the telegraph wires were to be cut between Harrisburg and Washington until it was clear that Lincoln had arrived in the nation's capital.

At three thirty a.m., the train passed through Baltimore without a problem and proceeded straight to Washington. "At six o'clock," a relieved Lamon recalled, "the dome of the Capitol came in sight." It was a discouraging and ominous beginning for the new president. Though Lincoln arrived safely, he was criticized and ridiculed in the press for the manner in which he had "crept into Washington." Later, considering the trials and tensions endured during his presidential transition and his first taxing weeks in office, Lincoln confessed to a friend: "They were so great that could I have anticipated them, I would not have believed it possible to survive them."

On the day of Lincoln's inauguration, the outgoing president, James Buchanan, of whom Lincoln had been fiercely critical, met Lincoln at the Willard Hotel in Washington, DC. As they moved arm in arm toward the open carriage—against the advice of Lincoln's advisers—the Marine Band played "Hail to the Chief." The carriage made its way up Pennsylvania Avenue, while cheering crowds and hundreds of dignitaries mingled uneasily with the hundreds of troops put in place to guard against an attempted assassination. Sharpshooters looked down from windows and rooftops. Troops mounted on horses were placed strategically throughout the entire route.

The appearance of Lincoln on the square platform constructed outside the Capitol building was met with loud cheers from more than thirty thousand spectators—the largest inauguration crowd the city had ever

---

Who was Kate Warne?

It is likely that detectives are known as "private eyes" because of Allan Pinkerton. Around 1850, Pinkerton, a Scottish immigrant, created America's first detective agency, with a focus on catching train robbers, and his agency's logo was that of a large, open eye.

In 1856, Kate Warne, a twenty-three-year-old widow, convinced Pinkerton to hire her as the country's first woman private detective by noting that she would have access to places where only women could enter, and that she would be able to coax out of them details and gossip that could be crucial to the agency's intelligence-gathering work. Pinkerton was so impressed by her and her work that he later created the Female Detective Bureau for her to lead.

To learn of and try to stop the plot to assassinate Lincoln ahead of his inauguration, Warne posed as an anti-Lincoln Southerner and befriended the wives and sisters of those planning to kill Lincoln. Then, for the train ride to Washington, Lincoln wore a disguise and pretended to be gravely ill, and Warne posed as his sister and caregiver, convincing the train conductor to allow her and her "brother" to have an entire train car to themselves. Warne remained alert all night until they arrived safely in the nation's capital. Her sleepless vigilance inspired the slogan of Pinkerton's National Detective Agency—"We Never Sleep."

seen. Mary sat behind her husband, their sons beside her. In the front row, along with Lincoln, sat soon-to-be-ex-President Buchanan, Senator Douglas, and Supreme Court Chief Justice Taney. Noting Lincoln's uncertainty as to where to place his stovepipe hat as he began to juggle it with his notes, Senator Douglas, the man Lincoln had defeated just a few months earlier, reached over, took the hat, and placed it on his own lap.

Lincoln then delivered his inaugural address, which included a direct appeal to the South to avoid a civil war. "In your hands, my dissatisfied fellow countrymen, and not in mine, is the momentous issue of civil war. The government will not assail you. You can have no conflict, without being yourselves the aggressors." He closed with the stirring assurance that "We are not enemies, but friends. We must not be enemies. Though passion may have strained, it must not break our bonds of affection. The mystic chords of memory, stretching from every battle-field, and patriot grave, to every living heart and hearthstone, all over this broad land, will yet swell the chorus of the Union, when again touched, as surely as they will be, by the better angels of our nature."

At the end of the address, Chief Justice Taney walked slowly to the table. The Bible was opened, and Abraham Lincoln was sworn in as the sixteenth president of the United States.

Chapter Six

*"If my name ever goes into history it will be for this act,
and my whole soul is in it."*

THE NEWS OF LINCOLN'S ELECTION had at first provided some desperately needed hope to abolitionist leaders like Frederick Douglass. Ultimately, though, they were disappointed and angered by what they considered an appeasing tone toward enslavers. Two major claims had run through every public statement Lincoln had made since he reentered public life in 1854: no extension of slavery into new US territories and no interference with slavery where it already existed. When Douglass read for himself Lincoln's inaugural address, beginning with the president's declaration that he had "no lawful power to interfere with slavery in the States" and, worse still, no "inclination" to do so, Douglass found little reason for optimism and was disgusted by what he described as Lincoln's impulse to beg and grovel "before the foul and withering curse of slavery."

Lincoln's inaugural address had not soothed or satisfied the breakaway states either. A month after Lincoln took the oath of office, Confederate forces fired their first shots at Fort Sumter on April 12, 1861, and ignited the Civil War, a wrenching conflict that would be the bloodiest in the nation's history. And it was never clear that the Union would win. Quite the contrary, over the course of the first year, Union forces lost one major battle after another. Confederate forces successfully repelled them throughout the South, inching their way northward, and leaving Washington, DC, vulnerable to attack. In the last week of June 1862, over a year into the war, Union forces suffered a crushing defeat. In a series of brutal battles, Confederate General Robert E. Lee's forces triumphantly defended against a Union attack on the Confederate capital at Richmond, Virginia, driving the Union army into retreat, leaving nearly sixteen thousand dead, captured, or wounded.

"Things had gone from bad to worse," Lincoln recalled of that midsummer, "until I felt that we had reached the end of our rope on the plan of operations we had been pursuing; that we had played our last card and must change our tactics."

In addition to the pressures of the war, Lincoln and his family were deep in mourning. A few months earlier, in February 1862, his eleven-year-old son Willie had died of typhoid fever after battling the illness for several weeks. Willie's younger brother, Tad, had also fallen sick, and Lincoln had spent as much time with his sons as possible. "This is the hardest trial of my life," Lincoln said. Several times during the long nights Tad would awaken and call for his father. "The moment [the president] heard Taddie's voice he was at his side." Tad, thankfully, survived. But Lincoln also worried about Mary, who remained in her bed, unable to cope with daily life.

Outwardly, the president appeared to handle Willie's death better than his wife. He had important work to engage him every hour of the day. He was surrounded by dozens of officials who needed him to discuss plans, make decisions, and communicate them. He also had been in a period of religious reflection for some time, beginning with his son Edward's death twelve years before, and attended services regularly at New York Avenue Presbyterian Church in Washington, DC. Yet, despite a more awakened spirituality and his relentless duties, Lincoln suffered an excruciating sense of loss. Ten months later, when he wrote to a young woman shortly after her father's battlefield death, he closed with the consolation of remembrance. In time, he promised her, "the memory of your dear Father, instead of an agony, will yet be a sad sweet feeling in your heart, of a purer, and holier sort than you have known before." Now, even more than ever before, Lincoln was able to identify in a profound and personal way with the sorrows of families who had lost their loved ones in the war and with the soldiers who were waging it.

Lincoln resolved to visit the troops in July of 1862 when the weakened Union army arrived back at its Virginia base at Harrison's Landing. He would comfort the wounded, talk with them in small groups, bolster their morale, and sustain his own spirits. Equally important, Lincoln asked his soldiers questions—which led to a major change in his thoughts about the role of slavery in the war. From the beginning of the struggle, Lincoln had stressed that the North was fighting solely to preserve the Union, not to interfere with slavery. Though he had long despised slavery, he felt constrained by the Constitution, which protected the institution of slavery in states where it already existed.

Through firsthand meetings with commanders and soldiers, however, Lincoln came to realize that Confederate forces were using enslaved people to support their war efforts—to dig trenches and build fortifications for the Confederate army. Enslaved people served as carriage drivers, cooks, waiters, and hospital attendants. On the home front, they tilled fields, raised crops, and picked cotton. The labor of enslaved people kept farms and plantations in operation, freeing Confederate soldiers to fight. If the rebels were stripped of the people they enslaved, the struggling North would thus gain a desperately needed military advantage.

"In the present civil war it is quite possible that God's purpose is something different from the purpose of either party," Lincoln wrote in his personal papers in September 1862. "[God] could have either saved or destroyed the Union without a human contest. Yet the contest began. And, having begun He could give the final victory to either side any day. Yet the contest proceeds." What would shift the balance of the contest? As Lincoln began to survey the darkening landscape of the war and think through a new strategy regarding abolishing slavery, he considered issuing an emancipation order to free enslaved people in any state that had broken away from the Union.

Lincoln believed the oath of office he had taken as president bound him to protect and defend the Constitution, which allowed slavery where it already existed. But, upon further thought, in his role as commander in chief of the United States Armed Forces, he believed he had found another path forward. By breaking away from and warring with the Union, the South had broken faith with the Constitution, making them traitors. Given the advantage enslaved people provided the Confederacy, a proclamation freeing enslaved people in any state that had seceded from the Union could be considered "a military necessity absolutely essential for the salvation of the Union." Emancipating enslaved people,

How does the Constitution work?

Together, the Declaration of Independence and the US Constitution are the two most important and enduring documents in our nation's history. In 1789, the Constitution created a federal government and determined its relationship with the citizens of the country. Its first three words—"We the People"—affirm that the government of the United States exists to serve its citizens and are the foundation upon which the entire Constitution depends, as it separates the government's powers into three branches to establish checks and balances for each branch over the other two: the legislative branch, which makes the laws; the executive branch, which executes, or carries out, the laws; and the judicial branch, which interprets the laws.

The founders did put into place a process by which the Constitution may be amended, and in the past 225 years, twenty-seven amendments have been added. The first ten amendments constitute the Bill of Rights. With the adoption of the Thirteenth Amendment, the United States found a final constitutional solution to the issue of slavery, and the Fourteenth and Fifteenth Amendments soon followed; this trio of Civil War amendments greatly expanded the civil rights of Americans.

"otherwise unconstitutional," might therefore become a lawful action and could help save the Union. The constitutional protection of slavery could be canceled by the constitutionally warranted war powers of the commander in chief. Thus, Abraham Lincoln was able to come to the decision that would free enslaved people, as well as define both his presidency and his place in history.

The life Lincoln had led, marked by both struggle and steadfastness, provided the best preparation for the challenges the country faced. His temperament was stamped with melancholy but lacked pessimism and was brightened by enormous wit and charm. He was humble and true and also confident in his capacity to lead. Most of all, he had a mind tempered by failure, a mind able to turn the appalling suffering of war into a sweeping story that would provide direction, purpose, and lasting inspiration. Abraham Lincoln's Emancipation Proclamation to free enslaved people in states that had broken away from the Union demonstrates how the man met the moment, a hallmark of great leadership.

When on September 17, 1862, General Robert E. Lee and his Army of Northern Virginia attempted to take the war North, they were forced by the Union army to retreat. It was at this point that President Lincoln made public his plans for the Emancipation Proclamation, explaining to his cabinet: "When the rebel army was at Frederick, I determined, as soon as it should be driven out of Maryland, to issue a Proclamation of Emancipation. . . . I made the promise to myself, and . . . to my Maker. The rebel army is now driven out, and I am going to fulfill that promise. . . . God had decided this question in favor of the slaves."

The scope of the proclamation, which was unveiled to the public on September 22, 1862, and would be put into practice in January 1863, was stunning. Eighty words in just one sentence would replace laws about property rights and slavery that had governed policy in the United States for nearly three quarters of a century: "All persons held as slaves within any state or states," that did not accept the US Constitution "shall then, thenceforward and forever, be free."

For the first time, a president tied Union and slavery into a single, transformative, moral force. Some three and a half million Black people in the South who had lived enslaved for generations were promised freedom.

But not all of Lincoln's bold efforts were similarly worthy. Though President Lincoln's initial opposition to the institution of slavery grew ever stronger over the years, as his views on race evolved, he did not always see Black people as equal to whites. And while he worked toward emancipation for all enslaved people, believing slavery was morally and politically wrong, he also proposed the concept of colonization, which would involve sending freed Black Americans to a location outside the United States—to Liberia or Central America—as the solution to their perceived difficulty in integrating into US society. He shared this belief with Henry Clay, a founder of the American Colonization Society, and former president Thomas Jefferson, a supporter of the movement.

On August 14, 1862, during the period in which he was preparing the proclamation, Lincoln held the first meeting of Black leaders at the White House so he could make his case for a voluntary emigration of Black Americans to a different country. "Your race suffer very greatly, many of them by living among us, while ours suffer from your presence," he told the five men of his long-held belief. "In a word we suffer on each side. If this is admitted, it affords a reason at least why we should be separated." His proposal was received with mixed results. However, Frederick Douglass, who was not invited to the meeting, objected vehemently, arguing that Black Americans were entitled to equality in their own country of origin, the United States. "There is no sentiment more universally entertained, nor more firmly held by the free colored people of the United States, than that this is their 'own, their native land,' and that here (for good or for evil) their destiny is to be wrought out," Douglass wrote in a published article, "The Colonization Scheme." "There is not now, there has never been, and we think there never will be, any general desire on the part of our people, to emigrate from this land to any other." Later that year, Lincoln made another case for colonization during his second annual message to Congress on December 1, 1862, during which he proposed a constitutional amendment to colonize Black Americans and provide for them better lives in "their long-lost fatherland," where they would have access to homes and schools. Abolitionists, both Black and white, were upset at the suggestion, believing too that formerly enslaved Black people should and could integrate into the US. Lincoln eventually realized that Black Americans had a legitimate and hard-fought claim to remain in the United States. Once the Emancipation Proclamation went into effect, he abandoned all efforts at colonization and trained his focus on freedom for the enslaved and keeping the Union whole.

As the first of January 1863 drew near, an "ill wind" of discontent about the Emancipation Proclamation swept through the North. Critics predicted that it would trigger race wars in the South, cause Union officers to resign their commands, and prompt one hundred thousand men to lay down their arms. The prospect of emancipation threatened to fracture the brittle coalition that had held Republicans and Union Democrats together.

Whether the president would follow through on his September pledge to activate his proclamation on New Year's Day was met with a "general air of doubt" across the land. "Will Lincoln's backbone carry him through?" wondered one skeptic. "Nobody knows." But those who knew Lincoln best would not even have posed the question. All through his life, the honor and weight of his word had been the "chief gem" of his character. His once-broken engagement to Mary had contributed to a life-threatening depression, as had his failure to deliver on his pledge to bring Illinois an economic boom through public works projects. His ability to make good on his promises, "his resolves," had been central to his healing and the resurrection of his confidence and career. Ever since, as a family man, friend, lawyer, and politician, he had reflected carefully before setting forth opinions and making promises. That he would hold firm his pledge to issue the proclamation was never in question. "My word is out," Lincoln told a Massachusetts congressman, "and I can't take it back."

Frederick Douglass had been fiercely critical of Lincoln's delay in issuing the Emancipation Proclamation, but he knew Lincoln's character and the strength of his word better than most, even though the two had not met in person. "Abraham Lincoln may be slow," he wrote, "but Abraham Lincoln is not the man to reconsider, retract and contradict words and purposes solemnly proclaimed over his official signature." To answer those who asked if Lincoln would back down, Douglass gave a forceful no. "Abraham Lincoln will take no step backward," Douglass insisted. "If he has taught us to confide in nothing else, he has taught us to confide in his word."

As the doors of the White House opened at noon for the traditional New Year's Day reception to ring in the year 1863, the general public was ushered in. For three hours, Lincoln stood in the Blue Room, "serene and even smiling," shaking hands with more than one thousand citizens, even though, as one reporter later noted, "his eyes were with his thoughts, and they were far away." Later that afternoon, he was scheduled to sign the Emancipation Proclamation.

The day before, Lincoln had gathered his cabinet for a final reading of the proclamation. The version he presented differed in one major aspect from the September draft. It included a new section declaring that the Union army would begin recruiting Black soldiers.

The signing took place in a simple ceremony attended by only a dozen people, including Secretary of State Seward and his son Fred. As the parchment paper was placed before the president, Fred Seward recalled, Lincoln "dipped his pen in the ink, and then, holding it a moment above the sheet, seemed to hesitate." But then he began to speak in a forceful manner: "I never, in my life felt more certain that I was doing right, than I do in signing this paper," Lincoln said. "If my name ever goes into history it will be for this act, and my whole soul is in it." His arm was "stiff and numb" from shaking hands, however, and he worried that his signature would look shaky, as if he had doubts about this decision. "Now, this signature is one that will be closely examined, and if they find my hand trembled, they will say 'he had some compunctions.'" So he waited for several minutes until he took up the pen once more and signed with an "unusually bold, clear, and firm" hand.

Across New England, immense crowds had gathered since early morning at churches, reception halls, and theaters to await the news that the president had signed the proclamation. In Boston's Tremont Temple and the nearby Music Hall, more than six thousand people waited. Speakers—including Frederick Douglass, abolitionist writers Ralph Waldo Emerson and Harriet Beecher Stowe, and future Supreme Court Associate Justice Oliver Wendell Holmes—addressed the large crowd as the day wore on and the suspense escalated. A "visible shadow" fell upon the crowd when it reached ten o'clock in the evening and still no word had arrived. Finally, a man raced through the crowd. "It is coming! It is on the wires!" Douglass recorded the "wild and grand" reaction, the "Joy and gladness," the "sobs and tears," and then the singing—"Glory Hallelujah"—that united them until the first light of dawn.

That night's jubilation was not shared by most white people in the states that bordered the South nor, for that matter, in much of the North. And yet he was certain, Lincoln told the swarm of doubters, that the timing was right for this moral reframing of the war. "It is my conviction that, had the proclamation been issued even six months earlier than it was, public sentiment would not have sustained it," Lincoln later said. He had carefully marked "this great revolution in public sentiment slowly but surely progressing." Lincoln was politically astute, an intuitive and careful listener, who studied the shifting opinions of his cabinet members, the emotions expressed in newspaper editorials, the tone of conversations among people in the North, and, most centrally, the opinions of Union troops. Although Lincoln knew opposition would be fierce when the proclamation was initiated, he judged that resistance would not be strong enough "to defeat the purpose." A determined stillness came upon Lincoln as he enacted the plan, sure that his lengthy decision-making process had yielded the right course for a country that would be ready and willing to follow him. "I have often wished that I was a more devout man than I am," he later wrote in remarks to be delivered at Baltimore Presbyterian Synod. "Nevertheless, amid the greatest difficulties of my Administration, when I could not see any other resort, I would place my whole reliance in God, knowing that all would go well, and that He would decide for the right."

As the war continued to drag on and the country grew weary, Lincoln drew strength from his moral victory. Where others saw the death of the founders' experiment, he saw the birth of a new freedom. Under Lincoln's leadership, recruitments to the army picked up, and Congress passed all the war-related bills the White House needed.

The recruitment and enlistment of Black soldiers drove home the transformative power of the Emancipation Proclamation. Black men responded in thunder to the enlistment call, signing up by the tens of thousands—including two sons of Frederick Douglass. Douglass argued that once a Black man served in the armed forces, "there is no power on the earth or under the earth which can deny that he has earned the right of citizenship."

This initial wave of enthusiasm soon faded, however, when the Black soldiers learned they would not receive pay equal to white soldiers; likewise they would neither earn a bonus for enlisting nor be eligible to become officers. Douglass decided to call directly upon Lincoln to explain why he could no longer in good conscience persuade soldiers to enlist.

Arriving at the White House and finding a large crowd assembled in the hallway, Douglass expected to wait hours before meeting for the first time with President Lincoln. But only minutes after presenting his calling card, Douglass was ushered into Lincoln's office. "I was never more quickly or more completely put at ease," Douglass recalled of that first meeting. As Douglass described the problem, Lincoln listened "with earnest attention and with very apparent sympathy." Lincoln explained that when Congress passed the bill allowing Black men to be soldiers, they put off the question of Black equality in order to gain the support of many white lawmakers. The discriminatory policy, Lincoln now agreed, was wrong and impractical. It would need to change to transform the war into a cause worth fighting for. He also said that he would agree to promote any Black soldier to the rank of officer at the recommendation of his secretary of war.

At this initial meeting a relationship of trust and respect was fostered between Lincoln and Douglass, which would prove crucial in the months and years ahead. "He treated me as a man, he did not let me feel for a moment that there was any difference in the color of our skins!" Douglass later said. "I am satisfied now that he is doing all that circumstances will allow him to do." Eventually, Congress eliminated

the discriminatory wage policy, and nearly two hundred thousand Black troops supported the Union war effort and fought with striking gallantry. Their valor changed the prejudices of white soldiers.

A year later, in the summer of 1864, Lincoln was running for reelection, the war had been raging for more than three years, and hundreds of thousands had died. The public appetite for continued conflict was shrinking. Lincoln turned to Douglass for advice, and the two met again on August 19, 1864. In a conversation that Douglass later shared, Lincoln explained the pressure he was under to set up peace talks with the South on the basis of restoring the Union, leaving emancipation for a later time.

Lincoln had thought the publication of his Emancipation Proclamation would have prompted enslaved people to leave the South, but, he noted with disappointment, "the slaves are not coming so rapidly and so numerously to us as I had hoped." Douglass suggested "the slaveholders knew how to keep such things from their slaves, and probably very few knew of his proclamation." So Lincoln proposed that the federal government might pay for an organized "band of scouts," made up of Black men who would "go into the rebel states, beyond the lines of our Armies, and carry the news of emancipation, and urge the slaves to come within our boundaries." Douglass promised to consult with leaders in the Black community about the possibility of enacting such a plan, and the meeting lifted Lincoln's spirits and strengthened his resolve. Lincoln accepted that he might lose reelection but declared that if he abandoned his commitment to the twin goals of Union and freedom, he "should be damned in time & in eternity."

This was the true mark of a leader. This second election mattered more to him than even his first because reelection would show that voters approved of the work his administration had done. His ambition for the cause and for the greater good overrode his ambition for himself.

And then within days came the stunning news that the Union forces had overrun Atlanta. "Atlanta is ours," heralded the *New York Times*, signaling that the arms and ammunition factories, the machine shops, the wagons, ambulances, harnesses, shoes, and clothing, which had all been accumulated at Atlanta, "are ours now." The end of war finally seemed within reach.

On Election Day 1864, Lincoln won a decisive victory. What pleased him most was the overwhelming support he received from the soldiers, who voted with their hearts for the president they loved and the twin causes of Union and emancipation that they were fighting for together.

On March 4, 1865, Lincoln delivered his second inaugural address, which was not the triumphant message the crowd was expecting. In keeping with his lifelong tendency to see all sides of the most difficult situations, Lincoln urged a more sympathetic understanding of the nation's citizens of the South. There were no unbridgeable differences, he insisted: "Both read the same Bible, and pray to the same God. . . . Let us judge not that we be not judged. The prayers of both could not be answered; that of neither has been answered fully."

And then drawing upon the rare wisdom of a temperament that consistently displayed

Long ABRAHAM LINCOLN a Little Longer.

A cartoon from 1864 showing famously tall Lincoln as being even taller after his reelection.

uncommon generosity toward those who opposed him, Lincoln issued his historic plea to all citizens of the land: "With malice toward none; with charity for all . . . let us strive on to finish the work we are in; to bind up the nation's wounds . . . to do all which may achieve and cherish a just, and a lasting peace, among ourselves, and with all nations."

The oath of office was administered by Chief Justice Salmon Chase, who Lincoln had appointed to the Supreme Court, and the crowd went wild, cheering loudly, the artillery firing a round of salutes, the band playing, and the peaceful ceremony that had become a hallmark of our democracy drew to a close.

That evening, as the gates of the White House were opened for a public reception attended by the largest crowd that had been there to date, the president tirelessly shook the hands of the more than five thousand people who came to show their respect and admiration. It was estimated that Lincoln shook the hands of one hundred people every four minutes.

But when Frederick Douglass arrived at the White House, he was stopped at the door by two policemen, who he said "took me rudely by the arm and ordered me to stand back, for their directions were to admit no persons of my color." Douglass assured the officers "there must be some mistake, for no such order could have emanated from President Lincoln; and that if he knew I was at the door he would desire my admission." His assertion was later confirmed when word came from the president to let Douglass in. "I walked into the spacious East Room, amid a scene of elegance such as in this country I had never before witnessed." Douglass had no difficulty spotting Lincoln, who stood "like a mountain pine high above the others," he recalled, "and in grand simplicity, and home-like beauty. Recognizing me, even before I reached him, he exclaimed, so that all around could hear him, 'I am glad to see you. I saw you in the crowd to-day, listening to my inaugural address; how did you like it?'" Douglass was embarrassed to detain the president in conversation when there were "thousands waiting to shake hands," but Lincoln insisted: "There is no man in the country whose opinion I value more than yours. I want to know what you think of it?"

For a moment these two remarkable men stood together amid the sea of faces. Lincoln knew that Douglass would speak his mind, just as he always had. "That was a sacred effort," Douglass finally was able to tell Lincoln. "I'm glad you liked it!" Lincoln replied as his face lit up with delight.

Theodore Roosevelt

Chapter Seven

"I'll make my body."

THEODORE "TEEDIE" ROOSEVELT WAS A NERVOUS, unhealthy, fragile child, whose boyhood was shaped by terrifying attacks of bronchial asthma. "Nobody seemed to think I would live," Roosevelt later recalled. Usually coming on in the middle of the night, these attacks made him feel like he was suffocating or drowning. When his father, Theodore Sr., known as Thee, would hear his young son coughing, wheezing, and struggling for breath, he would rush into Teedie's bedroom, scoop him up, and walk him around the house for hours—sometimes holding the child's head out an open window—until he could breathe and fall back asleep. If this didn't work, Thee would wrap the gasping child in a blanket and call for their servants to bring the horse and carriage around so he could take him out into the fresh air. Thee would drive the horse at a good clip through the gaslit streets, believing that the cool night winds would stir the child's lungs. "My father—he got me breath, he got me lungs, strength—life."

While asthma weakened young Roosevelt's body, it spurred the development of an already bright mind. "From the very fact that he was not able originally to enter into the most vigorous activities, he was always reading or writing," his younger sister, Corinne, recalled, and with a most unusual power of concentration. Under the guiding eye of his father, who encouraged his son's curiosity and intellectual and spiritual development, Teedie became a ferocious reader and storyteller, transporting himself into the lives of the adventurous heroes he most admired—men with extraordinary bodily strength, who were fearless in battle, explorers in Africa, hunters living on the edge of the wilderness. When asked years later whether he knew the characters in James Fenimore Cooper's Leatherstocking Tales, he laughed: "Do I know them? I have bunked with them and eaten with them, and I know their strengths and weaknesses."

Born in New York City in 1858 to a prominent and wealthy family, young Roosevelt read more broadly and had more access to books, newspapers, and magazines than most children of the era. He had only to pick a volume from the shelves of the vast library in his family's home or express interest in a particular book, and it would magically appear. Books became for him "the greatest of companions," and every day for the rest of his life, he set aside time for reading—at a minimum snatching moments while waiting for meals, between visitors, or lying in bed before sleep. During one family vacation, eleven-year-old Teedie proudly reported that he and his siblings had read fifty novels! Reading was valued by Teedie's father, and he read aloud to his children in the evenings after dinner. He spiced learning with family games and competitions and organized amateur plays for the children, urging them to recite poetry and encouraging them to follow their particular interests. His mother, Martha, known as Mittie, nicknamed Teedie her Butterfly and constantly entertained him with stories of "noble-hearted aristocrats who fought courageously for high ideals."

Above all, Roosevelt's father, who was greatly admired by his namesake son, shared principles of duty, ethics, and morality through stories, fables, and sayings, and instilled in Teedie a "hard work" ethic that he taught by example, along with a commitment to their religious faith. The family regularly attended the First Presbyterian Church, and Teedie's father put an emphasis on religion as service to others, and this applied to his devout patriotism. The elder Roosevelt, even though born into vast privilege too, worked hard in the family business of plate-glass importing and was a noted philanthropist, involved in a variety of charity work, including the Society of the Prevention of Cruelty to Children and a Newsboys' Lodging House.

Teedie Roosevelt at age eleven.

He was a founder of the American Museum of Natural History, the Metropolitan Museum of Art, and the New York Orthopedic Hospital.

Through his father's example, Teedie came to believe that anyone could be successful with ambition and hard, sustained work. However, his own achievements were aided by a remarkable mental energy and an extraordinary memory. When he talked about books he had read years before, the pages would appear before him, as if he were able to read them anew with his mind's eye. It seemed as if he could "remember everything he read," a friend marveled; he had only to read something once, and it was his forever, allowing him to recall not only whole passages but the feelings evoked in him when he first encountered them.

Due to Teedie's shaky health, his parents determined he should be schooled at home, which was isolating at the time and prevented him from developing relationships with boys his own age. He and his beloved older sister, Anna, nicknamed Bamie; younger sister, Corinne; and younger brother, Elliott, all of whom suffered from a range of serious physical ailments, were taught reading, writing, and arithmetic by tutors at home. Their playmates were mainly one another and members of their extended family, along with a few outside friends, all from the same wealthy class. Within this small circle of children, Teedie occupied the center as an "unquestioned leader," organizing their play, directing their games, entertaining the group with his talent for telling stories drawn from both his imagination and the many books he had read. "I can see him now struggling with the effort to breathe," Corinne recalled, as he told them stories that "continued from week to week, or even from month to month."

The privileged and unconventional Roosevelt family education extended beyond the boundaries of their winter and summer homes to include two separate, yearlong journeys abroad—the first to Europe, the second to the Middle East and Africa. The only downside of these trips for Teedie was that he would be away from his best friend, Edith Carow. As a five-year-old, Edith had joined the family's home school. Together, the Roosevelt siblings and Edith watched from the family's New York apartment as President Lincoln's funeral procession passed through lower Fifth Avenue in Manhattan. In the summers, Edith had been a frequent guest at the family's Long Island estate. There, she and young Theodore had become inseparable, discovering a first love of literature and nature, riding trails on horseback, and sailing in the bay. As Teedie was setting off with his family for their tour of Europe when he was ten years old, he broke down in tears at the thought of leaving eight-year-old Edith behind. She proved his most faithful pen pal over the long course of the trip, and he had plenty of highlights to share with her upon his return.

During all their travels, the Roosevelts stayed in exclusive hotels and inns, tents, and private homes. They spent two months in Rome, three weeks in Greece, two weeks in Lebanon, three weeks in Palestine, and an entire winter in Egypt. And always at night, Thee—attentive father, mentor, minister, and tour guide—would read aloud the poetry, history, and literature of the region they were visiting. On a later trip to Dresden, they lived for several months with a German family. Thee had made arrangements to hire the host's daughter to immerse the children in the German language, literature, music, and art. Teedie was so intrigued with his lessons, which lasted six hours of the day, that he pleaded to extend them further. "And of course," his younger brother, Elliott, complained, "I could not be left behind so we are working harder than ever in our lives."

By the age of ten, Teedie had developed a curiosity and passion for nature and the ambition to become a famous ornithologist like John James Audubon. As he roamed the woodland trails surrounding his family's summer retreats, searching for freedom to clear his lungs, he began to observe birds, listening to their songs, noticing their various shapes and plumage. When he was fitted with glasses to correct his severe nearsightedness, he was all the more astounded by what he saw. "I had no idea," he later said, "how beautiful the world was until I got those spectacles." He collected bugs, insects, and reptiles, which he kept in his dresser drawers. Noting his son's obsession with animals, Thee bought him a collection of books on natural history and provided private taxidermy lessons with one of Audubon's assistants, who taught

---

Where can you see young Theodore's museum today?

New York City's American Museum of Natural History is featured in the *Night at the Museum* movies. The real museum includes several memorials to Theodore Roosevelt: the grand entrance, the park that surrounds the museum, the rotunda, and the Theodore Roosevelt Memorial Hall. The markers at the museum honor Roosevelt's lifelong devotion to the natural world and wild places, from when he was a young boy through college and to the end of his life, when he explored remote habitats in Africa and Brazil. As president, Theodore Roosevelt conserved and protected 230 million acres of land throughout the country, creating parks and nature preserves. The museum, cofounded by his father, also contains some of the specimens young Theodore donated from his bedroom "museum." His collection included the skull of a seal acquired from a fishmonger neighbor of the family's and also birds' nests, insects, and mouse skeletons. "You can learn more about nature and life in the Museum than in all the books and schools in the world," Theodore Roosevelt told his young cousin Franklin Roosevelt.

him how to stuff and preserve dead animals. He applied that same keen focus toward skinning, dissecting, and mounting hundreds of carefully labeled specimens that he assembled in what he proudly called the Roosevelt Museum of Natural History. Oblivious to the mess he created in the bedroom—containers filled with the smelly, rotting remains of dissected creatures stood in every corner—he drove his brother, Elliott, to beg for a separate room.

But Teedie's chronic asthma required more and more days of bed rest. Thee worried that without physical activity Teedie's weak lungs would continue to worsen and that he would lose all physical ability, but Thee also believed that this outcome was not inevitable. His father said to him, "Theodore, you have the mind but not the body, and without the help of the body the mind cannot go as far as it should. You must make your body. It is hard drudgery to make one's body, but I know you will do it." Teedie responded enthusiastically, promising his father, "I'll make my body."

Thee had a fully equipped gymnasium built on their back porch and worked with his son to lift weights and pull himself up on horizontal bars, slowly, ever so slowly, expanding his physical capabilities and building the strength of his body. But change does not happen overnight, and the following summer, while traveling alone on a stagecoach to Moosehead Lake in the north woods of Maine, he met the fists of two bullies. They saw in Teedie a "victim," he remembered years later, and they "proceeded to make life miserable for me." Finding he was unable to fight back, he resolved that he would "not again be put in such a helpless position." When he told his father he wanted to learn how to box, Thee hired an ex-prizefighter to train his son.

Even when he began studying for Harvard University's entrance examinations, he would work long hours every day, focused on Latin, Greek, literature, history, science, and mathematics, completing in two years what normally took three years of preparation. His ability to concentrate, one friend recalled, was such that "the house might fall about

What were the social reform movements of Roosevelt's era?

Early American reform movements focused on promoting social justice and improving the human condition, including the antislavery movement, the temperance movement to outlaw alcohol, and women's suffrage to gain women the right to vote. Later social movements developed in response to America's Industrial Revolution, which greatly impacted the safety, health, and economic well-being of US citizens in the years leading up to and especially after the Civil War.

The invention of new machines spurred the construction of factories and mills to manufacture many goods quickly—shirts, stockings, shoes—that were previously made by artisans by hand. Operating the machines in these factories required masses of workers, and the population of cities exploded with immigrants, mainly from Europe, along with people who moved from the countryside to the cities for jobs. Gradually, fewer and fewer people were employed on farms, where their lives were ruled only by the changing seasons. Gone were the days when workers and their bosses came from the same community and knew each other personally. Now, men, women, and children worked around the clock in sometimes dangerous workplaces for little pay, while many absentee business owners became wealthy. Businesses were

his head," and "he would not be diverted." When given an assignment, he rarely waited until the last moment. He regarded procrastination as a sin. Preparing ahead, he recognized, freed him from anxiety—a habit of mind that would set an example for his colleagues in the years ahead. Easily passing all eight examinations, he was admitted to Harvard, eager to leave his mark on the world, though not knowing what form it would take.

While he was more than intellectually prepared for his studies at Harvard, Theodore lacked the social skills of many of his fellow students, for he had not been in a regular school environment and had not developed friendships outside his tight circle of family friends. One classmate remembered him as "studious, ambitious, eccentric—not the sort to appeal at first." Little wonder! The shelves in his room were filled with dead lizards and stuffed birds. He was forceful, passionate, and arrogant, often interrupting class in order to bombard professors with objections and questions and continuing those passionate discussions with his fellow students into the hallways. One classmate who witnessed Theodore arguing with two freshmen in the corridor remarked, "I was struck by the earnestness with which he was setting forth some point to the other two. He emphasized his points by vigorous movements of the head, and by striking his right fist into his left palm." At a time when it was trendy to act aloof, his overenthusiastic greetings from halfway across the Yard were generally considered in poor taste. Another classmate observed, "When it was not considered good form to move at more than a walk, Roosevelt was always running." Other students considered him straitlaced, and he looked down upon students who drank or smoked. He associated mostly with students who were wealthy like he was. Of course, most of Harvard's students at the time were wealthy white men—women were not admitted for many more decades, and very few men of color were allowed to attend. But even among that elite class, Theodore's family stood out for its wealth and fame.

As Theodore became more involved in clubs, sports contests, and recreational activities with classmates, he made friends outside his narrow circle. He wrestled and boxed, ran three or four miles a day, took up rowing and tennis, and continued to work out in the gym. While he failed to excel in any of these activities, he felt immense satisfaction in the sheer fact of overcoming his childhood weakness. Though he "never conquered asthma completely," suffering spasms at irregular intervals for decades,

not regulated, so owners could treat their employees however they wanted.

The growing economic inequalities between workers and business owners resulted in deep hostilities. Labor groups wanted the government to help employees by limiting the number of hours worked, setting minimum wages, and ensuring safe conditions. Most workers were paid so little that poverty became widespread. And because so many families were crowded into tightly packed, unventilated apartment buildings—landlords were not regulated by the government either—in neighborhoods without good sanitation, disease spread too.

Theodore Roosevelt Sr.'s philanthropic work of building schools and boardinghouses for poor children and their families was part of the new social reform movement, designed to solve the problems brought on by the Industrial Revolution. Women of all races and ethnicities were particularly active and effective in these social reforms, including Jane Addams, Lillian Wald, and Mary Church Terrell. Women founded organizations to provide education and medical services to poor families and pressed for the passage of laws to improve the lives of underprivileged children, including pensions for widowed mothers and the abolishment of child labor. The work of these humanitarian activists provided the foundation for modern-day social work.

he had strengthened his body enough to participate. "Funnily enough, I have enjoyed quite a burst of popularity," Theodore wrote to his parents.

While achieving honor grades each semester and participating in this wide array of extracurricular activities, he continued his interest in birds, tramping miles from Harvard to observe them, shoot them, and stuff them. In the midst of all this activity, he also managed to teach Sunday school and take weekly dance classes. Of course he danced awkwardly—"just as you'd expect him to dance," a classmate recalled; "he hopped." Overall, his life at Harvard "broadened every interest," Corinne noted, and his authentic personality eventually captivated his classmates, who marveled at his bursting energy and confidence.

"The story of Theodore Roosevelt," one biographer has suggested, "is the story of a small boy who read about great men and decided he wanted to be like them." But even more than the fictional and non-fictional characters he came to know and admire through his voracious reading, Theodore found in his own father the most powerful model of the heroic ideal. "My father was the best man I ever knew," Roosevelt later said. "He combined strength and courage with gentleness, tenderness, and great unselfishness." He was a public figure of great accomplishment in the world of charitable giving, committed to "every social reform movement"; yet, "I never knew any one who got greater joy out of living than did my father." Roosevelt considered Thee not only "his best and most intimate friend" but a beloved mentor whose advice he followed above all others. "I have literally never spent an unhappy day, unless by my own fault!" Theodore told his family.

In the middle of Theodore's sophomore year at Harvard, however, the streak of happiness he had long enjoyed was interrupted by the greatest sorrow he could have possibly imagined. That December, his forty-six-year-old father fell ill with colon cancer.

Chapter Eight

"I rose like a rocket."

THEODORE HAD NO IDEA how badly his father was suffering in that winter of 1878. After spending winter break at his father's side, Theodore returned to Harvard. His father's health had seemed stable, but in the weeks that followed, he deteriorated rapidly. Two months since learning of the cancer, Thee was gripped with excruciating pain. Being cared for at home, he shook the house with his groans, and his dark hair turned gray. Elliott was there to help, ever ready with a handkerchief drenched in ether for his father to inhale to hopefully dull his pain. But when Thee screamed, neither the ether nor any medications could provide relief, and the fear in his father's eyes was terribly hard for the teenage Elliott to behold.

On Saturday, February 9, 1878, the family, who had tried to shield Theodore from the worsening situation, sent an urgent message to Harvard for him to come home. He raced to catch the overnight train, but by the time he reached New York on Sunday morning, his father had died just hours earlier. "I was away in Boston when the man I loved dearest on earth died," Theodore wrote. Remembering how his father's devoted strength had comforted him throughout the worst of his childhood asthma attacks, he was filled with unbearable grief and guilt: "I never was able to do anything for him during his last illness."

Several days after his father's death, Theodore wrote in his diary: "I felt as if I had been stunned, or as if part of my life had been taken away." And then week after week, in his diary, he continued to lament, only mentioning his father, nothing else.

Theodore Roosevelt, age twenty-two.

"Every now and then it seems to me like a hideous dream. Sometimes when I fully realize my loss I feel as if I should go wild" for "he was everything to me; father, companion, friend. He shared all my joys, and in sharing doubled them, and soothed all the few sorrows I ever had. It is impossible to tell in words how terribly I miss him," Theodore wrote. Crushed, the younger Roosevelt read passages of Scripture, copied a hymn into his diary, and admitted "nothing but my faith in the Lord Jesus Christ could have carried me through this, my terrible time of trial and sorrow." Thee's death was also, as the *New York Times* stated, "a public loss." Flags were lowered in his honor. "Rich and poor followed him to the grave."

As Theodore considered his father's legacy, he began to take the measure of his own life. "Oh, how little worthy I am of such a father," he expressed in his diary. "How I wish I could ever do something to keep up his name."

But blessed with a positive temperament, Theodore was eventually able to recover his spirits. Engaging in nonstop activity, especially outdoors, he found some relief as well as an understanding of his own fundamental nature, influenced by his father. "I could not be happier, except at those bitter moments when I realize what I have lost. Father was so invariably cheerful that I feel it would be wrong for me to be gloomy."

"No one but my wife, if ever I marry," Theodore explained in his diary, "will ever be able to take [my father's] place." And then the following fall, his junior year at Harvard, he fell quickly in love with Alice Hathaway Lee, the seventeen-year-old daughter of a wealthy family from Massachusetts. "It was a real case of love at first sight," Theodore told a friend, "and my first love too." With the same single-mindedness he devoted to his books, his specimen collections, and the building up of his body, he launched a campaign to make Alice his wife. He escorted her to parties and to dances; he invited her skating and sledding, on horseback rides over trails and long hikes through the woods. He introduced her to his friends at Harvard and brought her to meet his mother and siblings in New York City. He charmed her family, playing cards with her parents, entertaining her younger brothers with ghost stories and tales of adventure. He was solely focused on "winning her." After only six months, he asked for her hand in marriage. She turned him down, fearful of taking such a big step at such a young age. Her rejection made him "nearly crazy," unable to study or sleep at night. He refused to give up, however, and eight months later, "after much pleading," she finally agreed to be his wife. "I am so happy that I dare not trust my own happiness," he recorded in his diary the night she accepted. And two months later he wrote: "I do not believe any man loved a woman more than I love her."

While in his last year of college, before he would graduate with the highest honors, Theodore began considering potential career options. He had initially thought he would train to become a naturalist, but Harvard's approach to the science would have kept him in the lab, instead of in the field studying birds, animals, trees, and the outdoor world that so invigorated him. For a young man who craved continual motion, the idea of a deskbound career, studying tissues under a microscope, held no appeal.

Theodore's recognition that he was not suited for science revealed a growing self-awareness—a deepening understanding of his own strengths and weaknesses—that over time would serve him well. Though he abandoned the prospects of a naturalist career, he never stopped pursuing outdoor adventures or his passion for the natural world. In the eighteen months after his father's death, he went on three expeditions into the deep wilderness regions of Maine, each trip further stretching the horizons of his narrow social world and bringing him into close quarters with people whose lives were so different from his own, ways of life he had encountered only through the books he had read.

The first trip had been arranged through his Harvard tutor, Arthur Cutler. "I want you to take that young fellow under your special care," Cutler told the Maine guide William "Bill" Sewall. "He is not very strong and he has got a great deal of ambition and grit. . . . Even if he was tired, he would not tell you so. The first thing you knew he would be down, because he would go until he fell." Cutler was right. While Theodore suffered from a serious asthma attack during the trip, he never once lost his good nature or seemed "out of sorts," whether canoeing five miles on the river, tramping thirty-five miles in the forest, helping to pitch the tents, or missing numerous shots at loons, ducks, and pigeons.

The thirty-four-year-old Sewall, who would become Roosevelt's mentor and lifelong friend, came to know Theodore beginning at age nineteen, "in that period in his life when a man's character, emerging from the shelter of home traditions and inherited beliefs, is most like wax under the contact of men and events." Sewall saw in young Roosevelt his fair-mindedness and directness, strong convictions that he was willing to stand up for—the makings of a leader. "He was different from anybody I had ever met," Sewall said. "Wherever he went, he got right in with the people," connecting with them, talking with them, enjoying them, without the slightest trace of snobbery. The teenager who had begun college only associating with those in his own wealthy social class now bunked in a lumber camp with a large crew of woodsmen. Though not formally educated, the crew, Sewall recalled, "knew the woods, the whole of them, and they knew all the hardships connected with pioneer life." That Theodore had the maturity to "find the real men in very simple men" and find ways to relate to them and learn from them suggested that he was beginning to chip away at the inherited elitism of his privileged background. He told Sewall he was thrilled to get "firsthand accounts of backwoods life from the men who had lived it and knew what they were talking about." He listened with rapt attention to their stories and in turn told them stories that he had read in the adventure books of his youth. Roosevelt was learning, Sewall said, what it meant to be an American, about the country's democratic character, the idea that individuals should be judged on their efforts, that "no man is superior, unless it was by merit, and no man is inferior, unless by his demerit."

In 1880, America had a long way to go to live up to the ideals of equality laid out in the Declaration of Independence. Native Americans and women still did not have the right to vote, and segregationist lawmakers were already chipping away at the rights and freedoms that Black men had secured in the aftermath of the Civil War, including the right to vote granted by the Fifteenth Amendment to the US Constitution, the promise of which would not be fully realized for many decades. Young Theodore's interactions in Maine gave him a sense of the unique experiences and

How did political corruption work in Roosevelt's time?

In big cities like New York, corrupt government officials were using their positions of power for their own personal gain, taking advantage of an unregulated political system. All power flowed from political parties and the "bosses" who led them, because these political "machines" controlled who got elected. These bosses collected money from owners of big companies to fund campaigns and help elect politicians who would stay loyal to the party, its wealthy backers, and the businesses and causes they championed.

Many elected officials used their positions of power and time in office not to serve the public that had helped elect them but instead to pass laws that would be helpful to their big-business supporters and to appoint party loyalists to civil service jobs—unelected positions in police, tax, postal, and other departments—rather than citizens who deserved those jobs. Further, corrupt government appointees accepted bribes, for example, from tenement landlords in return for overlooking violations of city housing codes; received campaign money from companies hoping to do business with the city; or used their insider knowledge for personal gain. At the same time, parties and their bosses pressured government civil servants to pay "the machine" a portion of their salaries or lose their jobs.

perspectives of rural Americans—farmers, ranchers, and their families—and how they lived through challenges and hardships. He began to realize what they might achieve if they had broader opportunities. This first-hand experience would inspire his next steps and lead him to reimagine his future and, later, that of the country.

Theodore had thought for a time to follow in his father's footsteps, carrying on the charity work Thee had so successfully undertaken to improve the lot of the poor. But he was too impatient, telling a friend, "I tried faithfully to do what my father had done, but I did it poorly." After accepting several leadership positions in charity organizations formerly held by his father, Theodore found he could no more sit in meetings for hours on end than he could sit in a laboratory, staring into a microscope. He concluded that he had "to work in his own way" to carry forward the moral character and passion to use his privilege to make society better that his father had instilled in him. The distant sense of duty he had inherited from his elite class felt too removed from the action of life, too indirect. Moreover, he began to suspect that charitable work might be less necessary if the political order—and the government—worked more efficiently and provided solutions for underlying social problems—of which he learned there were many, like poverty, hunger, and disease.

"I'm going to try to help the cause of better government in New York City . . . I don't know exactly how," Theodore told a friend. He enrolled at Columbia University Law School, not because he wanted to be a lawyer, but because he considered it a first step toward involvement in some aspect of public life. Though he impressed his professors and fellow students, he found the courses at law school ill-suited to his "irrepressible" temperament. He spent much time studying and writing in the Astor Library. But in the evenings before dinner he made his way to the corner of Fifty-Ninth Street and Fifth Avenue in Manhattan to Morton Hall, the headquarters of the Twenty-first District Republican Association, a large smoke-filled room over a saloon with shabby benches and poker tables. There he became immersed in the blood sport of working-class politics.

The needs of ordinary citizens were not being well represented. Who would stand up for workers who labored for inadequate salaries in dangerous conditions, the parents who couldn't afford a decent home to raise their children in and food to put on the table, the children who were trapped in dangerous factory jobs instead of going to school? These were some of the social problems President Roosevelt worried about, and he understood that a government free of corruption could help solve them.

"Who's the dude?" the local politicians wondered upon first setting eyes on this young law student, with his hair parted in the center, short whiskers on his cheeks, a monocle over one eye held in place by a gold chain over his ear, a waistcoat, and trousers "as tight as a tailor could make them." He certainly did not fit in. But once the oddity of first impressions faded and his visits became more frequent, he began to connect with the wide variety of Republican Party members—working-class Irish and German immigrants, butchers, carpenters, and horse groomers— listening to their stories, joining them in games of cards, thoroughly enjoying the lively, masculine atmosphere.

"I went around often enough to have the men get accustomed to me and to have me get accustomed to them," he later said. In time, those at Morton Hall recognized they were in the presence of an exceptionally good-natured, sincere, appealing, intelligent young man, who fought for what he believed but accepted defeat with good humor. To join the Republican Party then was "no simple thing," Roosevelt later recalled. "A man had to be regularly proposed for and elected into this club, just as into any other club." Watching Roosevelt over a period of months, the boss of the local Republican club, Joe Murray, a burly red-haired Irish immigrant, concluded that this twenty-three-year-old son of privilege could make a strong run for the state legislature.

The assembly district in New York City where Roosevelt dwelled was as diverse as the city itself, embracing both the elegant private brown-stone homes along Madison Avenue and the tenement apartment build-ings on the West Side of Manhattan crowded with impoverished and working-class tenants. Known as the Silk Stocking District, it was one of the few reliably Republican districts in the city. The boss "picked me as the candidate with whom he would be most likely to win," Roosevelt later said. "I had at that time neither the reputation nor the ability to have won the nomination for myself."

In selecting Roosevelt, Murray recognized the appeal of the Roosevelt name. Indeed, when the nomination of Theodore Roosevelt was announced, the *New York Tribune* suggested that in voting for the son of "one of the most loved and respected" figures in the history of New York, voters would have the opportunity "to show their regard for an honored name." The boss also understood that Roosevelt had the money to contribute to his own campaign.

Roosevelt's family and friends, however, deplored his entrance into politics. In his autobiography, Roosevelt wrote of their disapproval: "These men laughed at me, and told me that politics were 'low'; that the organizations were not controlled by 'gentlemen'; that I would find them run by saloon-keepers, horse-car conductors, and the like, and not by men with any of whom I would come in contact outside." Their denouncement only inspired Roosevelt, showing him clearly who worked in and for government. "I answered that if this were so it merely meant that the people I knew did not belong to the governing class, and that the other people did—and that I intended to be one of the governing class; that if they proved too hard-bit for me I supposed I would have to quit, but that I certainly would not quit until I had made the effort and found out whether I really was too weak to hold my own in the rough and tumble." He felt this was an opportunity, and he wanted "to take advantage" of it. "I put myself in the way of things happening, and they happened," he later said.

There was also the issue of there being only a week's time between the November nomination and the election, which was part of the reason the party machine was so important—parties had the power to get their supporters out to vote in a short amount of time. To open the campaign, Boss Murray planned to take Roosevelt "through the saloons along Sixth Avenue." Saloonkeepers in those days played an important political role, drawing up checklists of the "right" voters in the district, making sure those voters got to the polls. The first stop was Valentine Young's bar. No sooner had Roosevelt been introduced to Mr. Young than trouble began. It became clear that Roosevelt had no idea what he was doing.

Young told Roosevelt that if he won, he expected him to vote for lowering the cost of the liquor licenses that were issued by the state to allow saloons to sell alcohol, which the saloonkeeper considered much too high. Roosevelt replied that while he would treat all interests fairly, he actually thought that liquor taxes were "not high enough," and that he would vote to raise them. Boss Murray swiftly ushered Roosevelt out of there, deciding that he and his colleagues would take care of the Sixth

Avenue vote, leaving Roosevelt to gather votes among his wealthy neighbors and friends. On Election Day, the affluent "brownstone vote" came out in much larger numbers than usual, thanks to seeing the Roosevelt name—one of their own—on the ballot. Roosevelt won the assembly seat with a margin almost twice the size of the typical Republican vote.

From his start in the assembly, it was clear that Theodore Roosevelt had found his calling. Politics included the activities he found most enjoyable and fulfilling: public speaking, writing, connecting with people, being the center of attention. As one of his law school colleagues observed: "He was destined for politics . . . he could not escape the fate of being persistently in the public eye." Roosevelt charged into action, grilling his fellow assemblymen, soaking up everything they knew about how the assembly operated, taking on members of the assembly he considered corrupt.

He then won a second term in the assembly, and, despite his youth, he was chosen by his Republican colleagues as their leader. "I rose like a rocket," Roosevelt recalled of this period. But as his friend, journalist Jacob Riis, later observed, "if they do shoot up like a rocket they are apt to come down like sticks."

He instantly became "a perfect nuisance," constantly interrupting assembly business, yelling and pounding his desk with his fist, reveling in the headlines his colorful language inspired. After failing to mobilize support for several projects, however, he began to see that he "was not all-important," and "that cooperation from other people" was essential, "even if they were not so pure as gold." And he soon learned that "if he could not get all he wanted, he would take all he could." He turned to help others, and they, in turn, gave him a hand. The world was far more complicated than his black-and-white vision had led him to believe. The ability to learn from the excesses of his self-centered behavior, to change course and learn the art of compromise, was essential to his growth and to successful governing.

When a bill to stop the manufacture of cigars in overcrowded, filthy, and dilapidated tenement houses was introduced in one of the committees on which he sat, Roosevelt planned to vote against it, as he had voted against bills to limit the hours of the working day and to provide working people a minimum wage, believing that businesses should be permitted to operate without much government supervision. In the case of the cigar bill, he believed that tenement owners, who were also the cigar manufacturers, had a right to do as they wished with their own property. On the other side, the bill was supported by labor unions, workers who joined together to fight for their rights. And labor leader Samuel Gompers appealed to Roosevelt directly, asking him to come see the tenements before voting against them. You'd have to see these dreadful conditions to believe them, Gompers told Roosevelt.

So Roosevelt agreed to make a personal inspection, to see with his own eyes where thousands of families lived and worked—stripping, drying, and wrapping cigars. Roosevelt was stunned by what he witnessed: five adults and several children, all immigrants from Bohemia (part of the modern-day Czech Republic) who could barely speak English, living and working in a single room, making cigars sixteen hours a day. The tobacco was crammed in every corner, next to the bedding, mixed in with food. Roosevelt changed his mind entirely about the bill and even agreed to become the bill's champion. His investigation persuaded him "beyond a shadow of a doubt that to permit the manufacture of cigars in tenement-houses" was "an evil thing."

Roosevelt's sense of empathy was growing. By visiting places that a man of his background typically would not, and seeing with his own eyes the ugly truth about how millions of people were forced to live under squalid and substandard conditions, he expanded his

heart. Roosevelt came to believe that empathy, like courage, could be learned over time. He acknowledged that one might "at first feel a little self-conscious" associating with people who are different, "but with exercise this will pass off." Just as he had become acquainted with the woodsmen in Maine and the working-class Republicans at Morton Hall, Roosevelt understood that connecting with people who are different from yourself inspires "fellow-feeling." Indeed, he argued that distrust in politics and in life springs from the fact that different classes or sections "are so cut off from each other that neither appreciates the other's passions, prejudices, and, indeed, point of view."

This pursuit of "fellow-feeling" would inspire Roosevelt for the rest of his life as he came to know people all over the country. "I had grown into sympathy with, into understanding of, group after group, with the effect that I invariably found that they and I had common purposes and a common standpoint," Roosevelt wrote. "We differed among ourselves, or agreed among ourselves, not because we had different occupations or the same occupation, but because of our ways of looking at life." He came to believe that fellow-feeling and mutual understanding were the basis of "good government" and "the betterment of social and civic conditions."

By his third term in the assembly, Roosevelt had begun to soften his earlier self-righteousness. Working with Democrats, who he had previously labeled as "rotten," he brought the two parties together to pass a host of bills to benefit the city of New York. He had taken his weaknesses, his physical disadvantages, his fears, and the brash and self-centered aspects of his leadership style, and had carefully worked to overcome them.

Every weekend, Roosevelt rushed home from the state capital in Albany to New York City to be with his wife, Alice, who was expecting their first child in mid-February 1884. In diary entries, Roosevelt celebrated the pleasure of being "in my own lovely little home, with the sweetest and prettiest of all little wives—I can imagine nothing more happy in life than an evening spent in my cozy little sitting room before a bright fire of soft coal, my books all around me." At twenty-five years old he now felt, he told Alice, that he "had the reins" in his own hands, that he could chart his own destiny. He would soon be shown, in a heart-wrenching manner, how little control over life he actually had.

Chapter Nine

"The light has gone out of my life."

ON THE FLOOR OF THE ALBANY LEGISLATURE, Theodore Roosevelt was "full of life and happiness" when he received the joyful telegram that he was now father to his first child, a healthy baby girl. When shortly afterward a second telegram was delivered, all liveliness drained from his being. He rushed from the assembly floor and boarded a train to New York City, where his family had gathered to support his wife, Alice, and celebrate the birth of their child. In the next six hours, Roosevelt would be plunged into such an excessive nightmare of grief as to be found only in grand tragedy.

"There is a curse on this house," his brother, Elliott, told him upon his arrival. "Mother is dying and Alice is dying too." By midnight, both women were in a semiconscious state. His forty-nine-year-old mother, Mittie, still a youthful-looking, beautiful woman, had been suffering from what was considered to be a severe cold, but which turned out to be a deadly case of typhoid fever. Theodore was at his mother's bedside at three a.m. when she died. Less than twelve hours later, as he held his young wife in his arms, Alice died from what was later diagnosed as acute kidney disease, its symptoms masked by her pregnancy. In his diary that night of February 14, Valentine's Day, Theodore placed a large X, along with the simple words "The light has gone out of my life." Two days later, he recorded: "We spent three years of happiness greater and more unalloyed than I have ever known fall to the lot of others. For joy or sorrow my life has now been lived out."

In Albany, the legislature voted unanimously to end business until the following Monday night, a tribute to the popular assemblyman. At the double funeral service held at the Fifth Avenue Presbyterian Church, party bosses and dozens of assemblymen were present, along with members of New York society and scores of people who had attended Roosevelt Sr.'s funeral six years before. During the service, Theodore appeared to his former tutor, Arthur Cutler, "in a dazed stunned state. He does not know what he does or says." The pastor nearly lost command of his voice as he noted the especially sorrowful occasion. "Two members of the same family, of the same home were on the same day taken from life and were to be buried together," he said. He did not remember anything like this in the course of his long ministry.

Two days after the funeral, Roosevelt returned to the assembly, telling a friend, "I think I should go mad if I were not employed." He seemed "a changed man," remarked a colleague; "from that time on there was a sadness about his face that he never had before. He did not want anybody to talk to him about it, and did not want anybody to sympathize with him. It was a grief that he had in his own soul." Going back to work required him to have someone to care for his newborn daughter, Alice, and he found that loving guardian in his sister Bamie, baby Alice's aunt, who had assumed a motherly role when Theodore was growing up and became his close confidant. "We are now holding evening sessions and I am glad we are; indeed the more we work the better I like it," Theodore wrote to Bamie.

He had always worked at a fast and intense pace. Now, driven by the need to reduce his misery, Roosevelt was in a frenzy, pushing one reform bill after another, paying little attention to assembly rules, failing to weigh the criticisms of colleagues. It did not take long to blow the goodwill and sympathy of the old machine politicians and the young reformers after his devastating losses. Before the session came to an end, he decided that he could not bear returning to Albany for another legislative term. His career in the state legislature was over.

Feeling the need to escape the extreme pain of his personal life, Roosevelt headed for the Badlands in South Dakota, where he had purchased a ranch the previous year. "I am going cattle ranching in Dakota for the remainder of the summer and a part of the fall," he told a reporter who was hounding him. "What I shall do after that I cannot tell."

So began a stay on the western frontier that Roosevelt would come to regard as "the most important educational asset" of his entire life. During this western interlude, Roosevelt would gather material for the most accomplished writing ventures of his life—*Hunting Trips of a Ranchman*, *Ranch Life and the Hunting Trail*, and *The Winning of the West*. But by far the greatest and most enduring of the projects during these months and years of reaction to the devastating trauma he had experienced was the work of his own healing, growth, and self-transformation.

To partner with him in the demanding daily operation of the ranch, he called upon his old Maine guide and close friend, Bill Sewall, and Sewall brought along his nephew Wilmot "Will" Dow. Neither man had prior experience with cattle ranching, but that made small difference to Roosevelt. Knowing the character of both men, Roosevelt guaranteed them "a share of anything" the ranch might earn, while promising that he would absorb any losses. He also invited them to live with him in the ranch house they would together design and build. "He never was a man to hesitate to make a decision," Sewall recalled years later. Once he could detect "a streak of honor" in a man, that man could be trusted.

When Roosevelt first arrived in the Dakotas, Sewall recounted, he "was very melancholy—very much down in spirits." The landscape of the Badlands—its lonely plains, open spaces, and haunting beauty—mirrored the emptiness of his inner landscape. With Sewall, Roosevelt felt safe to express his emotions, confessing "that he felt as if it did not make any difference what became of him—he had nothing to live for." Sewall suggested he had his young daughter to live for, but Roosevelt countered that his sister was better positioned to take care of the child. "She would be just as well off without me."

Just as he had driven himself to exhaustion in Albany in the weeks after the deaths of his mother and wife, so now, with reckless abandon and reckless intensity, he pushed himself to do the hardest and most dangerous work of the cowboys, as if, through excitement and fear, he might once again feel alive. He rode his horse sixteen hours a day; galloped at top speed over rugged terrain; hunted blacktail deer, antelope, elk, and buffalo; and joined in the frenzied five-week roundups when the cattle were branded and gathered for market. By flinging himself into every aspect of the daily lives of the cowboys, Roosevelt "was not playing cowboy—he was a cowboy." The daily work of the ranch, companionship with his fellow cowboys, and the sustained pursuit of his writing distracted him from overthinking, and he was finally able to sleep at night.

The young reform-minded Republicans in the East, who had once idolized Roosevelt, knew nothing about this immersion in the West. "We only knew that the man who seemed to have the brightest opportunity and the most splendid career opening had disappeared," said Roosevelt peer Charles Evans Hughes. "He was out of politics altogether, he was no longer apparently available for anything. He had gone away, and it seemed like a candle light that had been snuffed out."

But neither was Roosevelt a snuffed candle nor had he altogether abandoned politics. He had retreated West seeking in a state of nature not gentle comfort but a test, a strenuous challenge where he might

confront his deadened heart and fear of intimacy and somehow renew confidence in himself and in a future where he might become a genuine guide, and leader.

And it worked. As the seasons passed, his depression slowly began to lift. By the end of his two-year break, Roosevelt had emerged from his trauma and grief stronger in body and resurgent in spirit. Even his lungs had improved in the cool mountain air, although he would occasionally have bouts of asthma the rest of his life. Sewall witnessed firsthand Roosevelt's transformation from "a frail young man" troubled by fits of breathless-ness and chronic stomach pains. "When he got back into the world he was as husky as any man I have ever seen who wasn't dependent on his arms for his livelihood." He had gained thirty pounds "and was clear bone, muscle and grit." The high voice that "failed to make an echo" in the legis-lative chamber was "now hearty and strong enough to drive oxen."

Transforming his body was but one step in the psychological struggle to overcome what Roosevelt still considered his own "nervous and timid" nature. When he arrived in the West, he acknowledged, "there were all kinds of things of which I was afraid at first, from grizzly bears to 'mean' horses and gun-fighters, but by acting as if I was not afraid I gradually ceased to be afraid." While some men, he believed, were naturally fearless, he had to train his "soul and spirit" as well as his body. So, "constantly forcing himself to do the difficult or even dangerous thing," he gradually was able to develop courage as "a matter of habit, in the sense of repeated effort and repeated exercise of will-power." Though only a mediocre horseman, he volunteered to ride "mean" horses, those likely to buck. As the owner of the ranch, he wanted to set a leadership example, even at the cost, on several risky occasions, of breaking his ribs. Similarly, while poor eyesight prevented his becoming a first-rate shot, he nevertheless joined professional hunters in the hazardous pursuit of bear, antelope, and buffalo.

"Perseverance," Roosevelt insisted, was the key to his success as both a hunter and a cowboy. With endless practice, he learned to shoot at a moving target with the same accuracy as one that stood still. Years of studying animals allowed him to identify, track, and anticipate the behavior patterns of his prey. He hoped his example of learned courage would persuade other people that if they could consider danger "as

Roosevelt ranching in the Badlands, in full cowboy gear.

something to be faced and overcome," they would "become fearless" by "practicing fearlessness." So completely was he able to tackle his own fears that in the years ahead, countless observers made reference to courage that seemed to them clearly "ingrained in his being."

But on the other hand, Roosevelt's single-minded focus on the difficult tasks at hand allowed him to bottle up his feelings and shut down emotionally. He had abandoned his baby daughter and refused even to speak her given name, Alice, the same name as his late wife's. He referred to her simply as "Baby Lee," confessing, "there can never be another Alice to me." Nor could he bear memories of his courtship and brief marriage. He destroyed almost all the pictures, letters, and mementos of their shared past. It was "both weak and morbid" Roosevelt said, to dwell on loss.

As Roosevelt began to feel better both emotionally and physically, his thoughts returned eastward to the home, family, and friends he had left behind. In the fall of 1885, Roosevelt came to visit his sister Bamie, who was caring for Baby Lee, and it was there he encountered

Who was Alice Roosevelt Longworth?

She was the only child of Theodore Roosevelt and his first wife, Alice Lee, known as "Sunshine" due to her cheerful personality. After her mother's death when she was two days old, Theodore was devastated and asked his sister Bamie to care for Baby Lee, as he called her. Under Bamie's loving guardianship, Alice emerged as a lively toddler who developed a force of personality equal to that of her father.

Theodore later reunited with his former girlfriend and lifelong family friend Edith Carow, and they married in 1886. Edith insisted they incorporate Baby Lee into their new household, creating a painful dilemma for Theodore, who well knew the devotion his childless older sister had shown her "blue-eyed darling." For Bamie, having Alice taken from her was devastating. "It almost broke my heart to give her up," Bamie confessed. Although she maintained her composure, conceding that it was best for Alice to be with her father, she avoided further emotional attachments for some time thereafter. Alice never forgot the wrenching and confusing day Theodore returned with his new wife: "I in my best dress and sash, with a huge bunch of pink roses in my arms, coming down the stairs at my aunt's house in New York to meet my father and my new mother." Theodore never spoke about his late wife. "In fact," Alice lamented, "he never ever mentioned my mother to me, which was absolutely wrong. He never even said her name . . . I think my father tried to forget he had ever been married to my mother. To blot the whole episode out of his mind. . . . He obviously felt tremendously guilty about remarrying. . . . The whole thing was really handled very badly. It was awfully bad psychologically."

Edith Carow again—although it is not clear if it was a chance meeting or Bamie's doing. Carow, the highly intelligent, intensely private young woman who had once been his closest childhood friend, was considered part of the family. As teens, Theodore and Edith had stayed close and were dancing partners and constant companions at social events, but the young couple had a mysterious "falling out," and their "very intimate relations," as Theodore described them, were suddenly over while he was at Harvard. Edith later confessed that she had loved Theodore "with all the passion of a girl who had never loved before." When he married Alice, Edith "danced the soles off her shoes" at the wedding, but she was certain she would never love again.

When Theodore and Edith met once more, the years in between seemed to evaporate, and the deep feelings they once held for each other were revived. Even they were "amazed and rather shocked to think that it could happen so soon," and in the following months they met whenever he was in New York and regularly wrote to each other when they were apart. Their contrasting natures livened and supported each other. Theodore approached everything head-on. Edith was composed and carefully observant. What they had in common was a strong moral core, strength of character, and powerful personalities, and both were used to getting their own way.

By the next summer, Roosevelt was ready to reenter the political world. In the two-year period of his West exploration, Roosevelt had transformed himself into a new kind of American man, a mix of the sophisticated Easterner and the hard-bitten Westerner. Healing change had come from within while he waited for the historical moment to turn. Life as a literary cowboy was not enough to fulfill his grand ambitions. "I would like a chance at something I thought I could really do," he told his friend, Massachusetts representative Henry Cabot Lodge.

Theodore and Edith went on to have five other children. Alice was considered headstrong and a wild child. At nineteen, her various exploits included late-night partying, unchaperoned motor car rides, smoking, and betting on racehorses. She was known to keep a pet snake in her purse, hide small flasks of whiskey in her long gloves, and play poker with men.

Later, Alice joined a delegation of government officials to the Philippines with Secretary of War William Taft. Friends and family had warned Taft that dealing with Alice—or "Princess Alice," as she had been dubbed by the press—would prove challenging. After all, her father once said, "I can do one of two things. I can be President of the United States, or I can control Alice. I cannot possibly do both!" Despite such warnings, Taft found her unspoiled and delightfully direct. At times, she could be "oblivious to the comforts of other people," he acknowledged, but considering "what she has gone through and who she is," the young woman managed to make herself extremely popular with the entire party.

When she married Nicholas Longworth, who became a Speaker of the House of Representatives, Alice became the center of Washington, DC, society. Her knowledge of Senate machinations and political intrigue and her awareness of issues charmed the future First Families she befriended, including the Kennedys, Nixons, and Johnsons. She kept a pillow by her tea table with the words "If you can't say something good about someone, sit right here by me."

He was ready to test himself again in the public arena, the world for which he was born and bred.

Chapter Ten

"Do what you can, with what you have, where you are."

ROOSEVELT WAS TWENTY-EIGHT YEARS OLD, having served four years in the state assembly, when he returned to New York City in 1886 and promptly ran for mayor. When he finished last in a three-way race, he told a friend, "This is the end of my political career." He then sailed to London, where he married Edith, and then they returned to New York, where Roosevelt set forth to determine his career and build a family.

The loss of his wife and mother on the same day in the same house became more than a catastrophic landmark in Theodore Roosevelt's personal life. The brutal twist of fate reshaped his life's philosophy, forged his resilience, and impacted the professional choices he would make and the leadership roles he would seek or accept. His expectation of a smooth, upward path, either in life or in politics, was gone forever, so he stopped worrying about the perceived status of a job, focusing instead on what he could accomplish in it. "Do what you can, with what you have, where you are," he liked to say. He would view each job as a test of character, effort, endurance, and will. He would keep nothing in reserve for some uncertain future.

Roosevelt also became painfully aware that death lurked around any corner. His intensified sense of passing time, his awareness that life could turn on a dime, made him impatient, sometimes unbearably so, to get things accomplished. The hectic speed with which he had introduced dozens of bills in the legislature following Alice's death became a lifelong pattern, a confrontational and often abrasive mode of leadership that put him at odds with the established procedures and sluggish tempo of government action. These jobs, however, were not merely an effort to satisfy a personal mission or fill an emptiness in his heart. In his hands they were attempts to ensure that the government to which American workers paid taxes and voters elected officials was worthy of the people who depended on it.

So the roles Roosevelt took on during the next decade may have seemed random to those who didn't know him well: a post heading the Civil Service Commission, police commissioner of New York City, and assistant secretary of the navy. What had become of the singular rising ambition that had driven young Roosevelt from his earliest days? What explains his willingness, against the advice of his most trusted friends, to accept jobs that they considered "low-level" or beneath his social class? He had absorbed his father's belief that public service was a demonstration of faith and patriotism, as he later wrote: "Unless we are thorough-going Americans and unless our patriotism is part of the very fiber of our being, we can neither serve God nor take our own part."

When Roosevelt was later asked how he was able to successfully lead such diverse departments as the Civil Service Commission, the New York Police Department, and the Navy Department, he insisted that the challenges he faced did not require "genius" or even "any unusual qualities, but just common sense, common honesty, energy, resolution, and readiness to learn." In fact, Roosevelt believed there were "two kinds of success," the first in the form of a gift or a talent that no amount of training will enable an ordinary person to do—perhaps like that of an Albert Einstein, William Shakespeare, or Babe Ruth. But much more common is the type of success that comes from developing ordinary qualities to an extraordinary degree by the application of relentless, hard, sustained work. Roosevelt put himself in the second category, and his leadership style was governed by that theory as well as a series of simple sayings: hit the ground running; consolidate control; ask questions of everyone wherever you go; manage by wandering around; determine the basic problems of each organization and hit them head-on; when attacked, counterattack; stick to your guns; spend your political capital to reach your goals; and then when your work is stymied or done, find a way out.

Friends had urged Roosevelt to turn down the post of Civil Service commissioner offered to him by President Benjamin Harrison because they considered it beneath the heir to the Roosevelt name. But they had failed to understand that the fight to enforce the controversial new Civil Service Law represented a signature battle in the war against corruption in government—which was widespread—and a battle ideally suited for this son of a reform-minded philanthropist with his own drive to effect change and serve the public. Americans were sick of corruption. No matter how difficult, Roosevelt intended to enforce a new anti-corruption law, the Pendleton Act, to the fullest, and to stop anyone, including leaders in his own party, who were standing in the way of it.

In one of his first acts, Roosevelt launched an unexpected raid on the powerful New York Custom House, which oversaw the port of New York and collected taxes on imported goods. Rumor suggested that violations of the new law were widespread there. Agency jobs required passing a written test, and Roosevelt had learned that some government clerks were selling the examination questions to favored party candidates for fees of fifty to one hundred dollars—which would give those cheating candidates an edge in gaining employment. So after hearing testimony and examining documents, Roosevelt demanded the immediate firing of three guilty employees, showing the public that the new law was "going to be enforced, without fear or favor." His investigation also uncovered that party leaders continued to collect "so-called voluntary contributions" from Custom House employees as the price for keeping their jobs.

Roosevelt walked the corridors to directly engage with entry-level employees—clerks, copyists, letter carriers, and the like. They revealed to him how hard it was to meet the party leaders' demand for 2 percent of their salary, which might mean "the difference between having and not having a winter overcoat for himself, or a warm dress for his wife." Roosevelt recounted stories like these in a blistering report about the corruption he uncovered as a way to show the public that civil service reform had a practical impact on people's real lives. Less than a month later, having heard that postmasters in several cities were manipulating examination scores to appoint favored party members, he began an investigatory tour of post offices.

To make the changes he thought necessary, Roosevelt essentially took over the three-person commission and became its public face. "My two colleagues are away and I have all the work of the Civil Service Commission to myself," he exclaimed to his sister Bamie. "I like it; it is more satisfactory than having a divided responsibility; and it enables me to take more decided steps."

What was the Civil Service Commission?

The Civil Service Commission was created by an anti-corruption law called the Pendleton Act, named for Senator George H. Pendleton of Ohio and passed in 1883, following newspaper reports of widespread corruption and incompetence in federal departments and the assassination of President James Garfield by a disgruntled job seeker. At first the law required 10 percent of all federal "civil service" jobs—positions that provide a service for the public—to be obtained by merit, meaning applicants would have to pass a test to be hired as a government employee. By the time Theodore Roosevelt was offered a role on the Civil Service Commission, it was in charge of filling positions for a quarter of all federal jobs. But the new process was not without its problems. Despite campaign promises of advancement for Black Americans, President Woodrow Wilson's administration (1913–1921) required applicants to attach a photograph of themselves to the application, further allowing for discrimination in the hiring process. Even after ongoing protests, the photo requirement was not eliminated until 1940.

Not surprisingly, Roosevelt's power play angered Republican Party bosses, produced tension with colleagues, and gained him criticism in the press. The *Washington Post* declared, "He immediately announced himself the one man competent to take charge of the entire business of the Government." Another critic recommended that he "put a padlock on his restless and uncontrollable jaws." But Roosevelt kept talking. He understood that he was accountable to the public and needed to keep the public informed and on his side.

By the time Roosevelt left the Civil Service Commission after six years, his leadership had ignited such public support for the new Civil Service Law that open violations were no longer tolerated; a true merit system was actually in the process of being born, so that, as Jacob Riis later summarized, job opportunities for every working person expanded: "The farmer's lad and the mechanic's son who had no one to speak for them should have the same show in competing for public service as the son of wealth and social prestige."

In the fall of 1894, a reform-minded Republican businessman, William Strong, was elected mayor of New York City in the wake of scandals showing a corrupt relationship between the city's dominant political machine, Tammany Hall, and the New York Police Department. Not long after he was sworn in in 1895, Mayor Strong offered Roosevelt the most challenging job in his administration: police commissioner, chief of the four-man police board, on which sat two Republicans and two Democrats. Roosevelt, now thirty-six years old, accepted. "I have the most important and the most corrupt department in New York on my hands," Roosevelt wrote about the difficulties ahead, clearly excited by the challenge.

Roosevelt literally hit the ground running, racing up the steps of the Mulberry Street police headquarters in order to dramatize for the reporters watching that he would act with speed at the police board. "It was all breathless and sudden," one reporter recalled. Still jogging along, Roosevelt fired off questions: Which higher officials should be consulted, which ones ignored, which ones punished? What were "the customs, rules, methods" of the police board? "What do we do first?"

In truth, Roosevelt needed no suggestions on what to do first—and that was to consolidate power into his own hands. Power "in most positions," he believed, should be concentrated "in the hands of one man." While this might suggest he sought to be like a dictator or a king, Roosevelt added, "so long as that man could be held fully responsible for the exercise of that power by the people." In other words, he understood the role of an executive was to take charge, but that he answered to the public. But the other members of the police board were not impressed. "Thinks he's the whole board," complained Democrat Andrew Parker. "He talks, talks, talks, all the time. Scarcely a day passes that there is not something from him in the papers." Parker failed to understand that for Roosevelt publicity was not merely about being the center of attention; public support, gained through public relations, was his single most powerful tool for driving change.

The first massive leadership task before Roosevelt was to analyze the basic problems of the organization and assault them head-on. An investigation by the state legislature had revealed corruption between the NYPD and Tammany Hall "from top to bottom"; the police force was found to be "utterly demoralized." Police recruits were forced to pay a fee to get their jobs. As they rose in the ranks, they would receive payments from a blackmail fund; businesses that paid into this corrupt fund could do as they wished without having to worry about police interference. For a monthly fee, gambling houses were guaranteed protection from police raids, grocery stores could display their wares on the sidewalk, and saloons could remain open on Sundays, the one day they were forbidden by law to be open. With each higher rank a policeman or a politician reached, his percentage of the blackmail fund grew.

Roosevelt decided he needed to fire leaders at the top, change the culture in which the individual policemen worked, and destroy the widespread system of bribery that enveloped the police, the politicians, and the managers of thousands of small businesses.

Within three weeks of his swearing in as police commissioner, Roosevelt forced the resignations of the powerful superintendent of police and his chief inspector, who could not explain how they had accumulated hundreds of thousands of dollars in their bank accounts. Roosevelt's bold action worried Republican Party bosses. They feared he was moving too far too fast and creating uproar wherever he went. But so long as Roosevelt could count on the full support of the public, he would stick to his guns.

Next, Roosevelt recognized that lasting reform would be determined by the behavior of the patrolman on the beat. Accordingly, he launched the second part of his strategy—to patrol the patrolmen. To learn firsthand the nature of the patrolman's work, he made a series of unannounced "midnight rambles." Disguising his identity with an oversized coat and a floppy hat drawn down over his forehead, he roamed the streets of a dozen or more patrol areas between midnight and sunrise to determine whether the policemen assigned to those zones were carrying out their duties. But what did Roosevelt find? Policemen relaxing in bars, eating at all-night restaurants, and the like. In each case, Roosevelt summoned the officer to appear at headquarters the following morning for disciplinary action. In one instance, he found a patrolman eating oysters at a Third Avenue bar. Without revealing his identity, he asked why the officer was not at his post on the street, where he belonged.

"What is that to you, and who are you anyway?" the officer asked.

"I am Police Commissioner Roosevelt," came the reply.

"Sure you are," the patrolman mocked. "You're Grover Cleveland and Mayor Strong, all in a bunch."

"Shut up, Bill," the bartender said to the officer, "it is his Nibs sure! Don't you see his teeth and glasses?"

Stories of Roosevelt's midnight rambles captivated reporters and the public alike. SLY POLICEMEN CAUGHT BY SLYER ROOSEVELT, one headline read. ROOSEVELT ON PATROL: HE MAKES THE NIGHT HIDEOUS FOR SLEEPY POLICEMEN, blared another. Cartoons of policemen crouching in fear at the sight of an enormous set of teeth, metal-rimmed glasses, and a mustache entertained the country and brought Roosevelt new national fame. The *Chicago Times-Herald* dubbed him "the most interesting man in America."

Even as Roosevelt disciplined individual policemen who were shirking their duties, he insisted that the majority of the police force were "naturally first-rate men" caught in a bad system. Maintaining that it was as important to recognize good behavior as to punish bad conduct, Roosevelt established a system to award certificates and medals to officers who exhibited "courage and daring"—men who risked their lives to catch criminals, save children from drowning, struggle with runaway horses, and perform countless other heroic deeds in the course of their everyday jobs. When he came upon an officer on proper patrol, he offered encouragement and thanks. While in office, Roosevelt introduced a range of technological improvements to the police department, including the use of fingerprinting and an expansion of telephone communications. The morale of the police force began the slow process of healing and restoration.

At the same time, Roosevelt worked to build a police force that represented the diversity of the city, where all the dominant ethnic strains were included—Irish Americans, German Americans, African Americans, Jews, Scandinavians, Italians, Slavs, and others. He acted swiftly when signs of prejudice or discrimination became visible. "When one man attacked another because of his breed or birthplace, I got rid of him in summary fashion," Roosevelt exclaimed.

The third element of his reform action, in the end, took the greatest personal and political toll on Roosevelt. Owners and managers of the more than ten thousand saloons operating in the city understood that so long as they continued making a monthly payment to corrupt police and politicians, they were free to

Roosevelt at his desk as New York's police commissioner, between 1895 and 1897.

remain open on the most profitable day of the week: Sunday. Those who refused to make payments to the machine were shut down and arrested for violating the law. "The result," Roosevelt argued, "was that the officers of the law, the politicians, and the saloon-keepers became inextricably tangled in a network of crime." By enforcing the law "fairly and squarely" against all saloons, Roosevelt hoped to eliminate the central source of the city's corruption.

Personally, however, Roosevelt did not agree with the Sunday closing law. For the working class, on the job six days a week, the local saloon was a place to relax with friends on their one day off, to drink beer, play cards, shoot pool, and talk politics. But the law was on the books, and as police commissioner, Roosevelt felt he had to enforce it.

While he became successful in shutting down the saloons, he was ill-prepared for the furious messages that flooded his office from angry working people. "You are the biggest fool that ever lived." "You are the deadest duck that ever died in a political pond." A box containing dynamite sent to his office detonated before reaching him. "A less resolute man" would have backed down, observed journalist Jacob Riis, "but he went right on doing the duty he was sworn to do."

Refusing to take "the howl" of criticism personally, Roosevelt astonished his critics when he accepted an invitation to attend what turned out to be a massive parade protesting the new enforcement policy for Sunday closing—and him. Escorted to the viewing stand on Lexington Avenue, Roosevelt stood for two hours, smiling and waving as decorated floats and more than thirty thousand marchers paraded by carrying angry-worded banners and signs. When he saw one banner that read ROOSEVELT'S RAZZLE DAZZLE REFORM RACKET, he asked the men carrying it if he could keep it as a souvenir. His good nature and ability to embrace criticism with his toothy grin won over the crowd. The *Chicago Evening Journal* summed up the day's event: CHEERED BY THOSE WHO CAME TO JEER.

Despite his willingness to peaceably accept responsibility, his war against the saloons was politically disastrous. Roosevelt was blamed when Republicans lost badly in the following election. He had failed to frame the issue as a necessary battle against corruption in such a way as to gain the people's confidence and support. It was one thing for Roosevelt to earn the anger of the political bosses and the saloonkeepers, quite another to be viewed as an enemy by the working class he had worked so hard to understand and champion. He needed to find a way out.

William McKinley's 1896 campaign for president provided Roosevelt with the perfect exit. Taking temporary leave from the police board, he campaigned far and wide for the Republican nominee from Ohio and swiftly became one of the most sought-after speakers on the stump. However unpopular he was as police commissioner in New York, his corruption- and crime-fighting efforts had made him a magnetic figure across the country. Already, Theodore Roosevelt had become a symbol and leader in the war against corruption that in the next decade would win the widespread support of his countrymen. Everywhere he went, he attracted great crowds at sites "jammed, people standing in masses in the aisles." By giving "all of his time, all of his energy, and all his towering ability to the work of the campaign," he once again earned the praise of the Republican bosses.

After McKinley's victory, the new president made an offer to Roosevelt—the job of assistant secretary of the US Navy, the second most powerful role in the organization. As so often before, friends cautioned Roosevelt not to settle for this lesser post, but in what had become a familiar pattern, he snatched up the offer, one that would lead to more unexpected twists and turns in his life, including his most daring and dangerous venture yet.

Chapter Eleven

"Speak softly and carry a big stick...."

As ASSISTANT SECRETARY TO NAVY SECRETARY JOHN DAVIS LONG, Roosevelt had, for the first time, and at age thirty-eight, an actual boss to whom he had to answer. Potential minefields surrounded the relationship from the start.

Roosevelt was convinced that a looming war with colonial Spanish forces in Cuba was on the near horizon. Spain had been mistreating the people of the island of Cuba—just one hundred miles from Florida's southern tip—who were fighting for their freedom from the Spanish colonizers. Roosevelt believed that the navy needed to be in a stronger position, better prepared, should war become a necessity. Two decades older than Roosevelt, Secretary Long was cautious. Having experienced the horrific years of the Civil War, Long, like President McKinley, was committed to preserving the peace.

How then, did Roosevelt, the man who took charge of every committee he joined, manage being second in command? For a start, Roosevelt built up "a reserve of good feeling" through repeated acts of courtesy, kindness, and helpfulness that secured the trust and confidence of Secretary Long. Recognizing that Long, who had no prior experience with the navy, was uncomfortable with technical naval details, Roosevelt swiftly mastered them, including the schedules for inspection, repair, and maintenance; the numbers of inactive vessels; the construction of new ships. He then translated the data into clear, readable reports delivered to Long's desk every morning.

Long was delighted with his hardworking young associate. Just as Roosevelt had instituted hands-on inspections in the Civil Service and extended his police oversight to the sidewalks of New York City, so now he left his desk to investigate, inspect, and review various aspects of the naval force. All the while, Roosevelt was carefully planning to build an expanded, war-ready navy. The summer of 1897 presented Roosevelt the opportunity for action when the exhausted Secretary Long retreated to Massachusetts for an eight-week vacation. This was not unusual in the days before air-conditioning. Government officials, including presidents, regularly escaped Washington during the summer for cooler climes.

Long's departure left Roosevelt in charge. "The Secretary is away, and I am having immense fun running the Navy," Roosevelt reported to a friend that summer. "As I am given a free hand when alone, I am really accomplishing a great deal," he told Bamie. Roosevelt figured out which fleets could play an important role if war broke out in Cuba.

What was the Spanish-American War?

Spain's colonization of the Americas began with Christopher Columbus's voyage to the "New World" in 1492. Spain became one of the largest, most brutal colonial powers in the world, acquiring territory in the Pacific, including the Philippines and Guam; in South, Central, and North America; and in the Caribbean, including Cuba, declaring control and killing and displacing many thousands of Indigenous people.

In 1895, Cuban revolutionaries reignited a fight for independence from Spain that had been decades in the making. The Spanish responded harshly, including placing the entire island under military rule and establishing concentration camps for Cubans in order to deprive the rebels of an opportunity to hide among civilians. Nearly one in three of the Cubans in the camps died. Americans were sympathetic to the Cuban people's plight, while American businesses were heavily invested in Cuba's sugar trade.

President William McKinley did not want to get entangled in a war with Spain. But ultimately the US did go to war after the USS *Maine*, an American battleship in Cuba's Havana Harbor, was blown up, killing 266 American sailors. The war resulted in Cuba's independence from Spain.

He then pulled every string to get Commander George Dewey appointed commander of that squadron.

At the same time, Roosevelt wrote frequently to the vacationing Secretary Long, assuring him that he had things under control. "You must be tired and you ought to have an entire rest," he wrote in early August. A week later, he wrote, "If things go on as they are now there isn't the slightest reason to you to come back for six weeks more." He then followed up: "I am very glad you have been away, for it has been the hottest weather we have had." Roosevelt could not have pressed harder against the bounds of deception and not broken them. "Speak softly and carry a big stick" was one of his favorite sayings.

When, on occasion, his public statements contradicted President McKinley's agenda and drew the anger of Secretary Long, Roosevelt immediately apologized to Long, accepted his scolding with grace, but then proceeded exactly as he'd intended. Roosevelt succeeded in keeping Long's trust by remaining "honest and open" about their differences of view. Of paramount importance to Long was simply to acknowledge who was in charge, and Roosevelt had no problem obliging.

On February 15, 1898, the USS *Maine*, stationed in Cuba's Havana Harbor, exploded, killing 266 Americans. Though the cause of the explosion was never determined, widespread rage and a call to declare war swept the United States. Still, President McKinley, who had fought at Antietam, the bloodiest battle of the Civil War, hesitated. "I have been through one war; I have seen the dead piled up; and I do not want to see another." While the president was anguished with indecision, Roosevelt took a series of actions that under any boss other than Long might well have triggered his immediate firing.

On February 25, Long left the office for a day's rest with clear and specific instructions for Roosevelt: "Do not take any step affecting the policy of the Administration without consulting the President or me. I am not away from town and my intention was to have you look after the routine of the office while I get a quiet day off. I write to you because I am anxious to have no unnecessary occasion for a sensation in the papers." Despite this warning, Roosevelt launched a series of orders—"distributing ships, ordering ammunition," purchasing tons of coal, "sending messages to Congress" to recruit more seamen, and finally, ordering Admiral Dewey to "keep full of coal" and be prepared if war came to take offensive action.

When Long returned to the office the next morning, he discovered Roosevelt's orders; Long wrote in his diary of Roosevelt: "He means to be thoroughly loyal but the very devil seemed to possess him yesterday afternoon." Reacting more from compassion than in anger, Long made excuses for Roosevelt, suggesting he had lost his head as a consequence of grave troubles at home. Edith was suffering from what doctors would finally diagnose as a massive infection in a muscle near the base of her spine, requiring an intensive and risky operation to remove. At the same time, Long knew that their ten-year-old son, Theodore Jr., the second oldest of their six children, was "just recovering from a long and dangerous illness." This combination, Long wanted to believe, had prompted Roosevelt to take unauthorized action, which he otherwise would not have.

Nonetheless, neither Long nor McKinley canceled a single one of Roosevelt's orders. Accordingly, when Congress finally declared war on Spain nearly nine weeks later, Commander Dewey was well-positioned to strike. US Army officer Leonard Wood later observed that "few men would have dared to assume this responsibility, but Theodore Roosevelt knew that there were certain things that ought to be done and that delay would be fatal. He felt the responsibility and he took it." Roosevelt may have had a boss, but he wasn't one to be bossed around.

No sooner had Congress declared war on Spain on April 25, 1898, than Roosevelt resigned from his navy post and volunteered for the army. Not a single friend agreed with what seemed to them an impulsive decision. "I really think he is going mad," one friend remarked. "It really is sad, of course this ends his political career for good." Secretary Long worried that Roosevelt had "lost his head in this unutterable folly of deserting his post where he is of most service and running off to ride a horse and probably, brush mosquitoes from his neck on the Florida sands."

Roosevelt's decision was, in his mind, anything but rash. His "usefulness" in the Navy Department, he suspected, would "largely disappear in time of war." Long would stay put, and there would be no chance for Roosevelt to rise to head the department. The time had come once more to find a way out. "My work here has been the work of preparing the tools," he told his friend Bill Sewall. "They are prepared, and now the work must lie with those who use them. . . . I would like to be one of those using the tools."

Despite the fragility of his own family—Edith had not yet recovered from her operation, and young Theodore seemed to be suffering a nervous collapse—Roosevelt felt compelled to serve in Cuba. "You know what my wife and children mean to me," he later told his military adviser, Archie Butt, "and yet I made up my mind that I would not allow even a death to stand in my way; that it was my one chance to do something for my country and for my family . . . I know now that I would have turned from my wife's deathbed to have answered that call."

Among our four leaders, only Theodore Roosevelt would command men in the heat of a military battle. Only he would personally face an actual enemy with his own life and the lives of his men teetering in the balance. When Roosevelt took command of his troops in Cuba, he was directly responsible for them—an experience that changed and vastly enlarged his confidence in himself as a leader.

Roosevelt's volunteer army regiment required the very skills he had developed during his years in the Badlands. He had willed himself to become a tireless hunter, a reasonable shot, a cowboy able to stay in the saddle for a dozen hours at a time, toughened to extremes of weather, equipped to tolerate all manner of unexpected hardships. Yet, when the secretary of war offered Roosevelt the top leadership post—colonel of this regiment—he said no.

Why, when Roosevelt had the opportunity to live out a lifelong fantasy of the heroic knight on horseback, leading a charge at the forefront of his men, would he decline and instead suggest his younger friend Leonard Wood? The answer reveals a crucial leadership attribute—the self-awareness to calmly analyze his own strengths and weaknesses. Roosevelt knew that he lacked the experience and knowledge that Wood possessed about how to speedily prepare, supply, and ready a regiment. If Wood were made colonel, Roosevelt said he would happily, without the slightest hesitation or competitiveness, accept the second-in-command post of lieutenant colonel. Central to Roosevelt's decision was not the title he would enjoy but the ultimate success of the regiment in which he would share command.

Colonel Wood and Lieutenant Colonel Roosevelt together formed an effective team leading the Rough Riders, the First US Voluntary Cavalry, consisting of 1,060 soldiers and 1,258 horses and mules, which trained at Fort Sam Houston in San Antonio, Texas. Projecting a vision of a unique fighting force, Roosevelt brought together from all forty-five states then in existence and four US territories Eastern elites and Ivy League athletes who "possessed in common" with Western cowboys, Native Americans, gamblers, and hunters "the traits of hardihood and thirst for adventure." This glamorous mosaic of the country's diversity was a reflection of his own experience: his willed athleticism, bodybuilding, Harvard education, engagement with hunters and woodsmen in Maine, ranching and riding in the West, and working with the police force in New York. The unit's official uniform was a slouch hat, blue flannel shirt, brown trousers and leggings, boots, and polka-dot bandannas. For himself, Roosevelt had his uniform carefully tailored by the high-society Brooks Brothers clothing shop in Boston.

Designed to help forge "fellow-feeling," which Roosevelt believed essential to the success of the mission, he deliberately arranged the tents at the training ground in such a manner that cowboys and wranglers slept side by side with the sons of wealthy bankers. He assigned members of fancy private New York social clubs to wash dishes for a New Mexico company and brought Easterners and Westerners together in the daily chores of washing laundry and digging and filling in toilets. Eventually, a common denominator emerged throughout the entire regiment—a leveling of the playing field—where money, social status, and education were meaningless under the umbrella of teamwork.

Roosevelt (center) with the Rough Riders on San Juan Hill in Cuba.

Roosevelt long understood that leadership had to be earned; it did not come solely from rank or title. As he had learned on the cattle drives in the Dakotas, being the one who issues orders and pays wages was not enough to become a real boss. He had to lead by sharing his life with the men, by his own willingness to do anything he asked them to do, by never asking them to suffer anything he wouldn't suffer first. "When we got down to hard pan, we all, officers and men, fared exactly alike as regards both shelter and food," Roosevelt later wrote. Grumbling stopped "when all alike slept out in the open."

But the on-the-job training that provided a formidable learning experience for Roosevelt and his men was not without mistakes. Roosevelt had to learn how to balance being one with his men without overstepping the line of familiarity, which could diminish their respect for him. After a successful day of drills in the oppressive heat of San Antonio, Texas, Roosevelt announced to his troops, "The men can go in and drink all the beer they want, which I will pay for!" Later that evening, Colonel Wood summoned Roosevelt to his tent. He explained that it became complicated to discipline soldiers after relaxing with them. Roosevelt took Wood's scolding to heart: "Sir, I consider myself the damnedest ass within ten miles of the camp." Humbled, Roosevelt realized that while he had gained the affection of his troops, he had not established the proper separation between himself and his men. "When things got easier I put up my tent and lived a little apart," he recalled, for "it is the greatest possible mistake to seek popularity either by showing weakness or mollycoddling the men. They never respect a commander who does not enforce discipline." Experience taught him to strike the right balance between reverence and respect.

As the troops moved from training grounds in Texas to Port Tampa to Cuba, Roosevelt revealed a sure-handed ability to calm confusion, impose order, and do whatever it took to protect his men. When trains to transport the heavy equipment for his regiment could not be secured, he paid from his own funds. When the canned beef they were fed proved rotten, he demanded and obtained better food. When the boat to ferry his men was not available, he occupied another regiment's assigned boat with stealth and speed. Despite filthy, cramped quarters on board, he imposed inspections and roll calls. In a matter of weeks, he had established the kind of leadership that is bonded by two-way trust. He had taken command of his men by assuming responsibility for them and had demonstrated that he was prepared to do anything he could to provide for them. They, in turn, were prepared to give everything he asked of them.

The first battle the Rough Riders faced at Las Guasimas in Cuba began in confusion. As the troops made their way through the tall grass and twisted brush, they encountered fierce fire from an unseen enemy. "What to do next I had not an idea," Roosevelt later confessed. When they came upon a cut in a barbed-wire fence indicating the route the Spanish had taken, however, Roosevelt's uneasiness vanished. Leading his men across the wire, heading straight toward shots of rifle fire, he suddenly became, according to a witnessing journalist, Edward Marshall, "the most magnificent soldier I have ever seen. It was as if that barbed-wire strand had formed a dividing line in his life." Leaving indecision behind, Marshall observed, Roosevelt found on the other side of the thicket "the coolness, the calm judgment, the towering heroism which made him, perhaps, the most admired and best beloved of all Americans in Cuba." Under Roosevelt's lead, the outnumbered Rough Riders charged triumphantly uphill and drove back the Spanish soldiers.

Then on July 1, 1898, the Rough Riders were ordered to advance toward the San Juan River, and as they neared, shrapnel from a Spanish shell that had exploded hit Roosevelt in the wrist and also wounded several other Rough Riders and army regulars. Colonel Wood then ordered the Rough Riders to advance up Kettle Hill. Roosevelt, riding his horse named Texas, urged his men forward as he pressed on. The Rough Riders found themselves pushing the troops in front of them, and Roosevelt bolted to the front of the entire advance—almost single-handedly leading the charge. "No one who saw Roosevelt take that ride expected he would finish it alive," the journalist Richard Harding Davis reported. Seated high on his horse with his blue polka-dot bandanna floating "out straight behind his head," he was "the most conspicuous object in the

range of the rifle pits." Another reporter marveled, "Up, up (the hill) they went in the face of death. It was an inspiring sight and an awful one." Roosevelt, sitting tall on his horse all the way, "shouting for his men to follow," finally forced the Spanish to retreat and reached the summit, "cheering and filling the air with cowboy yells." Within short order, the city of Santiago was captured, and the Spanish surrendered.

But 89 of 490 Rough Riders were killed or wounded in what came to be known as Roosevelt's "crowded hour." In newspapers, magazines, and journals across the country, Roosevelt was portrayed as the man who "had single-handedly crushed the foe." Although Roosevelt credited his regiment in military reports and conversations with journalists, carefully citing individuals he felt deserved special recognition, it was the iconic image of him on horseback that became the symbol of American bravery. "You are the next governor of New York!" reporters shouted at him when he returned to the state. On September 15, 1898, the victorious Rough Riders disbanded, and two days later, Roosevelt, their fearless leader, entered the governor's race.

The newly minted war veteran running for the highest office in New York State was not the same man who had volunteered to fight in Cuba. He had gained a deeper, more durable confidence in his leadership capacities after commanding men in combat, earning not only their trust but their devotion. He had come to believe that leadership itself was his greatest talent. Less than three months after returning home, Theodore Roosevelt was elected governor of New York.

He wrote to a friend: "I have worked hard all my life, and have never been particularly lucky, but this summer I was lucky, and I am enjoying it to the full. I know perfectly well that the luck will not continue, and it is not necessary that it should. I am more contented to be Governor of New York," he added, using words psychologically necessary to him throughout his career, and always ending with "I shall not care if I never hold another office."

In typical Roosevelt fashion, he hit the ground running. Within his first few weeks as governor, Roosevelt got to work on one of his great lifelong passions: conservation of wild lands and protection of endangered species. "When the blue birds were so nearly destroyed by the severe winter a few seasons ago, the loss was like the loss of an old friend, or at least like the burning down of a familiar and dearly loved house," he wrote in a letter to the New York State Audubon Society, read at their annual meeting on March 23, 1899. "When I hear of the destruction of a species I feel just as if all the works of some great writer had perished. . . ." In the course of his two-year term, Roosevelt convinced the state legislature to preserve tens of thousands of forested acres in the Catskills and the Adirondacks in upstate New York. He created the Palisades Park and promoted awareness of the state's unique natural resources and the need to conserve them.

True to his roots and in accordance with the long line of his career, Roosevelt also pressed hard to root out corruption, taking on some of the state's most powerful companies and politicians. While the public loved this, business interests made it clear to New York's Republican Party bosses that if Roosevelt were nominated for a second term, businesses would pull their support for Republicans. Since it was risky to outright deny the popular governor a second term, the Republican Party machine devised what they thought was a perfect solution. They would promote Roosevelt to "the most dignified and harmless position": vice president of the United States, since Vice President Garret A. Hobart of New Jersey had died in office. Roosevelt would then be removed from New York politics, and at the same time, the Republican Party and President McKinley would be energized by Roosevelt's celebrity as a war hero and charisma on the national campaign trail.

The scheme attracted the support of all the bosses in the Republican Party save one—Mark Hanna, national Republican Party chair. "Don't you know that there's only one life between that madman and the White House?" he warned. But although Hanna eventually came around, Roosevelt himself initially resisted the so-called promotion. He had no desire to be the "figurehead" in a job then considered a wasteland for political ambitions. At the time, not a single vice president had been elected to the presidency in over sixty years. But when the convention nominated him, Roosevelt felt he had no choice but to accept with gratitude and grace. And when McKinley won reelection by a large margin, Roosevelt was elected vice president of the United States.

Roosevelt's daughter Alice humorously observed that her father so fiercely craved being at the center of action that he wanted to be the baby at the baptism, the bride at the wedding, and the corpse at the funeral; but Roosevelt knew the vice presidency would not allow for his abundant energies. Frustration, depression born of inactivity, grew by the day in that "useless and empty position," where Roosevelt was deprived of the spotlight he craved as a plant craves sunshine. The president gave him no responsibilities, nor did he seek Roosevelt's advice. Roosevelt grew so bored that he considered returning to law school.

Friends advised him to be patient. They remained fully confident that he would rise to become president one day, that the White House would be his future home. But Roosevelt was restless. Little could he have known that on September 6, 1901, an assassin's bullet would bring President McKinley's life to an end. At the age of forty-two, Theodore Roosevelt was "shot into the presidency," the youngest man to occupy the White House in the history of the country.

Chapter Twelve

"A square deal for every man, great or small, rich or poor."

"IT IS A DREADFUL THING to come into the Presidency this way; but it would be a far worse thing to be morbid about it," Roosevelt wrote a friend days after President William McKinley's death. "Here is the task, and I have got to do it to the best of my ability; and that is all there is about it."

Roosevelt's outsized personality was quickly on full display, as he made it immediately clear that a new leader was in charge, one who understood the country's challenges in a very different way than his predecessor. "Probably no administration has ever taken such a curious hold upon the people as that of Theodore Roosevelt," remarked the longtime White House usher Irwin "Ike" Hoover of the new president. Indeed, Roosevelt's first few months as chief executive were less remarkable for political accomplishments than for his impact on the public consciousness. "The infectiousness of his exuberant vitality made the country realize there was a new man in the White House," noted reporter Mark Sullivan. Roosevelt was actually responsible for naming the presidents' home the White House, changing it from the Executive Mansion in 1901 by executive order.

Roosevelt began each day in the White House by darting "into the breakfast-room with a cheerful hail to those already there"; then he rushed to his office before the official workday started to tackle his loads

Who visited Roosevelt in the White House?

Not long after Theodore Roosevelt was catapulted into the presidency following President William McKinley's assassination, he invited the prominent Black educator Booker T. Washington to dine with him and his wife, First Lady Edith Roosevelt, in the White House on October 16, 1901—making Washington the first Black person to share a meal with a president in the White House. Activists Sojourner Truth and Frederick Douglass had visited President Lincoln but never dined with him. When news got out that Washington, a formerly enslaved man, had joined the Roosevelts for a meal, many white people were aghast, while Black Americans were pleased by the event. Newspaper editorials throughout the South viciously attacked the president's attempt to show the world that a Black man was and should be considered the social equal of a white man by sharing the same dinner table. Vulgar political cartoons including the First Lady were widely circulated. The nasty reaction in the Southern press stunned and saddened President Roosevelt.

of letters, dictating "one letter after another" to his secretary. From ten a.m. to noon, except on cabinet days, the second-floor reception room was crowded with senators, with whom Roosevelt met for all manner of official and political business. At noon, the White House doors opened to the public, "an overflowing stream" of people eager to see the most colorful president that ever lived. For an hour, Roosevelt moved speedily around the room, giving each person a dazzling smile and a warm handshake. At one p.m., Roosevelt generally excused himself from the crowd for his midday shave. During the "barber's hour," reporters were invited in, permitted to ask questions—or more likely listen—as Roosevelt talked animatedly about any number of subjects while the skillful barber tried not to cut the president's famous face.

Following the shave, lunchtime was always a lively affair, featuring guests rarely seen in the White House—"Western bullwackers, city prize fighters, explorers, rich men, poor men," or authors who had written something that had intrigued Roosevelt. Late afternoon was devoted to exercise—a horseback ride or boxing match, a raucous game of tennis or a strenuous hike along the cliffs in nearby Rock Creek Park. Dragging visitors and friends through the wooded sections of the park, Roosevelt had one simple rule: you had to move forward "point to point," never going around any obstacle. "If a creek got in the way, you forded it. If there was a river, you swam it. If there was a rock, you scaled it." The French ambassador Jean Jules Jusserand provided a celebrated account of his first jaunt with the president. After presenting himself at the White House at 1600 Pennsylvania Avenue "in afternoon dress and silk hat," he soon found himself in the countryside, following Roosevelt "at break-neck pace" through fields and over rocks. When they approached a broad stream, Jusserand assumed the contest had finally ended. "Judge of my horror when I saw the President unbutton his clothes and heard him say, 'We had better strip, so as not to wet our things in the Creek.' Then I too, for the honor of France, removed my apparel, except my lavender kid gloves." To be without gloves, he insisted, "would be embarrassing if we should meet ladies." Reporters soon discovered that the hour when the president returned from these excursions and continued sorting his correspondence was "by far the best time to see him." He would chatter away unfiltered as he went through the mail.

After the workday was done, Roosevelt left his office and returned to the living quarters, where he could relax and dress for dinner. There he was "allowed to become again husband, father and playmate." He talked over the day's events with his wife, Edith, and read to their children or, more often, engaged them in fun and physical games. "I play bear with the children almost every night," he wrote, "and some child is invariably fearfully damaged in the play; but this does not seem to affect the ardor of their enjoyment."

Under Edith's guidance, new life was breathed into the presidential residence. "It was the gloomiest house," she recalled, referencing President McKinley's assassination and his wife Ida's longtime serious illness, "with the shadow of death still over it." Edith opened windows, rearranged rooms, brought in fresh flowers, had new carpet laid, and replaced the heavy canopied beds in the children's rooms with their familiar white bedsteads from the Roosevelt summer home.

Not since Willie and Tad Lincoln scampered through the hallways and played hide-and-seek in closets had there been such liveliness in the old mansion. The Roosevelt children, ranging in age from three to seventeen at that point, gleefully made the White House their own. They dashed across its wooden floors on roller skates. They hid live reptiles in sofa cushions, walked upstairs on stilts, waded through the fountains on the landscaped grounds, and coaxed their pony to ride the elevator to the second-floor bedroom when seven-year-old Archie was sick. The Roosevelt family has "done more to brighten and cheer the White House than a whole army of decorators," it was written in the *Atlanta Constitution*, "and the merry prattle of children echoing through the corridors and apartments impart a homelike atmosphere which every caller is quick to notice and appreciate."

Despite the whirlwind of activity and fresh energy that Roosevelt brought to every endeavor and interaction—which captured the country's imagination—conservatives were not convinced that the transition was going smoothly. To calm the fears of powerful congressional leaders, the new president reached out to the conservative political boss Mark Hanna, McKinley's closest friend, who was now face-to-face with the situation he had dreaded when he cautioned fellow Republicans against putting "that madman" Roosevelt into the vice presidency. Roosevelt had pledged to "continue absolutely unbroken the policy of President McKinley for the peace, prosperity, and the honor of the country."

Yet, despite these promises, Roosevelt understood that the country was looking to him to meet the enormous challenges America was facing during this new industrial age: the rise of gigantic trusts that were rapidly swallowing up their competitors in one field after another, increasing prices on household goods; the invisible web of corruption linking political bosses to the business community; the growing gap between the rich few and the majority of people, who were poor or struggling; the filthy conditions in city slums; the justified mood of rebellion among the working classes. Divisions between various groups were deepening and hardening: Between workers and the business owners, who were increasingly

How did trusts have the money to buy all these smaller coal operations? The investment money came from people like J. P. Morgan, Wall Street's most respected and powerful financier, who was creating many such trusts all over the country, monopolizing industries, putting ownership of essential services (like railroads) and goods (like oil and coal) into the hands of a few wealthy men. These owners had so much money that they easily bought influence over powerful and corrupt government officials, who agreed to keep government out of their business.

In 1901, Roosevelt issued a State of the Union message to Congress calling on lawmakers to limit the power of trusts. "Great corporations exist only because they are created and safeguarded by our institutions," President Theodore Roosevelt asserted. Therefore, he added, it is "our right and our duty to see that they work in harmony with these institutions." The Roosevelt administration sued successfully to break up such monopolies as John D. Rockefeller's Standard Oil Co. and J. P. Morgan's railroad conglomerate, Northern Securities Co., resulting in the creation of dozens of separate companies.

disconnected from their mills and factories. Between the established, bustling East Coast and the hardscrabble, vast frontier West. Between city dwellers and farmers. Between immigrants who were pouring into the country by the millions, Americans whose families had arrived generations earlier, and Native Americans. Between people of different races and ethnicities. Between those who believed women deserved the right to vote and those who did not. Roosevelt knew that it was up to him to try to knit together these diverse elements into one United States, using new tools for a new era.

Calling for a "square deal," Roosevelt would lead the country in a different kind of war, a progressive battle designed to restore fairness to America's economic and social life. And he would do it in the same way he had done every other job in his life—by going out and meeting with people, to hear from them directly what they were thinking and feeling, and to see with his own eyes how they were living, thus ensuring that he was accountable, first and foremost, to them.

During the summer of 1902 while traveling in the Northeast, Roosevelt encountered anger about the growing gap between the rich and the poor, between the captains of industry and everyone else. He understood that many looked back with nostalgia upon the preindustrial era, "when the average man lived more to himself" and had more control over his destiny. He challenged his audiences to look not backward but forward—to a national government that was ready, willing, and able to find constructive ways to help people adjust to the changing economy by policing businesses, empowering workers, and protecting customers.

That fall, he took the opportunity to make good on those promises during a strike led by coal miners that threatened to leave the Northeast without coal, the major fuel source that provided heat in homes and buildings. The strike started because coal mine owners and operators would not pay the miners what they considered fair wages. Like a shortage of bread, a coal famine would cause great suffering and upheaval.

Damp and frigid schoolhouses would be forced to send children home to freezing houses with empty coal stoves. Hospitals throughout the region would experience a rise in deadly respiratory infections due to the bitter cold conditions. Factories faced shutdowns without the essential fuel to keep them going, which meant workers would lose their jobs.

Roosevelt's spirit could not tolerate "any implication that the government of the United States was helpless," so he got involved in the strike as no president ever had before. In fact, it was the first time a president had ever intervened in a domestic confrontation between business and workers. He invited the workers' representatives and the coal mine operators to meet together at the White House, appealing to each side's "spirit of patriotism." He opened the meeting insisting that he championed "neither the operators or the miners"; he was the advocate for "the general public." While the representatives of the miners came to the table hoping for a good-faith compromise, the mine owners, believing that they were superior, refused to "waste time" negotiating with the union men, who

---

Did you know that Theodore Roosevelt saved football?

Football was a fairly new sport during Roosevelt's presidency, and it was extremely violent, sometimes leading to deaths on the field. Players would choke, kick, and hit each other, and doctors waited on the sidelines to treat them. After an investigative report detailing the dangers of the sport and a public outcry that would have ended the game, Roosevelt agreed that football required changes to improve safety.

So, in what had become a signature leadership tool of his, Roosevelt invited football coaches to the White House in October 1905 to urge them to come up with rules that would make the sport safer for its players. That season turned out to be particularly bloody as eighteen players died, and Roosevelt's own son, a Harvard freshman, suffered a broken nose that required surgery. A few months after the meeting, several coaches formed the Intercollegiate Athletic Association (it would eventually become the NCAA, the National Collegiate Athletic Association) to establish rules for play and safety measures to help protect players, who still today suffer from body blows, concussions, and spinal injuries.

---

they called "goons" and "outlaws." The White House talks summarily failed. But Roosevelt, a natural-born fighter, would not give up.

As the crisis intensified, to the point where mobs hijacked coal cars as trains moved through villages and towns, Roosevelt proposed that the American military take over the coal mines. "I am Commander in Chief of the Army," he flatly declared. "I will give the people coal." While it was impossible to know if he was bluffing, it was just the push the parties needed to come to an agreement to reopen coal operations. As he explained to his old friend Bill Sewall, "I believe in rich people who act squarely, and in labor unions which are managed with wisdom and justice; but when either employee or employer, laboring man or capitalist, goes wrong, I have to clinch him, and that is all there is to it." This experience showed him that the people wanted an activist president, one who used the powers of the office to fight for a "square deal" for all of them.

A few months later, on the morning of April 1, 1903, Roosevelt embarked in high spirits upon the longest tour ever taken by a president—a nine-week transcontinental journey by train that would cover fourteen thousand miles across twenty-four states and territories. The specially equipped, fancy, mahogany-finished train consisted of six cars and would be the president's home throughout the trip. This "traveling palace" boasted three staterooms, a kitchen staffed by expert chefs, a private dining room, an observation parlor, quarters for the servants, and a rear platform from which he would address the massive crowds gathered at little stations along the way. The remaining cars included spacious sleeping quarters for the president's guests, stenographers, reporters and photographers, and the Secret Service crew that had expanded after McKinley's assassination.

During this tour, the president "gave himself very freely and heartily to the people," a guest noted, his arrival sparking a festive spirit in each village and town. Whenever Roosevelt spotted a group of men or

women waving from a distance, he raced out to lift his hat and return the greeting. Once, the president was lunching as the train passed by a small schoolhouse where the teacher had ushered her students outside. Clutching his napkin, Roosevelt raced to the platform. "Those children," he said, "wanted to see the President of the United States, and I could not disappoint them. They may never have another chance." Another time, possibly due to his extreme nearsightedness, "he found himself waving frantically at a herd of cows." With dry wit, Roosevelt remembered that he had been "met with an indifferent, if not a cold, reception."

Recognizing that people would come "to see the President much as they would come in to see a circus," Roosevelt also guessed that in many small towns the train—rather than the president—was the main attraction. Nonetheless, he was convinced that "besides the mere curiosity there was a good feeling behind it all, a feeling that the President was their man."

Jostled by frantic crowds as he made his way to crude bandstands erected along his travel route, Roosevelt never seemed impatient or irritated, even radiating delight as he accepted an array of unique gifts that included an infant badger, a lizard, a horned toad, a copper vase, a Native American basket, two bears, a horse, and a gold-inlaid saddle. Through it all, Roosevelt maintained good humor and gratitude. Since active campaigning by a presidential candidate was considered undignified at the time, this extended tour represented Roosevelt's best chance to solidify "the people's trust" before the 1904 election.

It was during this western tour that Roosevelt began to flesh out what the square deal really meant for particular segments of the population. A product of his time, Roosevelt was not always a progressive leader on the issues of race, and his legacy on race relations and civil rights is uneven. While he made some advancements, he also fell short. In one shameful incident during his presidency he issued a sweeping presidential order discharging without honor an entire battalion of Black soldiers for an incident in Brownsville, Texas. Racial tensions had been brewing at Fort Brown for a while: white soldiers forced Black soldiers off the sidewalk and hit them with revolver butts, and local white barkeepers denied them access to public bars. Later, a group of Black soldiers allegedly entered town and fired into buildings, killing a saloonkeeper and injuring the chief of police, whose arm was amputated as a result. When interviews with battalion members failed to reveal the identities of those involved, the president directed that all 167 battalion members be dishonorably discharged from the army—a status that not only prevented them from reenlisting but prohibited them from any civil service position. The battalion included several Medal of Honor winners, soldiers with twenty-five years of distinguished service, and men who had fought beside Roosevelt in the Spanish-American War. It took six decades for the army to clear their records. Regarding Native Americans, Roosevelt strongly defended the rights of white Americans to settle Native American lands, using violence if necessary, and he hoped that Native Americans would assimilate into white culture and forego their traditions.

Even so, Roosevelt recognized the contributions of men and women from various racial and ethnic groups and their rights to equal opportunity. In Arizona, he praised Native Americans in his Rough Riders regiment, which included members of the Cherokee, Chickasaw, and Pawnee Nations: "They were good enough to fight and to die, and they are good enough to have me treat them exactly as square as any white man. . . . All I ask is a square deal for every man." In Montana, he expressed a similar sentiment about the Black troops who fought beside him in Cuba. The notions of basic fairness, of common sense, of striking a workable balance between competing interests were at the heart of every aspect of Roosevelt's agenda. "We must treat each man on his worth and merits as a man. We must see that each is given a square deal, because he is entitled to no more and should receive no less." Roosevelt sought to widen the circle of opportunity to Americans who had been left out, and always with an eye toward future generations.

Roosevelt's train arrived at the Grand Canyon as a great contest was raging over whether to preserve the landmark as a national monument or open it up to mining for precious metals. Deeply moved by this "great wonder of nature," the president resolved to ensure the designation of the Grand Canyon as a national park. "Leave it as it is," he urged his countrymen. "The ages have been at work on it, and man can only mar it. . . . Keep it for your children, your children's children and for all who come after you, as one of the great sights which every American . . . should see." The historian Douglas Brinkley observed, "If Roosevelt had done nothing else as president, his advocacy on behalf of preserving the canyon might well have put him in the top ranks of American presidents." During his nearly two terms in office, Roosevelt created 150 new national forests, "five national parks, eighteen national monuments, and 51 wildlife refuges."

Inspired by Lincoln, Roosevelt considered the president "the steward of the people." As such, it was not only the president's right but his responsibility "to do whatever the needs of the people demand, unless the Constitution or the laws explicitly forbid him to do it." It was why he had intervened in the coal strike, protected the Grand Canyon, and taken on the powerful trusts. He considered it a "danger to American democracy" that power was concentrated in the hands of a few wealthy men; they manipulated the political system to serve their narrow interests and weakened the rights, opportunities, and freedoms of the vast majority of Americans to have a government, as Lincoln proclaimed in the Gettysburg Address, that was "of the people, by the people, for the people."

A regular churchgoer, Roosevelt also framed his efforts to do as much good as possible in spiritual terms, as he wrote in a Thanksgiving proclamation in 1908. In return for America's great wealth and abundance, he urged Americans to give thanks and continue their good works: "we owe it to the Almighty to show equal progress in moral and spiritual things. . . . I recommend that the people . . . meet devoutly to thank the Almighty for the many and great blessings they have received in the past, and to pray that they may be given the strength so to order their lives as to deserve a continuation of these blessings in the future."

Whether cleaning up corruption, regulating the activities of businesses if they threatened to disrupt the lives of millions, preserving America's beautiful wild lands from ruin by industry, or championing laws that ensured that food and medicine were safe to consume, Roosevelt expanded and transformed the responsibilities and expectations of the chief executive for future generations. Though he declined to run for a third term in 1908, Theodore Roosevelt's leadership would prove to be the dawn of a new era. Under the banner of his Square Deal, a mood of progressive reform swept the country, creating a new vision of the relationship between government and the people, one inspired by the promise of equal opportunity in the Declaration of Independence. "All law must be so administered as to secure justice for all alike—a square deal for every man, great or small, rich or poor."

Franklin Delano Roosevelt

Chapter Thirteen

"All that is in me goes back to the Hudson."

WHEN FRANKLIN ROOSEVELT SPOKE OF HIS HUDSON ORIGINS, he didn't mean simply the peaceful river that runs through New York State and Springwood, the rural estate in Hyde Park, about fifty miles north of New York City, where he was raised, but the atmosphere of love and affection that enveloped him as a child. The boy's personality flourished in the warmth of his environment. His maternal grandfather described him as "a very nice child, that is, always bright and happy. Not crying, worrying." Others described him as radiant, beautiful, uncommonly self-confident.

"All that is in me goes back to the Hudson," Roosevelt later wrote. For his first eight years, Franklin enjoyed a childhood of extraordinary stability and balance, with little disruption except for rare instances when his parents, James and Sara, would travel without him. James Roosevelt, a widower with an adult, married son, met Sara Delano in 1880 at the New York City home of his distant cousin Theodore Roosevelt when James was fifty-two and Sara twenty-six, half his age. After a whirlwind romance they married and, from all accounts, had a genuine love marriage despite the difference in their age and over the objections of Sara's father, who thought James was too old for his daughter. James was courtly, good-humored, and gentle; Sara, beautiful, strong-willed, and confident. They both were well educated. The Roosevelt money had been made years before in real estate and the sugar trade, allowing Mr. James, as he was known, to lead the life of a country gentleman. Sara brought even more money to the household from her family; her father, Warren Delano, had made a fortune in trade in China.

The estate where Franklin was born in 1882 and grew up resembled an English country manor, "with class lines separating" the Roosevelts "at the top from the nurses and governesses, and these in turn from the maids and cooks indoors, and these in turn from the stable boys and farm hands outside." As a child, Franklin, seated on his pony, had ridden with his father every morning to survey the plantings and the various construction projects underway on the estate. He graduated from a donkey when he was two to a pony at six and a horse at eight. As father and son rode by, employees "tipped their hats." Franklin's family worshipped at St. James' Episcopal Church in Hyde Park, where he was christened and later served as senior warden. Franklin's parents observed a liberal Episcopal form of Christianity that embraced the Social Gospel, the philosophy that the churches should be actively engaged in social reform, which was reinforced later at his boarding school.

Franklin's vigorous father introduced him to the outside world. In winter, father and son went sledding and tobogganing down the steep hill that stretched from their home to the Hudson River far below. With his father by his side, Franklin learned to ice-skate and ice-boat on the frozen river. In spring, walking in the woods with his father, he learned to observe birds and identify trees and plants, fostering a life-long love of nature. In summers, the family went to Campobello, the small Canadian island near the border of Maine where they owned land and built a cottage. It was there he learned to fish and sail. In the fall, father and son went hunting together. Franklin viewed his father as his best companion and friend. While James encouraged Franklin's love of the outdoors, Sara organized the indoor world of books, hobbies, and governesses. And Franklin himself handled the pranks and jokes, which he would practice on his governesses and tutors. Most notably, Fraulein Reinsberg, Franklin's full-time tutor, received quite a scare after he had snuck in her room and sprinkled fizzing powder into her chamber pot. In the middle of the night when she used the convenience to pee, "the resultant bubbling and hissing sent her screaming down the hall." When Franklin's father questioned him about the incident, the boy confessed. "His father, convulsed with laughter, told him to consider himself spanked and sent him away."

Raised as a single child, "the problem of juvenile squabbles virtually dispensed with itself," his mother noted. The focus of his parents' lives, Franklin lived in a place from which unpleasantness and conflict seemed banished. Protected from the slightest fight, he never learned how to deal with conflict when it arose, as it inevitably would, later in life. He did begin practicing leadership traits during play dates, explaining, "Mummie, if I didn't give the orders, nothing would happen!"

But if the young boy's independence was compromised by the close care of both his parents, Franklin Roosevelt's temperament and character would bear the permanent stamp of his optimistic spirit—a general expectation that things would turn out well, proof of the overwhelming sense of security and confidence that he gained during these early years of his life.

Franklin was forced to summon that inner strength at the age of only eight, when his world was shaken to its core. In November 1890, Mr. James suffered a heart attack that left him essentially an invalid, unable to care for himself for the remaining decade of his life.

An uncommonly intuitive child, Franklin worried that if he appeared sad or troubled, he might be responsible for damaging further his father's heart. When a steel curtain rod fell on him, producing a deep gash on his

A photograph of Franklin and his mother, Sara, taken when he was eleven.

head, Franklin insisted that his father not be told. For days, he simply pulled his hat down over his forehead to hide the wound. The desire to protect his father's failing health required Franklin to practice secrecy, deception, and manipulation—skills that would later prove troubling but were at this moment designed only to protect a loved one from harm.

In the absence of his father's companionship, and with the lack of nearby playmates, Franklin spent more and more time inside the house, devoting hours each day to what became an impressive assembly of collections: stamps, maps, model ships, birds' nests, coins, naval prints. His stamp collection came to be his central hobby, and each day Franklin spent quiet time poring over stamp catalogues, selecting and arranging his stamps into albums, creating a sheltered space where he could be free from the demands of an overprotective mother who had developed an increasing dependence on her only son in her husband's diminished state. Mr. James had been their protector; together, she and her son were now responsible for protecting him.

When Franklin was young, his mother regularly read aloud to him, although he did not develop into a big reader. He learned more from listening and had the ability to absorb great quantities of information by hearing people talk. One night, Sara recalled, she was reading to Franklin while "he lay sprawled on his tummy, sorting and pasting" his beloved stamps. Thinking that he was not listening, she put the book down. "I don't think there is any point in my reading to you anymore," she said. "You don't hear me anyway." He looked up, "a whimsical smile on his face," and "quoted verbatim the last paragraph of the essay." With "a mischievous glint in his eye," he said, "Why, Mom, I would be ashamed of myself if I couldn't do at least two things at once." It was clear even in early childhood that he possessed a problem-solving intelligence, a patience and determination, coupled with a flexible, and often cheerful, manner.

Franklin's education was casual and haphazard. While a series of governesses tutored him in childhood, even this irregular instruction was interrupted by three lengthy stays in Europe, where James and Sara sought the healing powers of mineral spas in Germany. Focused entirely on restoring his health, James could not take his son on expeditions to battlefields and historic sites. Instead, Franklin attended a local German school for a short time, where he picked up the German language with remarkable ease.

When Franklin turned twelve, his parents hired for him a tutor, Arthur Dumper, who later remarked that he went about learning in a curiously "unorthodox" manner. He preferred to engage his tutor in conversation, talking over what he was learning and spending more time with his stamps than with his books. It was through his passionate interest in stamps that Franklin gained a great deal of knowledge, along with endurance and focus. Each stamp was like a passport to the world, each with its own story—from the place and date of issue to the postmark providing the time and location of its travels. In Franklin's mind these stories were alive, meanwhile teaching him about geography, biography, history, culture, and art. The original collection his mother had given him had been assembled during her family's long stay in Asia. Other stamps came from Europe; still others from South America. When asked years later how he had gained such familiarity with far-off places in the world, Roosevelt explained that "when he became interested in a stamp, it led to his interest in the issuing country." Digging through the encyclopedia, he would learn about each country, its people, and its history. Encountering words he didn't know the meaning of, he carried a massive dictionary to bed at night, at one point telling his mother he was "almost halfway through."

Roosevelt continued to learn in his own way, revealing a unique intelligence that cut naturally across subjects. A fascination with maps and atlases developed next, fixing in his mind an astonishing range of facts about the topography of countries, their rivers, mountains, lakes, valleys, natural resources—information that would prove crucial when he was called upon in future years to explain to his countrymen how and where two wars would envelop the entire world. In fact, many of his childhood hobbies would serve later as valuable tools nourishing his leadership—providing a habit for his curiosity, lessons in patience, a means to create a meditative state, and a space in which he could turn things over in his mind, as well as a way to relax and replenish his energy. But first he had to survive the rigors and humiliations of high school.

Franklin's ability to adapt to changing circumstances was put to a punishing test when he was sent to the exclusive Groton School for Boys at the age of fourteen, while most of his classmates started at the Massachusetts boarding school at age twelve. But Sara and James, unable to part with him, had kept him back for two years, which made it difficult for him to fit in with the circles of friends that had already formed. He was unaccustomed to the ordinary give-and-take of schoolmates, and the studied charm and manners that had impressed adults struck

fellow students as stiff and insincere. To make matters worse, Franklin was not athletic enough to participate in varsity team sports and was quickly assigned to the second worst of eight ranked schoolwide football squads and the Bum Baseball Boys, made up of the worst players. He was more successful, however, at individual sports, including the high kick, which "required more pluck and patience than skill."

As a student, he did well enough, having been sufficiently prepared academically by his tutors and governesses. Within a month of his arrival, Franklin stood fourth in his class of nineteen. His highest marks came for his neatness and punctuality, which he worried would give him a bad name with the older boys. So he tested school discipline. "I have served off my first black-mark today [for talking in class] and I am very glad I got it," he explained to his parents, "as I was thought to have no school-spirit before."

He later confessed that he "felt hopelessly out of things" at Groton. He fiercely desired to be popular but had no idea how to gain the favor of his fellow students, mistakenly assuming that he would be respected if he was a model student. Never once, however, did the lonely teenager share his true feelings with his parents. On the contrary, in a string of cheerful and informative letters, he insisted he was adjusting splendidly "both mentally and physically," that he was "getting on very well with the fellows" and receiving good marks in his classes. He wrote about a visit from cousin Theodore Roosevelt, who "gave us a splendid talk on his adventures when he was on the Police Board." The following year when Theodore Roosevelt became governor of New York, Franklin described himself as "wild with delight" and went with his parents to the inauguration in Albany. The image Franklin projected was meant to soothe his mother and not worry his father, but also to cheer himself, blurring the mismatch between things as they were and things as he wished them to be.

His expectation that things would somehow turn out positively allowed him to move steadily forward, to adjust and persevere in the face of difficulty; and in time, he found his place as a member of the debate team. Franklin prepared hard and long for each of his debates, asking his father for advice, information, and pointers. His excellent memory allowed him to speak directly to the audience without notes. Franklin enjoyed considering an issue from different points of view, demonstrating a persuasive reasoning talent to express whatever side he was given. He connected emotionally with his audience and celebrated in victory.

Franklin also connected deeply with the influence of the school's headmaster and cofounder, the Reverend Endicott Peabody, whose "repeated theme, inside chapel and out, was service, particularly public service." He would say, "If some Groton boys do not enter political life and do something for our land it won't be because they have not been urged." Franklin joined a society that helped underprivileged boys at summer camp and at a club in Boston. One winter, during this era when Black Americans faced intense discrimination, Franklin was responsible for helping care for an elderly Black woman, to whom he brought food. He later recalled, "As long as I live, the influence of Dr. and Mrs. Peabody means and will mean more to me than that of any other people next to my father and mother."

While his philanthropic work and academic and other accomplishments did little to mark him yet as a leader, the success allowed him to relax more with his classmates, and by his final year, he had made some good friends. Although he had dreams of joining the navy and fantasized about running away to do so, when he achieved high enough scores on the entrance examinations for Harvard University and another of Groton's cofounders recommended him as "a fellow of exceptional ability and high character," his "immensely proud" parents decided he should attend.

During Franklin's first semester at Harvard, his father's health deteriorated, and he returned home to be by his father's side. On December 8, 1900, Mr. James suffered a fatal heart attack and died. Sara was crushed, and Franklin stayed with her until the new year to console her, while grieving quietly, alone in his room during sleepless nights. Together, mother and son took walks and gathered flowers for Mr. James's grave.

Having spent the last decade acting to protect his ailing father, Franklin was now expected to be the man of the family. The long-established bond with his mother was profound and mutually dependent. Without the focus and buffer of Mr. James, they were alone together. Unable to bear the "unthinkable" idea of living by herself at Hyde Park, Sara rented a town house in Boston to be near her son. "She was an indulgent mother," observed a family friend, "but would not let her son call his soul his own." Franklin's quest to achieve independence without wounding his mother required new levels of manipulation and cunning, a deeper resourcefulness, persistence, and willfulness. Even when he wrote in his diary, he resorted to creating a secret code in case his mother decided to spy on him and read his private thoughts.

As a college student, Franklin was forced to take stock of his own position, desires, and ambitions. Sara could not imagine that her eighteen-year-old son was beginning to form dreams of his own, visions of a life beyond that of a country gentleman who would lead a regular seasonal existence, managing the estate, dabbling in local affairs, and summering on Campobello. In later years, when Sara was asked if she ever envisioned her son becoming president, she replied, "Never, no never! That was the last thing I should ever have imagined for him, or that he should be in public life of any sort."

But beneath his breezy exterior, the young man's family background and faith, upbringing and education, confidence and sense of self, resulted in his desire to accomplish something worthy. For the first time, Franklin began to chart his own course, seeking a place where he could shine on his own, free from parental burdens and expectations. While being an average student and not an athlete, he found that

THE HARVARD CRIMSON, SENIOR BOARD

W. Drinkwater   H. Otis   W. E. Sachs   A. V. de Roode   A. A. Ballantine   R. T. Holt   E. B. Krumbhaar
    C. W. Blossom   W. R. Bowie   F. D. Roosevelt   P. Dana   H. de H. Hughes

Franklin (seated, center) as president of Harvard's student
newspaper, the *Harvard Crimson*, age twenty-two.

place at the *Harvard Crimson*, the student newspaper run by under-graduates. Franklin began at the lowest level, one of seventy freshmen trying out for a position on the staff. "The competition was tough," a classmate recalled. The challenge demanded his full attention, providing legitimate reasons to decline his mother's constant invitations to dinner or the theater. He worked harder than he had ever worked before, harder than he did on his studies, for which he received barely passing grades. "My Dearest Mummy," he wrote, "I am working about 6 hours a day on [the *Crimson*] alone and it is quite a strain." Though he failed to make the first group of five freshmen selected in February, he refused to give up.

Two months later, he learned from the cousin he so admired, vice president and Harvard alumnus Theodore Roosevelt, that he had a lecture scheduled at Harvard that had not been made public. Franklin hurried to the *Crimson* to break the news. "Young man," the managing editor told him, "you hit page one tomorrow morning." The lecture hall was jam-packed. Weeks later, Franklin was elected to join the *Crimson* staff. The following September, President William McKinley was assassinated, and Franklin's cousin Theodore Roosevelt became president of the United States.

Franklin worked his way up the *Crimson* ladder from assistant managing editor to managing editor, and when he finished all his college requirements in only three years, he took graduate courses in the fall of 1903 so he could stay on an extra year and head the paper as president. During this time he wrote the editorials and became known as a crusading journalist who "always had an issue to campaign for." In one revealing editorial, Franklin recommended that students interested in politics would learn more "in one day" by venturing into Boston to observe local politics—"the machinery of primary, caucus, convention, election and legislature"—than by listening to abstract lectures on government. Experience, he believed, was the "best teacher."

It was during these last years in college that Franklin also began to emerge as a student leader as the elected chairman of the Class Day Committee, a founder of the Political Society, and the secretary of the Glee Club. He also experienced during this time what he would later call "the greatest disappointment of my life" when he was rejected for membership into Harvard's most prestigious society, the Porcellian, to which cousin Theodore had belonged—"considered a mark of distinction one carried for life." Despite this rejection, Roosevelt would later look back with prideful nostalgia on his Harvard years, especially his first leadership position at the *Crimson*, where many colleagues agreed that he was "quick-witted and capable as an editor," "energetic, resourceful, and independent," with an optimistic spirit and an infectious sense of humor. While some thought he was cocky and a show-off, it was clear "he had a force of personality . . . he liked people, and he made them instinctively like him."

At Groton, he had managed to survive; at Harvard, he had begun to thrive. For what would he strive next? And how would his mother react to the fact that he was growing more independent, carving out for himself his own achievements, and enjoying his own life experiences?

Chapter Fourteen

"I know my mind, have known it for a long time. . . ."

A SIGNATURE OF FRANKLIN ROOSEVELT'S developing leadership style—an ability to make decisions without hesitating or looking back, coupled with an instinct to keep his process under wraps—emerged during his secret courtship of Eleanor Roosevelt. Early on in his time at Harvard, Franklin had worried about his mother's reaction to his romantic interest in women. In letters and conversations, he would exhaustively share with his mother details of his daily activities, skillfully leaving out his innermost feelings, those that might have interfered with their close relationship. In the wake of his father's death, Franklin felt that that need for concealment had intensified, because he did not want his mother to feel left out.

No one, not a single friend, and surely not his mother, knew that he had fallen in love with his distant cousin Eleanor in the spring of his junior year at Harvard. While Eleanor later recalled she had first met Franklin when she was just two years old and he was four years old, in the summer of 1902 they ran into each other on a train ride out of New York City. Franklin spotted Eleanor sitting alone on the way to her grandmother's home in Tivoli, New York—not far from his Hyde Park home—and invited her to join his mother and him in a different train car.

Eleanor was unlike any other girl Franklin had met. She was highly intelligent, sincere, deeply absorbed in social causes, and wholly uninterested in the privileged world of fancy dresses and debutante balls. Eleanor's early years had been as filled with sadness as Franklin's were filled with joy. She was eight when her mother, Anna, with whom she had had a difficult relationship, died suddenly from the infectious bacterial disease diphtheria. Two years later, when she was ten, her beloved father, Elliott, Theodore Roosevelt's younger brother and Franklin's godfather, died from alcoholism. Eleanor and her two brothers were sent to live with their grandmother, and at fifteen, she was sent to England to attend the elite girls' boarding school Allenswood Academy, which emphasized social responsibility and independence. During her time at Allenswood Academy, Eleanor started "a new life," free from the customs and traditions of her wealthy social class. Basking in the maternal love, guidance, and teachings of the legendary feminist headmistress Marie Souvestre, Eleanor became "everything" in the school, the most popular and respected student among faculty and students alike. "She is full of sympathy for all those who live with her," the headmistress reported to Eleanor's grandmother, "and shows an intelligent interest in everything she comes in contact with."

"The surest way to be happy," Eleanor wrote in an essay at school, "is to seek happiness for others." When she began seeing Franklin, Eleanor had just returned to New York and, at the urging of her headmistress, become involved in social work, teaching classes to Italian immigrants at the Rivington Street Settlement on the Lower East Side. She joined a group of female activists who were investigating working conditions in factories and department stores. "I had a great curiosity about life," she wrote, "and a desire to participate in every experience."

During their hidden romance, Franklin and Eleanor shared their unfolding dreams to leave a mark on the world. Eleanor's social consciousness and urgent sense of social justice—the awakening of a caring for the other, a championing of the underdog—had started earlier and ran deeper than his. Franklin admired her distaste for the debutante world she was about to enter, her rebellious desire to find something meaningful to do. She was a serious person, and so was he, despite the shallow "featherduster" impression he sometimes left. The life he might lead, as reflected and encouraged in Eleanor's eyes, was a life involving a "broad human contact" with all manner of people. One afternoon, when he picked Eleanor up from the settlement house, she enlisted his help in carrying home a young girl who had fallen ill. Although he had occasionally volunteered to teach at a boys' club in Boston, he was astounded when they reached the girl's decrepit tenement. "My God, I didn't know anyone lived like that," he told Eleanor, who later held the belief that the experience at Rivington had had a "lasting and powerful impact on him."

With Eleanor by his side, Franklin believed "he would amount to something someday." And he enjoyed her company immensely. He invited her to vacation with him at Campobello in the summer, to dances and football games at Harvard in the fall, and to his family home at Hyde Park in the spring, where they rode horses together in the woods and sat on the porch at twilight reading poetry to each other. As the days and months passed, Eleanor recalled, she came to realize she was happiest when she was with him. After a weekend together in New York, Eleanor wrote, "It is impossible to tell you what these last two days have been to me, but I know they have meant the same to you so that you will understand that I love you dearest and I hope that I shall always prove worthy of the love which you have given me. I have never known before what it was to be absolutely happy." Though he was only twenty-two and she only nineteen when he asked her to marry him in November 1903 during his senior year at Harvard, she was absolutely sure that it was right. "When he told me that he loved me and asked me to marry him, I did not hesitate to say yes, for I knew that I loved him too."

Franklin and Eleanor had been together at all manner of family events, but Franklin's mother, Sara, had no inkling they shared anything more than a friendship when, at Thanksgiving, he delivered the shocking news of their engagement. Sara was not pleased and tried to convince Franklin to change his mind. She thought them too young to marry and that "neither had a clear life plan." She also urged Franklin to keep the engagement secret for a year so he would have time to reflect, and she would have time to try to control how and when he and Eleanor would continue to meet up. Eleanor tiptoed carefully around her future mother-in-law's hurt feelings, writing to her, "I do so want you to learn to love me a little." But in her letters to Franklin she bristled at Sara's attempts to meddle in their plans and stake a claim on Franklin: "I suppose I ought not mind, only I do mind terribly."

For his part, Franklin was delayed but not discouraged. He was absolutely certain of his decision to marry Eleanor. "I know what pain I must have caused you, and you know I wouldn't do it if I really could have helped it," Franklin wrote his mother after returning to Harvard. "I know my mind, have known it for a long time and know that I could never think otherwise. Result: I am the happiest man just now in the world; likewise the luckiest—and for you, dear Mummy, you know that nothing can ever change what we have always been & always will be to each other—only now you have two children to love & to love you."

The secret courtship became a pattern for how Franklin would later deal with political colleagues as well as challengers. "Never let the left hand know what the right is doing" was a way he did business when the situation called for it. In saying that he knew his mind, had known it for a long time, and could never think otherwise, Franklin declared that his decision was not up for discussion. As would be true the rest of his life, once he made a decision, he rarely second-guessed himself.

When Franklin and Eleanor's engagement was announced on

December 1, 1904, President Theodore Roosevelt, Eleanor's uncle, wrote Franklin: "We are greatly rejoiced over the good news. I am as fond of Eleanor as if she were my daughter; and I like you, and trust you, and believe in you. . . . You and Eleanor are true and brave, and I believe you love each other unselfishly; and golden years open before you." Franklin and Eleanor traveled to Washington together on March 4, 1905, to celebrate Theodore Roosevelt's inauguration, joining the inner circle at an intimate lunch and sitting with the family at the reviewing stand during the parade, and then they "danced away the evening" at the inaugural ball. Shortly afterward, on St. Patrick's Day, President Roosevelt, standing in for his deceased brother, gave the bride away at the wedding, officiated by Groton's Reverend Peabody. "Well, Franklin," President Roosevelt said with a smile, "there's nothing like keeping the name in the family."

During a grand honeymoon in Europe, Franklin wrote home to his mother about how the Roosevelt family name was being celebrated there. "Everyone is talking about Cousin Theodore saying that he is the most prominent figure of present day history." Upon Franklin and Eleanor's return to New York, the family they would go on to build would ever after include Sara on close, personal terms. While Franklin's mother recognized she had lost the battle to keep her only son from marrying Eleanor, she was unable to back off, and he was

Franklin and Eleanor with the wedding party of Franklin's niece, Helen R. Roosevelt (not pictured). This was taken after Franklin and Eleanor became engaged but before they were married.

unable to make her go. Instead, Franklin allowed her to compete with Eleanor for his devotion. Sara's vast inherited wealth enabled her to control the finances for the family and furnish for Franklin and Eleanor a lavish lifestyle—which came at a price for the young newlyweds.

While Franklin was in law school, and less than fourteen months after they married, their first child, Anna, was born, and over the next decade, Eleanor would give birth to five more children: James in 1907, Franklin Delano Jr. in 1909 (who died of the flu later that year), Elliott in 1910, a second Franklin Jr. in 1914, and John in 1916. Three years into the marriage, Sara moved them all to adjoining town houses in New York City, with "doors giving access to their respective drawing and dining rooms" so she was always close by, as were the cook, maid, butler, nurses, and nannies. Sara inserted herself to help Eleanor in the task of raising the children, or rather, she took over.

It seemed to work to some degree. Eleanor was largely overwhelmed and unsure of herself in the early days of motherhood and therefore "allowed her ever-confident mother-in-law to take charge of hiring the nurses and setting up the nursery, accepting Sara's intervention both grudgingly and gratefully, intimidated by inexperience and fear." And there was the death of baby Franklin Delano Jr.; Eleanor blamed herself and was filled with grief. Sara became more and more involved, referring to the kids as "her" children, her grandson Jimmy later recalled. She told them, "your mother only bore you, I am more your mother than your mother is." Even as a young boy, Jimmy recognized that this was a cruel thing for his grandmother to say, but he loved her and needed her too much to condemn her. Since Sara had been unable to prevent her son's marriage, Eleanor observed in an unpublished article, "she determined to bend the marriage to the way she wanted it to be. What she wanted was to hold onto Franklin and his children were more my mother-in-law's children than they were mine."

In contrast to the tangled feelings about their mother, the children would remember for the rest of their lives the adventures they shared with their father. "Franklin loved his small children," Eleanor recalled. "They were a great joy to him; he loved to play with them and I think he took great pleasure in their health and good looks and in their companionship. He made the children feel that he really was their age." With the father acting as more of a playmate, discipline was always a source of trouble in the Roosevelt household. "I was the disciplinarian, I'm afraid," Eleanor recalled. "[Franklin] found punishing a child almost an impossibility. He just couldn't do it."

Franklin never did graduate from Columbia Law School but passed the New York Bar Examination and became a law clerk, ostensibly following an expected path for a member of the privileged class by joining an old, conservative Wall Street law firm. But when he and his fellow clerks discussed their hopes and plans for the future, Franklin shared that "he wasn't going to practice law forever, that he intended to run for office at the first opportunity," that he had "dreams of high political station." Indeed, he had begun to visualize his path, having made up his mind to duplicate cousin Theodore Roosevelt's career: election to the state legislature would come first, leading to an appointment to a senior post at the Navy Department, before becoming governor of New York and then, with good fortune, president of the United States. A key difference between the two men: Franklin was aligned with the Democratic Party, not the Republican Party of Theodore Roosevelt.

So when at age twenty-eight Franklin was offered the chance to run for a seat in the state legislature from the Hyde Park area with the full backing of the party, he was quick to accept. He knew something about himself that others might not—that he craved adventure, a desire for freedom from the confines of his insulated world. By this point,

What did it mean to be a Democrat or a Republican at the turn of the twentieth century?

FDR quite admired his distant cousin Theodore Roosevelt, a star in the Republican Party, but while at Harvard, FDR declared himself a member of the Democratic Party, as was his father. The makeup and priorities of the two major political parties has shifted over the decades. After Theodore Roosevelt left office, there was still a split within the Republican Party between traditional conservatives and progressive reformers who believed in his Square Deal activist government agenda, but over time, more and more of the reformers switched to the Democratic Party. The priorities of the remaining Republicans were largely to support the business class and keep government activities and oversight limited. Republicans then believed that government should not interfere with the free market, letting businesses operate as they wished. The priorities of Democrats were to meet the needs of working people, which meant passing laws that regulated businesses, ensuring decent wages and working conditions. There was another side to the Democrats at the time too. Many Democrats, especially those from the South, supported Jim Crow laws that cruelly discriminated against Black people and enforced racial segregation, while Republicans held on to the legacy of Lincoln, the president who ended slavery.

Eleanor was seriously outnumbered at home, having given birth to three of their six children. When Franklin was approached to run, Eleanor was pregnant with Elliott, who would be born a few weeks before Election Day.

To kick off his campaign, Franklin's first order of business was to meet with the local Democratic committeeman, Tom Leonard. Consequently, one August afternoon, Franklin went looking for Leonard, a housepainter at work inside one of the houses on the Roosevelts' country estate. Never having been formally introduced to the housepainter, Roosevelt rang the bell. "There's a Mr. Franklin wants to see you," the housekeeper told Leonard. "I thought for a moment," Leonard said, but after searching his memory, he concluded, "I don't know any Mr. Franklin." Nonetheless, he stepped out to meet the gentleman—surprised to find none other than Mr. Franklin Roosevelt. "Hello, Tom," said Franklin, smiling warmly and extending his hand in greeting. "How do you do, Mr. Roosevelt?" asked the puzzled painter. "No, call me Franklin. I'm going to call you Tom," he declared, telling him that he had come to ask his advice about getting into politics. That Roosevelt was able to seek advice with such good-natured spirits and without a trace of snobbery won over Tom Leonard as his naturally easygoing nature would soon win over thousands in his county. Franklin's friendliness and his sincerity conveyed something authentic. With this first foray into politics, he had bridged, symbolically at least, a lifetime of social distance.

The state senate seat Franklin sought had been long held by Republicans. The Roosevelt name might help overcome the Democrat's disadvantage—after serving nearly two terms in the White House, Franklin's Republican cousin Theodore Roosevelt remained the most dominant figure on the national scene. Still, the local Democratic boss, John Mack, thought that the race was a long shot. From the start, Franklin "had a distinct feeling that in order to win he must put himself into direct personal touch with every available voter" in the large district. As he thought the challenge over, he came up with an innovative strategy. He would be the first candidate to crisscross the district in an automobile instead of a horse and buggy. Veteran advisers cautioned him. "The automobile was just coming into use," Mack recalled. "Get a horse!" farmers jeered when passing frequent automobile breakdowns. Furthermore, Mack explained, "horses were terrified of the new 'contraption' and, when meeting one on the highway, would bolt, frequently upsetting the farmer's wagon with occasional injuries."

Despite such hazards, the idea of breaking precedent, of doing what had never been done before, captivated Franklin, as it would again and again in the years ahead. Locating a driver and a splashy red Maxwell touring car, he invited two fellow Democrats running for other offices to accompany him on what turned into a rollicking circuslike adventure. Citizens of all ages were drawn to the sight of the newfangled vehicle, decorated with flags and campaign banners, riding the rough country roads at a startling speed of twenty miles per hour. Meanwhile, Franklin turned the potential trouble the car could cause into an advantage. He ordered the driver to bring the car to an immediate stop whenever they encountered a horse and buggy or wagon. Such a show of respect not only impressed the farmers but gave Franklin the opportunity to personally introduce himself and shake as many hands as possible.

Everywhere he traveled, people were struck by Franklin's warmth, charm, and broad grin. On Saturdays and Sundays he stumped throughout the district, attending political meetings, talking with people in general stores, stopping in village squares, standing outside manufacturing plants, shaking hands. He made a good impression, Tom Leonard recalled, "because he wouldn't immediately enter into the topic of politics"; instead, he encouraged people to talk about their work, their families, their lives. He had always learned by listening, and now he was actively listening, his head nodding in a welcoming way. "There was something incurably sociable about this man," Frances Perkins, the future first female cabinet secretary, later observed, "he was sociable in his intellectual as well as his playful moods."

Every aspect of the barnstorming process excited Franklin. He designed his own posters and buttons; placed ads in county newspapers; and, most important, delighted in direct contact with people from all walks of life. At crossroads, train stations, general stores, saloons, and front porches, he delivered short speeches, sometimes as many as ten a day. Franklin "spoke slowly" then, Eleanor recalled, "and every now and then there would be a long pause, and I would be worried for fear he would never go on," but he always did, and when he finished, Tom Leonard recalled, he moved easily and naturally among the crowd, flashing "that smile of his," introducing himself as Frank, approaching every person "as a friend."

"I know I'm no orator," he liked to say of his simple, casual speaking style. "You don't have to be an orator, Roosevelt," someone in the audience yelled back. "Talk right along to us on those lines, that's what we like to hear." When the votes were tallied on Election Day, Franklin learned that he had crushed his opponent, winning by the largest margin of any Democratic candidate in the state. The cheerful, friendly, disarmingly good-looking gentleman had out-worked, out-traveled, and out-strategized the Republicans simply by listening to the hopes, dreams, and needs of whoever crossed his path.

No sooner had Franklin entered the state senate than he charged into battle against the entrenched Tammany political machine that had held a grip on the state Democratic Party for more than a hundred years, making headlines just as Theodore Roosevelt had a generation earlier. And further following Theodore Roosevelt's path, Franklin served as assistant secretary of the navy a few years later starting in 1913. Indeed, Theodore had recognized the similarities in his congratulatory note to Franklin when he got the job. "It is interesting that you are in another place which I myself once held. I am sure you will enjoy yourself to the full." Over the course of his seven years there, Franklin was charged with managing the giant Navy Department, which employed sixty-five thousand men, with a budget representing one fifth of all federal spending. He was responsible for securing supplies and equipment, supervising docks, navy yards, and workers. And beyond those daily responsibilities, he was determined to build bigger and better-equipped ships and to strengthen the navy's readiness for battle should the necessity arise. His preparation proved of great importance. Franklin had laid the foundation for America's entry into World War I years in advance and was praised as a visionary.

Then, climbing the next rung on the ladder to the presidency he had uncannily visualized for himself, Franklin was tapped as the vice presidential nominee for the Democrats in 1920. The Democrats ultimately lost the election for president that year, but Roosevelt had campaigned day after day with great energy and exuberance for his party, building a vast account of goodwill that would be drawn upon in the future. And while he continued to rely on his mother's fortune, he was also determined to make his own income. Consequently, he became partner in a New York City law firm and ran the New York office of an insurance company.

Franklin Delano Roosevelt had begun to make his mark on the national stage. But it was Louis Howe, a close adviser since FDR's years in the New York State Senate, who first saw in him presidential potential. "At that very first meeting," Howe told a reporter, "I made up my mind that he was Presidential timber and that nothing but an accident could keep him from being President of the United States."

Chapter Fifteen

"I hope to be back in the game before so very long."

FRANKLIN ROOSEVELT AWOKE on a late August day in 1921 with a mild sensation that something was wrong. His back ached, and he felt oddly drained of energy. Nothing serious, he assumed; exercise would surely shake off this peculiar exhaustion. From youth, Roosevelt had taken keen pleasure in a large range of physical activities. His earliest letters expressed the thrill of sledding, skating, and fishing with his father. He developed into an avid golfer, tennis player, sailor, and horseback rider. While neither particularly strong nor muscular, he was flexible and graceful and always active.

So, rather than surrendering to his weariness by remaining in bed, he launched upon a day of strenuous physical activity at Campobello, the island retreat where he and his family enjoyed the same pursuits he had as a child. First, he went for a long sail with Eleanor and their two oldest sons, James and Elliott. On their return home, they spotted a brush fire on one of the neighboring islands. Bringing the boat close to shore, they jumped out and spent an hour slapping down smoldering flames. Eyes "bleary with smoke," they no sooner had reached their cottage when Franklin challenged the boys to jog a mile and a half to their favorite swimming spot, a freshwater pond on the other side of the island. Still unrefreshed and uncomfortable after swimming, he raced the boys back home and plunged into the ice-cold Bay of Fundy. Then, suddenly so lethargic he was unable to take off his wet bathing suit, he slumped on the porch and tried to sort through mail. Abruptly he announced that he had a severe chill and would go straight to bed. "I'd never felt quite that way before," he recalled.

Within forty-eight hours, a shocking paralysis spread to his limbs, thumbs, toes, back, bladder, and rectal sphincter, which controls bowel movements. Excruciating pain shot up and down his legs. Misdiagnosis by the first attending doctors worsened his dire condition. Fear, confusion, and persistent agony followed. Finally, a specialist arrived who correctly diagnosed his condition—poliomyelitis, better known as polio, an infectious virus that attacks the central nervous system and can cause temporary or permanent paralysis. At the time, the other name for polio was "infantile paralysis," because the virus had mostly targeted children. Just five years earlier, there had been a devastating outbreak in New York City that left 9,000 paralyzed and caused 2,400 deaths, with 80 percent of the fatalities being children under the age of five. Every day the newspapers published the names and addresses of people identified with the disease. Placards were nailed to their doors, and their families were quarantined. Franklin's age, thirty-nine, was likely why he had been misdiagnosed at first and why he didn't receive essential treatment quickly enough.

In the days that followed, Eleanor, with the support of Franklin's close adviser, Louis Howe, a guest at Campobello, had to lift Franklin off the bed onto a bedpan so he could relieve himself. Eleanor administered enemas to clear his bowels and learned how to use a catheter tube so he could urinate without the bedpan. The doctor mandated complete bed rest, save a daily tub of soothing warm water. Everything Franklin had taken for granted his entire life—walking, sitting up, using the toilet, his very independence—had disappeared in an instant.

For weeks, Franklin lay in bed, unable to perform many of the most basic bodily functions on his own. Until the most severe phase passed, no predictions could be made about the future course of his illness. Some muscles might return; others would recover only partial strength or remain totally paralyzed. In mid-September, Franklin was transferred from Campobello to New York Presbyterian Hospital, where he remained for six weeks. While his bladder and sphincter muscles returned, his shoulders remained remarkably weak, his back could not support a seated position, and his legs showed no response at all. The physicians generally agreed that Franklin would not walk or stand on his own power again.

In 1920s America, polio sparked intense fears—especially among parents. Even though paralytic polio was relatively rare, it seemed to strike children and infants randomly and without warning. Almost no one at that time had health insurance, so polio treatments—doctors visits, hospital stays, physical therapy, braces, splints, wheelchairs—were too expensive for most people. A year of treatment often cost more money than most Americans earned in a year. One stricken girl wrote about the burden her father faced to treat her polio: "He was a very hardworking, proud man, and he had to beg for money from the county to take care of me and pay the hospital bills. He spent years paying the county back by cutting brush along roads and under telephone lines. . . . He would never accept charity without paying it back."

Though Roosevelt was privileged with access to doctors, specialists, medical devices, and household help, he still had to consider whether the ambitious path he had envisioned as a twenty-five-year-old—climbing from the state legislature to assistant secretary of the navy, up to governor of New York, and then to the presidency itself—was still possible.

Roosevelt's physician, George Draper, worried that his remarkably upbeat patient, despite his courage and ambition, would be unable to cope once he fully understood the gravity of his situation. "It will take all the skill which we can muster to lead him successfully to a recognition of what he really faces without utterly crushing him," Dr. Draper told a fellow doctor. Roosevelt, throughout his hospital stay, was always smiling and cheerful. In letters and conversations with friends, he predicted that he would be upright on crutches by the time he left the hospital, walking without a limp by the following spring. Then it was simply a matter of time before he could resume playing golf. "The doctors tell me I am getting along splendidly and I hope to be back in the game before so very long," read one of his letters from the hospital. A sharp contrast to his chart upon release from the hospital, which read "Not improving."

But Dr. Draper was not the first to miscalculate the resourceful depths of Roosevelt's perseverance. In the face of traumatic illness, the positive image and irrepressible optimism Roosevelt projected, his tendency to expect the best outcome, was so starkly at odds with the ordeal he was confronting. He was not simply protecting others but lifting his own spirits, and this provided the keystone strength that carried him through this harrowing experience. FDR also always had maintained a deep, personal inner faith, despite the fact that he rarely attended church as an adult, much to Eleanor's disappointment. "I think he actually felt he could ask God for guidance and receive it," Eleanor wrote in her memoir *This I Remember*. His speechwriter Robert Sherwood noted that "his religious faith was the strongest and most mysterious force in him."

From the outset, he set an objective: a future in which he would fully recover. Although necessity forced Roosevelt to modify the timetable for attaining this goal, he never lost his belief that he would eventually succeed. This too was a mark of the time. Published accounts of people who survived polio and recovered use of their paralyzed limbs credited their recuperation to good medical care and a positive, can-do attitude.

FDR's daughter, Anna, remembered that when he first returned from the hospital, her "knowledge that he was suffering made me shy with him." Some days were harder than others. In time, however, acting cheerful bred real cheer, as Anna came to understand. "I watched his courage, his suffering, his humor. I learned fast that he wanted no maudlin sympathy." If there was something fake and theatrical about the relentless sunniness he conveyed—a willful whistling in the dark— he radiated warmth, hope, and confidence that would, in the end, prove contagious. His immediate future included months and years of rehabilitation, accompanied by fear, anxiety, and concealed bouts of depression; but eventually, the sustained effort Roosevelt directed toward spiritual, mental, emotional, and physical recovery led him to a spectacular, albeit risk-filled return to public life.

Told by doctors that his upper body had the greatest likelihood of recovery, Franklin endured punishing exercises to remake his chest, shoulders, neck, arms, and back. Hour after hour he pulled himself up on a set of rings installed in "a trapeze-like contraption" above his bed, slowly and painfully strengthening his muscles until his upper body came to resemble that of a champion boxer or wrestler. With powerful arms, he could manipulate a wheelchair and push himself into a sitting position. Everything below his waist, however, remained paralyzed according to one of his doctors, preventing him from getting into or out of the wheelchair without help. Day after day he would ask to be lifted from the wheelchair and set down on the library floor so that he could further exercise his back and arms by crawling around the room, like a child would. He then proceeded to tackle stairs, grabbing railings on either side with his hands, hoisting up his body—step-by-step— to the top, sweat pouring from his face. He insisted that family members be on hand to witness and cheer on each of these triumphs. Praise and encouragement from his children made him feel better about his

condition, as Eleanor remembered: "The perfect naturalness with which the children accepted his limitations though they had always known him as an active person, helped him tremendously in his own acceptance of them."

He reveled in every small "win," Eleanor observed. "He regained his joy in living," she later wrote, "his hearty laughter, his ability to be happy over little things." The day he was at last able to move one of his "frozen" toes called for a grand celebration. When asked during his presidency how he dealt with continuing national problems, he half-jokingly observed, "If you spent two years in bed trying to wiggle your big toe, anything would seem easy!" Each bit of increased mobility led to new hope. After being fitted with heavy steel braces to keep his legs rigid, he met the difficult challenge of learning to totter awkwardly on crutches. Through it all, FDR adamantly refused to give up on his ultimate goal of walking on his own.

In his never-ending search for improvement, Roosevelt used a "trial and error" method, enthusiastically embracing dozens of novel contraptions for treatment: an electric belt, an oversized tricycle, a specially designed shoe, a children's double swing. Over time, he even invented his own devices to deal with "a number of mechanical problems" that obstructed his mobility. He designed a small wheelchair without arms to exercise his thigh muscles and fastened pincers to a stick to reach his library books on the bookcase. He loved to drive, but without the use of his legs, he had the first hand-operated throttle and brake installed in his car. He was able to return to work, too, joining the boards of several organizations and eventually forming a new law practice. FDR was unique in having these tools at his disposal. Society and government at the time were generally unaccommodating to people with disabilities, unable or unwilling to recognize and support their needs, their potential, and their capabilities for employment and even, in many cases, to treat them with dignity and respect. It would be more than three decades before a polio vaccine would be developed and almost seven decades before the landmark Americans with Disabilities Act was signed into law to pave the way for Americans with disabilities to be fully included in society.

But FDR was ahead of his time, carrying on an extensive personal correspondence with fellow polio survivors, comparing ideas for overcoming common dilemmas. The shared vulnerability revealed in these letters represented the first flowering of a new humility, a concern for the pain and suffering of others that would later grow to maturity during his years at Warm Springs, Georgia.

The nature of Roosevelt's paralytic polio was such that he had to seek help and depend on others as he struggled to recover his physical and mental strength. Aside from his family, the handpicked circle around FDR, mostly gathered in their New York town house on Sixty-Fifth Street, was extremely small. This unorthodox, fiercely loyal team assembled during his seven-year rehabilitation was composed of Eleanor, his children, his mother, adviser Louis Howe, and indispensable secretary Missy LeHand, who had been hired by Eleanor to work for Franklin a year before he contracted polio and would become one of his closest friends and advisers for twenty years. Together, this intimate group reduced the isolating impact of FDR's paralysis. It also helped hide the extent of his paralysis from the public; while most knew that he had survived polio, few realized that he remained disabled. Franklin's long period of recovery and transformation was also a time of change for those closest to him, a time when they discovered previously undeveloped interests and talents of their own.

If he didn't have political hope, Eleanor believed, "he would die spiritually, die intellectually, and die in his personality." Working side by side, the team mobilized a strenuous campaign to sustain FDR's political dreams. Anxiously at first, and then with genuine enthusiasm, Eleanor took on the task of keeping her husband's name alive in political circles. She stood in for him at public events, joined various Democratic Party committees, volunteered for the victorious campaign of Al Smith to become New York's governor, and spoke at luncheons and dinners. Having little experience in public speaking, her son James recalled, she gave more than a hundred practice speeches to an audience of one—her mentor and coach, Louis Howe. Howe taught her to restrain her nervous giggle, lower her high-pitched voice, say what she wanted to say, and then sit down. When she began to speak before packed audiences, Howe would sit in the back row, using a series of hand signals to indicate where she was reaching her audience and where she had fallen into nervous mannerisms. Before long, she was recognized as a powerful public speaker.

Entering public life proved a liberating force for Eleanor. Her marriage to Franklin had been rocked two years before he contracted polio, upon her discovery of a packet of love letters to her husband from a young woman named Lucy Mercer, who had worked as Eleanor's social secretary when FDR was assistant secretary of the navy. When Franklin pledged never to see Lucy again, Eleanor agreed to remain in the marriage. From that moment on, she later told friends, she no longer loved him in the same way, though they remained joined by unbreakable ties and retained "a deep and unshakeable affection and tenderness" toward each other.

Now, in the wake of Franklin's paralysis, Eleanor could support her husband's political plans and simultaneously create a role for herself—stirred once again by the ambitions that had been stifled by the responsibility to care for a husband and five children. In the course of her political activities for Franklin, she joined a circle of progressive feminists dedicated to abolishing child labor, passing protective

Franklin's affair permanently altered the Roosevelts' marriage. Instead of romantic partners, they became political and social partners. This crisis turned out to be a liberating force in Eleanor's life. It opened a new path for her, providing the opportunity for a more independent life, in which she sought fulfillment outside the conventions of marriage and family at that time.

A decade later, when Franklin was running for president, Eleanor became friends with Lorena Hickok, a thirty-nine-year-old journalist who was the most widely known female reporter in the country, respected for her political savvy, her passionate convictions, and her superb writing style. At poker games with her colleagues, Hick, as she was known, looked and acted like one of the "boys," with her flannel shirt, trousers, and a cigar hanging from her mouth.

During the last weeks of the 1932 campaign, Hick convinced her Associated Press editors that she should cover Eleanor on a regular basis. In the time they spent together—on the presidential train, in a car from one event to the next—Hick shared stories about her childhood days on a poor dairy farm in Wisconsin. Her father was a physically abusive man, prompting her to leave home as soon as she could. Her mother died when she was a teenager, and Hick put herself through high school by working as a servant in rooming houses. She won every school prize possible and became a

laws for female workers, and fighting for the minimum wage and maximum work hours. She further developed the leadership traits she had exercised during her days as a star student in boarding school: organizing people, inspiring them to loyalty, articulating their goals. With FDR's paralysis, a new opportunity had opened up whereby she might help him and realize her own dreams of leaving a mark on the world.

Franklin's paralysis transformed Louis Howe's world in equally dramatic fashion. Howe had first encountered Roosevelt during his time in the New York State Senate, and the two immediately hit it off. A former reporter for the *New York Herald* whose unique appearance inspired descriptions as a "gnome-like" creature, "a singed cat" with thinning hair and "luminous eyes," clothed in wrinkled suits perpetually covered with cigarette ashes, he was never shy about his opinions. While the good-humored and optimistic Roosevelt generally avoided confrontation, Howe was tough and cynical by nature, happy to battle opposing people head-on. Howe would tell Roosevelt flatly when and where he had gone wrong. Remaining largely behind the scenes, he let Roosevelt absorb credit when things went well and readily accepted blame when they did not. For nearly a decade, while married with two children, Howe had served as Franklin's adviser and close friend.

Franklin's illness, Howe told an interviewer, "changed everything." From the moment his boss was stricken, Howe never lived with his family again, choosing instead to make the Roosevelt family his own, visiting his wife and children only on occasional weekends. He had his own room at the Roosevelt family's Campobello cottage, their New York town house, the governor's mansion, and ultimately, the White House. "He had one loyalty in life and it was a kind of religion," White House speechwriter Sam Rosenman said: "Franklin D. Roosevelt." Howe courted politicians on Franklin's behalf; held private conferences with Democratic governors, mayors, and congressmen; attended local and state party conventions; and put together a twice-weekly roundup of interesting articles and gossip about politics, business, and world affairs—creating in effect a newspaper designed for a readership of one—FDR. "Father was too busy with his fight for his life to think of his political future," Roosevelt's son James

reporter. Her rise through the world of journalism was exceptional.

Hick's story moved Eleanor deeply, prompting her to share the story of her own sad childhood. Eleanor further confided in Hick the devastation of her husband's affair with her social secretary Lucy Mercer and the slow, painful process of reconstructing herself through her work after deciding to stay in the marriage. As they became closer, Hick resigned from her job due to her conflict of interest and went to work for the government as an investigator for the Federal Emergency Relief Administration.

When Franklin was first inaugurated president in 1933, Eleanor was worried that her role as First Lady would be largely ceremonial. It was Hick who advised and boosted her, giving her ideas about how to fill her new role, helping Eleanor become one of the most active, effective First Ladies in American history. Hick encouraged Eleanor to start a daily newspaper column, edited Eleanor's drafts, and suggested she host her own press conferences to which only female reporters would be invited—launching a whole generation of women newspaper reporters.

Hick's support for Eleanor provided a mix of tenderness, loyalty, confidence, and courage that sustained her in her struggle to redefine her sense of self and her position on the world's stage. Over a thirty-year period, three thousand letters between Eleanor and Hick were exchanged, revealing a deep love they shared in a friendship that lasted until Eleanor's death in 1962.

said. According to Howe's biographer, "Howe's solution to balance the two priorities—Roosevelt's physical well-being and the resumption of his public life—was to lift one of them off of his shoulders." Howe's belief in Roosevelt's destiny was a matter of faith. Soon after Franklin was stricken by polio, when Eleanor asked Howe whether her husband could navigate the rough-and-tumble world of politics, Howe assured her that nothing had altered his belief that one day Franklin would be president of the United States.

Meanwhile, Roosevelt continued to pursue his own consuming vision of full recovery. While grudgingly he agreed to wear the bulky twenty-pound braces and practice using crutches, he never stopped searching for a cure that would allow him to regain the power of walking, the necessary condition, he believed, for him to fulfill his political ambitions. He continued the difficult task of experimentation to figure out which treatments worked most effectively. He found that his "leg muscles responded more quickly" when he could sit outside in the summer sun; on cloudy days they would "freeze up from about 5 p.m. on." In swimming he found the most promising therapy of all, one allowing him to exercise his legs without the weight of gravity.

Roosevelt held an almost mystical belief in the healing power of sun and water. He had been enchanted from early childhood by sea tales of his grandfather's clipper ship days and thrilled at learning to sail with his father, and he considered his model ships and naval prints among his most prized possessions. When he needed a break from the relentless rehabilitation at their New York town house, his endless search for a cure led to the peaceful waters off Florida, where he spent some of the winter cruising, fishing, and enjoying the sun on the *Larooco*, an aging but spacious houseboat, in the company of a few of his close friends, including secretary Missy LeHand. Eleanor did not enjoy the lazy lifestyle aboard the houseboat, but she was supportive of LeHand accompanying Franklin, and with her blessing, LeHand, like Howe, was absorbed into the Roosevelt family and would later live in both the governor's mansion and the White House with the family. More important than the role LeHand played in sustaining Franklin's high spirits was the fact that he was able to reveal to her his darker fears. "There were days on the *Larooco*," she later told his secretary of labor Frances Perkins, "when it was noon before he could pull himself out of depression and greet his guests wearing his lighthearted façade." Slowly but surely, those bad days began to dwindle. While "F-D," as

"F-D" while living and convalescing aboard the *Larooco*, in Florida here.

LeHand called him, and friends were aboard the *Larooco*, Eleanor was happier to stay in New York to cultivate prospective political allies and pursue the network of new friendships that had grown central to her own social and intellectual existence.

FDR would replicate the strengths of this inner circle in the years ahead, as he expanded his working team as governor and then president. There was not a yes-man or yes-woman in the group. The team offered Roosevelt a range of opinions. From the earliest days of their relationship, Howe had never hesitated to argue with Franklin. LeHand handled disagreement in a more fun-loving but equally effective manner. Eleanor added the most essential moral heft to FDR's leadership. "He might have been happier with a wife who was completely uncritical," she observed in her memoirs, adding, "That I was never able to be."

She was uncompromising, straightforward, more deeply involved with activists who pushed against traditional boundaries. "I sometimes acted as a spur even though the spurring was not always wanted or welcomed," she later wrote of her relationship with FDR. Her constant pressure and lack of humor made it difficult for Franklin to relax. "We're not going to do that now," he would often say, cutting her short. "I don't want to hear about that anymore." And yet, inevitably, he would return to her unwanted suggestion.

This remarkable team, locked together in a complicated dance around the same center, succeeded so well in keeping FDR's spirits up and his political name alive that in 1924, three years after the onset of polio, New York's governor Al Smith offered Roosevelt the New York chairmanship of his preconvention campaign for the presidency. FDR hesitated at first, feeling far too vulnerable still to appear in public, but when told they simply needed his name, not his body, he agreed to head the campaign. Two months later, Governor Smith presented Roosevelt with a far more challenging proposition: Would he agree to place Smith's name in nomination at the Democratic National Convention to be held at Madison Square Garden in late June?

Chapter Sixteen

*"With this fine courage and determination
you are bound to win."*

IF EVER THERE WERE AN EXAMPLE OF POLITICAL COURAGE, of an enormous risk taken, it was Roosevelt's acceptance of Al Smith's offer—given the looming prospect of literally falling on his face in front of twelve thousand delegates.

That Franklin was not yet able to walk unassisted, even with braces and crutches, had been made clear months earlier when he'd ventured forth for the first time since the polio attack to meet with business colleagues at a private luncheon on Wall Street in New York City. An elevator would take him upstairs, but first he had to cross a slippery marble lobby floor to reach the elevator bank. With his chauffeur's assistance, FDR had reached the halfway mark when a crutch slid out from under him. He collapsed in a heap, his hat rolling off to the side. Spectators gathered round as he tried to prop himself into a seated position. "Nothing to worry about," Franklin announced to reassure the concerned onlookers, bursting into a sudden peal of laughter. He then called for help from two young men who eventually pulled him to a standing position. "Let's go," he said to his chauffeur. Someone put his hat on his head. Wearing a big smile, he acknowledged the crowd, and made his way toward the elevator.

The convention speech was to be his first public appearance in three years. It was one thing to fall in a lobby, quite another to risk embarrassment and jeopardize one's political ambitions at a national party convention that would be broadcast nationwide for the first time on radio. To minimize the immense risk, he carefully rehearsed and trained for the "walk" he would have to make. "Nobody knows how that man worked," Eleanor's close friend Marion Dickerman recalled. "They measured off in the library at the 65th Street house just what the distance was and he struggled, and struggled and struggled." With the support of his then sixteen-year-old son, James, FDR alternately shifted his weight from his son's arm on the left to the crutch under his right arm. James remembered how his father's fingers dug painfully into his arm "like pincers" as he hoisted and dragged his legs, locked in heavy steel braces, along the narrow line between potential pity and awe toward the imaginary podium.

On the night of the actual event, Franklin directed a friend to shake the podium in order to assure him that it was stable enough to support his weight, as he would grab its edges and hold on once he reached it. When his moment of introduction came, he replaced his son's arm with another crutch and approached the lectern alone. "There was a hush and everybody was holding their breath," recalled Frances Perkins, a commissioner of the New York State Industrial Commission at the time. After what seemed a long-drawn moment of tension, he reached the podium, handed off his crutches, gripped the lectern edges with his powerful, viselike grip, tilted back his head, and "across his face there flashed a vast, world-encompassing smile." Twelve thousand voices exploded with cheers and admiration for the courage he epitomized even before his speech had begun. His stiffened legs and strained shoulders supported a head thrown back with hard-earned pride and perhaps a touch of theatrical confidence, the confidence of having overcome the fear of humiliation, a confidence born of making a great effort, of taking a great risk—and triumphing.

His rich tenor voice had a musical quality as he asked delegates to unite behind Governor Al Smith, "the 'Happy Warrior' of the political battlefield." This phrase—drawn from a William Wordsworth poem about how one confronts life's difficulties, how one "doomed to go in company with Pain . . . Turns his necessity to glorious gain"—would from that moment forever attach itself to Smith; with striking force, however, it described Roosevelt himself. Seated in a front row, Perkins observed that he was "trembling" and "shaking" from the "extreme pain and tenseness with which he held himself up to make that speech," but his delivery "was strong and true and vigorous." He stood as the living emblem of a man who had truly transformed his own pain and necessity into glorious gain.

When he finished, the crowd "just went crazy," igniting an hour-long demonstration, according to Eleanor's friend Marion Dickerman. "They howled, yelled, screamed and sang from densely crowded galleries," the Hagerstown, Maryland, *Morning Herald* reported. "I have witnessed many heroic deeds in my lifetime," the reporter for the *Syracuse Herald* wrote, "but I never was present at so fine a display of mental courage." Later that evening, Eleanor hosted a reception at their New York town house. Exhausted but exhilarated, Franklin kept to his room. When Marion Dickerman went to see him, "he held out his arms and he said, 'Marion, I did it!'"

Though four years would pass before Franklin returned in earnest to his political calling, this speech was a vital way station. He had made great progress, but his greatest growth as a man and as a leader lay ahead—on a road that led through Warm Springs, Georgia.

The story of Warm Springs, the pioneering rehabilitation center Roosevelt built from a ramshackle resort, begins with his "discovery of a place" where he believed he would learn to walk again. Instead, he experienced a different kind of recovery, developed a more profound level of humility, and provided inspiration for—and was inspired by—the vibrant community he created with his fellow polio survivors.

Told about a spa in Georgia where a young man had restored strength to his legs by swimming in a giant pool fed by mineral water that gushed from the hillside at a soothing eighty-six degrees, Roosevelt traveled to the Meriwether Inn to find out for himself. "Almost everything was falling to pieces," Roosevelt later recalled, the hotel dilapidated and the roofs of the surrounding cottages leaking. But the buoyant water of the T-shaped thermal pool delivered on its promise, allowing him to exercise his muscles for an extended period of time without throbbing fatigue. "Every morning I spend two hours in the most wonderful pool in the world," he told a friend. "There is no question this place does more good than all the rest of the exercising put together."

Within a matter of weeks, he had "a hunch" that "a great 'cure' for infantile paralysis and similar diseases could well be established here." He envisioned a renovated hotel with bright, sunny rooms; spruced-up cottages; and a medical staff of doctors, nurses, and physical therapists; along with a host of recreational and social activities designed to let the patients "live normal lives and at the same time receive the best treatment known to science at the time." Furthermore, the place he imagined held out the healing promise of the great European spas he had known so well as a child, without the necessity of wealth—here was therapy within a rustic and democratic simplicity. Meditating years afterward on Roosevelt's leadership strengths, Frances Perkins marveled that "there were times when he could truly see it all," when he instinctively understood how one decision or one undertaking related to another. Warm Springs was such a time.

Against the advice of his wife, mother, and friends, he decided to invest $200,000 (roughly two thirds of his fortune) to buy the hotel, the springs, and the cottages along with twelve hundred acres of land. This would be the first major project he ran completely on his own.

He worked directly with architects to build a completely accessible, remodeled campus and provided suggestions for manicured lawns. He oversaw the planting of trees and flowering garden arrangements. He designed the layout of golf courses, riding trails, a dance hall, and a movie theater. During the construction phase, he drove around encouraging the crew with a contagious enthusiasm, just as he had made the rounds with his father surveying the various construction projects at Springwood. He staffed the facility with great care. Recognizing the importance of support from the medical establishment, he persuaded the American Orthopaedic Association to use the site for research to measure outcomes and deliver a report. When the report proved positive, he placed the entire enterprise into a nonprofit foundation, allowing him to raise additional funds to carry out improvements and to provide for those who could not afford to pay for their visit in full, making a reality of his initial democratic impulse, save for one ugly aspect: Georgia was in the segregated South, and at the time, "local customs" required Warm Springs to be a segregated institution. Black people could work there, but Black polio patients could not be treated there. Years later, a separate facility was created at the Tuskegee Institute in Alabama with funds from the nonprofit March of Dimes to care for Black polio patients and train Black physicians, nurses, and physical therapists in the most up-to-date methods.

At Warm Springs, FDR became known as old Doc Roosevelt, head counselor, spiritual director, "Vice-President in charge of picnics," and therapy pioneer "all rolled into one." He directed morning exercises in the therapy pool and then led patients to a separate pool, where they laughed and shouted as they engaged in swimming contests and played tag and water polo. During the afternoons and evenings, "there were bridge tournaments and poker games, classes, movies, excursions,

amateur theatricals," as well as festive cocktail parties and dinners. Roosevelt aimed not merely to restore the bodies of the patients but to return the possibility of joy and pleasure to their lives. "We mustn't let the fun go out of our program," he insisted. "We've got to make these patients more alive every day." He took pride, he told a reporter, in having created "a remarkable spirit of cooperation and competition among the patients to see who can improve the most," adding that "the spirit of the place has an extraordinary effect on the progress they make. Here they find people just like themselves. They get over their self-consciousness."

While micromanaging the grand scheme at Warm Springs for almost four years, Roosevelt underwent what Perkins called a "spiritual transformation." An "old priest" had once told her that "humility is the first and greatest of virtues. If we don't learn it on our own, the Lord will surely teach it to us by humiliation." The humbleness FDR learned at Warm Springs was of a different order than merely accepting one's limitations. By sharing those limitations with his fellow polio survivors, by listening to and learning from them, he had, Perkins believed, lost the elitist aura that had once surrounded him. He emerged from the experience "completely warmhearted, with humility of spirit and with a deeper philosophy."

He had developed a powerful new empathy, allowing him to connect emotionally with all manner of people to whom fate had also dealt an unkind blow. He had inspired the entire Warm Springs community with his optimistic spirit, infusing his fellow polio survivors with his own boundless courage. "You are making a brave fight for recovery and with this fine courage and determination you are bound to win," he wrote in a letter to a fellow polio survivor. "It was," one patient recalled, "a place which changed forever our feelings about ourselves and the man who made this . . . possible." And FDR, in turn, had experienced the intense fulfillment of linking his ambitions to the betterment of others, of creating an institution from the ground up that would serve for generations as a model for the treatment of people with disabilities.

At Warm Springs, FDR had found a cure different from what he had initially sought. He had come to restore his ability to walk—a condition he had thought crucial to run for public office. He knew that no one so paralyzed had ever been active and successful in politics. Could a propped-up leader, a wheeled or carried leader, lead and uplift? He knew the answer to this question now. He had developed a different concept of leadership. The deep affection and respect he felt from the shared community he had created at Warm Springs made it clear that a polio survivor who needed help to walk was fully able to exercise leadership of the highest order. He had made a separate peace with his own recovery and in his heart was ready to restart a life fully in the public glare.

FDR swimming at Warm Springs.

Chapter Seventeen

"Above all, try something."

OPPORTUNITY KNOCKED IN 1928, when Al Smith, having won the Democratic nomination for president, pressured Roosevelt—as a service to both the party and himself—to run for governor of New York. The Roosevelt name, Smith figured, would boost voter turnout in a state that had to be won in the presidential race. All the Democratic Party expected from Roosevelt, Smith assured him, were four or five radio addresses. As soon as the campaign was done, Roosevelt could turn over the heavy lifting to the lieutenant governor and return to Warm Springs and recuperation.

While Smith had rightly calculated the positive impact of the Roosevelt name in New York, he had badly miscalculated the man himself. Once Roosevelt agreed to be drafted and assumed the responsibility of running for governor, he was in it for keeps. "When you're in politics you have to play the game," FDR told a friend. He resolved to prove to himself and to the public that he had the physical vigor and the mental capacity for sustained hard work that would outperform any ordinary campaign effort. He got to work immediately. Often speaking fourteen times a day, he delivered thirty-three major speeches in thirty different locations, together with dozens of informal talks and clusters of meetings.

"It was a dreadful physical business to make this campaign," Perkins observed. "He really was kind of scared." As she watched him being carried up a fire escape to enter a third-floor hall, "a perilous, uncomfortable" ordeal, she said to herself, "My God, he's got nerve." Moreover, he accepted help with grace and dignity, though that didn't make his dependence on others easy or pleasant. "If you can't use your legs and they bring you milk when you wanted orange juice, you learn to say, 'That's all right,' and drink it." Seemingly trivial oversights like this can feel demoralizing, but Roosevelt chose to overlook them and preferred not to push back. "There were certain things that he never really talked about—that he would just shut up, and it made him very, very much alone in some ways," Eleanor once wrote. It was part of his lifelong tactic to mask the pain that lurked beneath his dazzling smile.

When the results were in, Roosevelt had won a narrow victory in the governor's race. But in the national election Smith was defeated when a Republican wave swept Herbert Hoover into the White House. Stunned by the devastating loss, Smith retreated to Albany, determined to be the power behind the new governor. Smith's plan, however, did not sit well with Roosevelt. "I realized that I've got to be Governor, and I've got to be myself," Roosevelt explained to Perkins. When he first agreed to run, he recalled, he wasn't sure if he could handle the rigors of the campaign, "but," he proudly noted, "I made it." Nor had he been certain that he was "sufficiently recovered to undertake the duties of Governor of New York, but here I am." When Roosevelt declined to hire Smith's top aide, it provoked a furious response from Smith: "I created you and now what are you doing to me!" This difficult, personal and professional struggle at the start of FDR's term as governor, Eleanor recalled, "ended the close relationship between my husband and Governor Smith." And it broadened opportunities for Eleanor as New York's First Lady.

FDR went to work on forming his own team in his own way, which was particularly important for Roosevelt because, as he had realized early on, his team would be a vital extension, given his restricted mobility—its members serving as his "eyes and ears," going forth to places that would be physically inaccessible to him, gathering information in the form of stories and human anecdotes that would illustrate New York's issues and problems. When the narrow corridors and stairways of state "institutions," as they were called then—for the blind, the elderly, the mentally ill, and the deaf—made those places difficult for him to navigate, he encouraged Eleanor to go as his surrogate, to gather information and return with insights on how well the institutions were carrying out their stated missions.

"At first my reports were highly unsatisfactory," Eleanor acknowledged. But she learned to probe further: to sample pots on the stove, notice if beds had been folded up and placed behind doors to hide overcrowded sleeping quarters, observe the patients' interactions with the staff. Before long, under Roosevelt's mentoring, Eleanor proudly became a first-rate investigative reporter.

FDR sought team members whose experiences and specific knowledge amplified his own wide-ranging curiosity. He filled the governor's mansion with a steady stream of visitors from all walks of life who joined him at lunch and dinner, and frequently stayed overnight. Going back to early childhood, Roosevelt had learned best by listening and could absorb and process large swaths of information. And now that he couldn't go out into the world in the same way, he would funnel the world into him. Having been away from state politics for a decade and a half, he asked Sam Rosenman, a young lawyer who had recently served three terms in the state legislature, to be his counselor and speechwriter. Rosenman brought in three Columbia University professors to form the nucleus of what would become known as the "brain trust," to help Roosevelt develop his policy agenda. This inner circle, in turn, reached out to experts in various fields—in business, agriculture, labor—who then filled the governor's mansion with a parade of interesting and useful guests.

"The routine was simple," one of the Columbia professors, Ray Moley, recalled. The atmosphere at dinner would be pleasant and casual. Roosevelt encouraged his visitors to talk about their work, their families, and themselves, making each person feel that "nothing was so important to him that day as this particular visit, and that he had been waiting all day for this hour." Dessert done, they moved to the governor's small study, where "random talk came to an end." There Roosevelt would throw questions to the experts "at an exciting and exhausting clip." Moley marveled at "the amount of intellectual ransacking Roosevelt could crowd into the evening." In hindsight, it was clear to Moley, who also became a speechwriter for Roosevelt, that he "was at once a student, a cross-examiner, and a judge."

FDR began to serve as governor in January 1929, as the decade of the Roaring Twenties was drawing to a close. World War I was in the rearview mirror, and 1920 to 1929 was a time of dramatic social, economic, and political change. For the first time, more Americans lived in cities than on farms. The nation's total wealth more than doubled. US industry was thriving, and the increased production and availability of cars, radios, and silent movies changed citizens' leisure time, if not their lives. The stock market had climbed to unprecedented levels, but the signs of stress on the economy were starting to show. The very operating method Roosevelt had devised from the beginning of his governorship—sending surrogates out to inspect and retrieve information while simultaneously bringing in a stream of hand-selected experts—clued him in early on that something was fundamentally wrong.

From Frances Perkins, who he put in charge of the state's labor department, which catalogued working conditions and job trends, FDR learned of a puzzling "irregularity" in the labor market during his first months in office: "Many people were out of work for longer periods than was comfortable." Perkins's inspection of the State Public Employment

What is a stock market, and how did it crash?

When the people running a company decide to turn it from one that is privately owned into one that is publicly owned, they sell stocks, which are tiny pieces of the company's ownership. A public company is owned by lots of people—all the folks who buy stock in the company. The owner of a company's stock has invested in that company. The stock market is where stocks of public companies are bought and sold, or traded.

During the 1920s, the economy seemed strong. A lot of people had jobs and were making money. Investors in the stock market were typically wealthy, with a lot of money to spare, but in this period, more middle-class people began investing in stocks too. A new industry arose that lent people money to invest in the stock market. In some cases, buyers only had to put in one dollar for every ten they were investing—the remaining nine dollars came in the form of a bank loan; without getting loans, these people otherwise would not have been able to afford to buy so many stocks. Banks also poured loans and investments into companies that were traded on the stock exchange, making it seem like those companies had a lot more money on hand than they really did. These loans—to stock buyers and the companies

Service revealed that many of its offices were overwhelmed by people who had lost their jobs and were looking for help. FDR immediately agreed to overhaul the system, which meant updating the offices and hiring more staff to deal with what would soon be a tsunami of unemployment cases—in a ten-week period, stocks on the New York Stock Exchange lost 50 percent of their value, causing the stock market crash of 1929 and ushering in the Great Depression.

Billions of dollars were lost, thousands of investors were ruined, businesses failed, and unemployment rose dramatically—and quickly. As had become his standard, Roosevelt was spurred into action by the individual stories of specific needs and grievances. He could understand a problem better when baffling statistics and facts could be translated into a human story. Upon visiting a sweater mill in a small village near Poughkeepsie after the Great Depression had started, he found both the owner and the workers "frightened and confused." Before the crash, the mill had employed 150 people making high-quality knitted sweaters. The workers received good wages, the owner made a good profit, and the community thrived. As the Depression deepened and demand for sweaters fell, because people could no longer afford to buy them, the owner was forced to cut his workforce in half, reduce wages, and use a lower-quality yarn to produce cheaper sweaters. He kept the mill going as long as he could, even to the point of losing any personal profit. He lived in the village; his employees were his friends. Still, demand continued to drop and was soon not enough even to cover costs. This small sweater mill, which eventually was forced to close, told the story on a human scale of what was happening in every sector, in every community, in every state.

Roosevelt had no single solution for the Depression in New York State. He began with trial-and-error methods to spread available jobs to a greater number of people: part-time work, a shortened workweek, a reduced workload, small projects that improved communities. "What was clear to Roosevelt," Perkins recalled, "was that we must find some answers and stimulate some immediate activities." Although he mobilized charities to respond, coordinated local relief efforts, and called on local towns and cities to borrow money to provide citizens with much-needed services and relief, the

themselves—inflated the stock value of those companies like a balloon. But many of those companies could not produce and sell as many goods as they promised they would, could not pay workers enough wages, and ultimately could not pay back the loans they'd received from banks. The same thing happened to the stock buyers who bought stocks using loans; there was no way they could make enough money to pay those loans back.

Over the course of September and October 1929, the prices of stocks began to drop to reflect the actual value of the companies on the stock exchange—not the inflated values. This caused a panic, and on October 29, 1929, owners of stocks started selling off their stocks wildly. The balloon popped, and this stock market crash was considered the start of the Great Depression. The stock market was flooded with stocks, because so many people were panic-selling at once. Sellers had a hard time finding buyers, so they sold their stocks at very low prices, and the companies on the stock exchange lost a lot of their stated value (which had been fake anyway due to all the loans). The trading was so intense that the ticker machines tracking trades could not even keep up.

growing magnitude of the Depression burst the bounds and capacities of all these institutions.

After waiting through the winter and spring of 1931 for solutions that never came from President Hoover and the Republican administration, Roosevelt resolved late that summer to "assume leadership for himself and to take action for the State of New York." He summoned the Republican-led state legislature into an extraordinary session to pass what was then considered a radical idea—a state-sponsored comprehensive program of unemployment insurance, a government program that would provide relief to people who had lost their jobs. He knew from the start that the Republican majority would block his proposal. Like President Hoover, the state Republican leaders believed that businesses, charities, and local governments were the only institutions capable of meeting the economic challenge. Relief brought from the distant level of the state or federal government, they insisted, would only worsen the problem.

Roosevelt spent several days preparing his message to the legislature. He had schooled his speechwriters Rosenman and Moley on how to communicate to the people directly: avoid dull facts; create memorable images; translate every issue into people's lives; use simple, everyday language; never use big words when small words will do. An example: simplify the concept that "we are trying to construct a more inclusive society" into "we are going to make a country in which no one is left out."

"What is the State?" Roosevelt began. The state was created by the people for their

What was the Great Depression?

The Great Depression was different from other economic downturns that began with the Industrial Revolution. It was declared the worst economic calamity the country had ever experienced, lasting a decade and doing more damage than any previous hard times. Job loss, hunger, homelessness, and business and bank failures became so widespread that the public demanded a new kind of government leadership that would find ways to help improve the lives of people suffering the effects of the Depression.

The era of Franklin Roosevelt's New Deal set a precedent and changed the federal government's role in the economic and social welfare of the country's citizens. FDR's policies used the government as a tool to protect Americans from businesses that operated without regard for the damage they might do if they failed. For example, Roosevelt "mutual protection and well-being." One of its central duties is to care for its citizens who are unable, during hard times, to maintain their lives without help. In normal times, such aid would be provided by private or local contributions, by charities. But these were not normal times. The prolonged unemployment had exhausted the savings of millions of families. The state had a responsibility to do its share, not out of charity, but out of duty. He pushed through a tax on citizens fortunate enough to be able to pay, to "provide public work for its unemployed citizens" and, "if no work could be found," to provide unemployment insurance in the form of "food, clothing and shelter from public funds."

> created the Federal Deposit Insurance Corporation (FDIC), which watches over banks to make sure they don't take depositors' money and use it in risky ways. It also insures bank deposits, so that even if a bank fails, people who put their savings in the bank won't lose their money. Another example was FDR's Fair Labor Standards Act, which abolished child labor and set minimum wages and maximum hours for workers. Since the New Deal, the US economy has experienced other recessions, but none as deep or painful to Americans as the Great Depression, thanks to policies like these.

First in the country, New York's comprehensive relief program became a model for other states, establishing Governor Roosevelt as the leading spokesman for the progressive wing of the Democratic Party. In a celebrated radio address in April 1932, Roosevelt called on the country to rebuild its lost prosperity from "the bottom up and not from the top down," to "put their faith once more in the forgotten man at the bottom of the economic pyramid." For Roosevelt, the forgotten man "was a living person"—a farmer facing crushing debt, a small businessman unable to compete against huge trusts, a housewife too strapped to put food on the table.

On a national level, President Hoover accomplished little to help the country. But in New York, Governor Roosevelt determined that "there is a duty on the part of government to do something about this," and he did. And then, cast as a voice for the everyman, Roosevelt sought the nomination for president at the 1932 Democratic National Convention in Chicago. He won on the third ballot. As soon as Roosevelt received word that he had won, he took the unprecedented action of traveling to the convention to accept the nomination in person. At a time when airplane travel was still uncommon, he flew from Albany to Chicago in a tri-motor plane. Traditional methods and old remedies would not help the country now. He had come in person to show that he was ready and eager to lead the battle against inaction, fear, and close-minded ideas. "I pledge you, I pledge myself, to a new deal for the American people," he concluded. "This is more than a political campaign; it is a call to arms."

The battle between Hoover and Roosevelt showed how strikingly different characters, temperaments, and leadership styles responded to the enormous stress and uncertainty of the country. Hoover's profound belief in individualism, volunteering, and the fundamental strength of the American economy prevented him from realizing, until too late, that it was necessary for government to help people through what was fast becoming the worst depression the country had ever known. At the slightest uptick in the stock market, Hoover believed and proclaimed that the worst was over. When the economy continued to sink, he still would not admit that voluntary activities had failed. He adopted a bunker mentality, refusing to face the worsening situation.

By contrast, Roosevelt had adapted all his life to changing—if not worsening—circumstances. The routine of his easy childhood had been disrupted forever by his father's heart attack and eventual death. Told he would never walk again, he had experimented with one method after another to improve his mobility. So now, as Roosevelt campaigned for the presidency, he built on his own long encounter with hardship: "The country needs and, unless I mistake its temper, the country demands bold, persistent experimentation. It is common sense to take a method and try it: If it fails, admit it frankly and try another. But above all, try something."

Roosevelt campaigning in Georgia with daughter Anna (center) and Eleanor.

On Election Day 1932, by an overwhelming majority, the people chose Franklin Delano Roosevelt as their president. In a time of national distress, it was Roosevelt's confident cheer and powerful shoulders—symbols of his resilience—that made it possible for ordinary people not only to believe and trust him but to identify with him as well. As a young man, Franklin had daydreamed of rising step-by-step to the presidency. That climb had been disrupted by paralysis. He had come through a dark time. And so would the country.

Chapter Eighteen

"The only thing we have to fear is fear itself. . . ."

"LOOKING BACK ON THOSE DAYS, I wonder how we ever lived through them," Secretary of Labor Frances Perkins said of the deepening Great Depression. "It is hard today to reconstruct the atmosphere of 1933 and to evoke the terror caused by unrelieved poverty and prolonged unemployment." The economy had reached "rock bottom." American industry had tanked; one in four workers was unemployed, and the hours—and thus the wages—of those who were working had been radically reduced. People had lost farms, homes, and small businesses that had been in their families for generations. The relief funds of cities and states were exhausted. Soup kitchens were running out of food, leaving tens of thousands of Americans hungry and millions more ill-fed. Starving people wandered the streets. Food riots broke out. The rate of suicides had tripled over the course of the four years of President Herbert Hoover's time in office. The future of capitalism, indeed of democracy itself, appeared grim. There did not exist any federal government "safety net" programs to catch the multitudes who had fallen off the economic cliff. "We are at the end of our string," President Hoover said despairingly as he was handing the reins to President-Elect Roosevelt.

"Panic was in the air," Roosevelt's incoming cabinet member Harold Ickes recalled of this frightening stage of the Great Depression. In mid-February, weeks before Roosevelt's inauguration, "the full brunt of the Depression" struck when banks in one state after another began to bolt their doors. During the early years of the economic downturn, some five thousand small, mostly rural banks had collapsed, wiping out the savings of millions of Americans, ransacking not only their security but their hopes for the future. With no recovery in sight, people in villages and cities all over the country rushed to withdraw their savings, standing in long lines with satchels in their hands, demanding the immediate release of funds that they planned to stash under mattresses or bury on their property. Banks rarely had the money on hand to meet the sudden, overwhelming demand. Faced with increasingly unruly customers lining up at bank doors, governors in one state after another ordered all the banks in their states closed for an indefinite period.

"When the American people feel they are doing all right for themselves they do not give much thought to the character of the man in the White House; they are satisfied to have a President 'who merely fits the picture frame,'" said Roosevelt aide and speechwriter Robert Sherwood. However, "when adversity sets in and problems become too big for individual solution," then, Sherwood argued, the people start looking anxiously for guidance, calling for a leader to "step out of the picture frame and assert himself as a vital, human need."

Mere opportunity is not enough, however. A leader must be ready and able to meet the challenges presented by the times. And no leader was more prepared to diagnose the national illness and repair the beleaguered nation than Doc Roosevelt—ready to minister with honesty, warmth, near-mystical confidence, and an unshakable determination. FDR was prepared to provide a shot of new leadership for the paralyzed and hopeless nation. After all, in a searing and personal way, he had been through all this before.

On the morning of his inauguration, accompanied by his entire cabinet, staff, family, and friends, Roosevelt attended a special prayer session at St. John's Episcopal Church. "A thought to God is the right way to start off my Administration," he told them. "It will be the means to bring us out of the depths of despair." After the twenty-minute service came to an end, Roosevelt remained on his knees, "his face cupped in his hands." As Eleanor later said, her husband always considered religion "an anchor and a source of strength and guidance." Later that morning, as he waited at the Capitol for the ceremony to begin, the president-elect improvised a new opening sentence to his address: "This is a day of national consecration." Clearly, the address he was about to deliver was a civil sermon designed to provide "the larger purposes" that would bind the people together "as a sacred obligation."

Roosevelt's inspired resolve was glimpsed by the wife of Alabama senator Joseph Hill, Henrietta McCormick Hill, who observed the president-elect's "tremendous effort" as he slowly maneuvered himself to the podium to take his oath of office on March 4, 1933—the last presidential inauguration to be in March, since the date was moved to January 20 after the Twentieth Amendment to the Constitution went into effect in 1935. "It gave me a feeling of his greatness that he could conquer such a physical handicap. Never have I seen an expression as he wore on his face—it was faith, it was courage, it was complete exultation!"

Roosevelt began his inauguration speech by "honestly" facing the facts of the country's dire situation. "Only a foolish optimist can deny the dark realities of the moment." But, he famously asserted, "the only thing we have to fear is fear itself." Intuitively, he understood that what the people needed to hear was that they were not to blame for the misery of their individual circumstances—or of their collective condition. "The people of the United States have not failed," FDR insisted. Failure of the economic system, he said, was due to a lack of leadership that had left citizens unprotected against greedy and reckless bankers and businessmen. Then, as the downward spiral deepened, leaders refused to offer practical government solutions, remaining passive at the very time robust leadership was needed most. Restoration would come through "a leadership of frankness and vigor," just as such leadership had carried the people through "every dark hour of our national life." With such a renewal, FDR was certain that the American people would once again rise. At the center of his speech, he called for a new contract between the leader and the people, a contract built upon the recognition of our dependence on one another. And in that spirit, he pledged, "On my part and yours we face our common difficulties."

Foremost, FDR understood that "the Nation asks for action, and action now." He told the country he was asking Congress to pass a series of emergency measures that "a stricken Nation" required. Here he harkened back to the tradition of Abraham Lincoln and to Theodore Roosevelt—using his power to do whatever the people needed, unless expressly forbidden by the Constitution or the laws. This was no dictator or king holding forth. Franklin Roosevelt spoke in the name of the people for a resurgence of the strength of democracy, for a constitutional system capable of meeting "every stress" without losing its essential form.

The magic of his leadership was contagious. A young lawyer who had joined his administration remembered that it was as if "the air suddenly changed, the wind blew through corridors." A half a million letters of encouragement and support were on their way to the White House. This atmospheric change, "the sense that life was resuming," was noted in headlines and commentary across the country:

THE ERA OF INACTION HAS COME TO AN END.

THE GOVERNMENT STILL LIVES.

PERHAPS A LEADER HAS COME!

What did Eleanor do as First Lady?

Once in the White House, Eleanor succeeded in transforming the role of First Lady. She became an important part of FDR's New Deal agenda—a leading advocate for programs to assist often-neglected people: women; people of color; and the poor, forgotten, and disfranchised. She pressured FDR's administration to appoint women to positions of influence within New Deal programs and to create new opportunities for women, as she did with her press conferences.

She continued to be Franklin's eyes and ears—traveling on average two hundred days a year as First Lady, bringing him back reports from New Deal projects, including the Civilian Conservation Corps created to employ about three million men with forestry and conservation jobs around the country. Some women also needed work, but opportunities for them were few and far between. They were not permitted to participate in the CCC, as much as Eleanor pushed. So she founded the She-She-She camps as an opportunity for the two million women who had lost work after the stock market crash of 1929. In the South, she sought to right the wrongs of Black people being discriminated against in New Deal programs, which led to a series of executive orders barring such unfair treatment.

One of President Roosevelt's very first actions in office was to declare a weeklong shutdown of all banks; ironically he called it "a bank holiday." The holiday provided a window of time, "an anesthetic before the major operation," a breathing space to devise a plan to reopen the banks in an orderly way. The coordinated closing, historian Arthur Schlesinger remarked, gave the long economic slide "the punctuation of a full stop, as if this were the bottom and hereafter things could only turn upward."

In that brief space of the weeklong holiday, Roosevelt's team had to prepare, rehearse, and produce what would amount to the staging of a national drama aimed at restoring public confidence in the nation's failed banking system. What if the emergency laws were not passed by Congress and enacted in time? What if the people did not believe in the soundness of the plan? What if on the morning of the banks' reopening, mobs of people all over the country stormed their banks demanding their money? The outcome was anything but certain—for both the banking system and for the new administration.

The marathon week called for a military-style operation complete with coordinating deadlines—getting Congress to return to Washington for a special session, drafting an emergency bill to stabilize the banks, inviting the nation's governors to the White House to build support around the country. Night after night, Roosevelt was still in his office after midnight, consulting with aides, cabinet officials, and members of Congress. Every detail had to be considered and a plan of action executed, down to the actual dollars and cents. The Bureau of Engraving was ordered to begin printing new currency immediately, and a fleet of airplanes was commandeered to stand by, ready to carry the money to banks across the country. Within nine hours after the special session of Congress convened, the Emergency Banking Act was passed. Such swift congressional action had no equal.

Roosevelt understood, however, that the true test would come the following Monday morning when the banks reopened—leaving him only three days to present and solidify his case before the public.

As a first step in educating the public during those critical days, FDR held two free-flowing press conferences that little resembled those held by previous administrations. "I am told that what I am about to do will become impossible," he told the 125 members of the press who crammed into his office, "but I am going to try it." Similarly, First Lady Eleanor Roosevelt held her own first press conference on March 6, 1933—the first press conference

Eleanor Roosevelt boldly broke precedent after precedent and modeled courage with her line "You must do the thing you think you cannot do." She became the first First Lady to speak at a national convention, testify before Congress, drive her own car, travel by plane alone, and help Black soldiers serve as pilots in World War II. She earned her own money through some of the speeches, radio appearances, books, and magazine and newspaper articles.

Eleanor was controversial, too—for the content she created and also due to the commercial nature of her endeavors, although she donated much of her earnings to causes that mattered to her. She promoted civic organizations, government programs, and progressive politics in dozens of speeches broadcast live on local and national radio. Her causes included polio research, civil rights, the need for low-income housing, the hardships of jobless young people, and demands for women's political involvement and equality. Over time, the American public grew accustomed to their unusually active and outspoken First Lady, and, increasingly, they not only respected her but also loved her.

ever held by a US First Lady. She made a rule that only female report-ers could attend her press conferences, which meant that all over the country conservative publishers had to hire their first female reporters, and those who already had jobs would keep them. Indeed, because of Eleanor Roosevelt's weekly press conferences, an entire generation of female journalists got their start.

The front page of the *New York Times* characterized this first week of FDR's administration as "so swift-moving and momentous that it contained as many major events as have occurred in the entire adminis-trations of some Presidents." The "strong, cheerful, more than hopeful" new president was just getting started. "The feeling is spreading," the *Times* article continued, "that the 'leadership' which was promised, and for which so many people voted, has arrived."

On the Sunday eve of the decisive Monday morning of the bank reopen-ings on March 13, Roosevelt delivered the first of what became known as his "fireside chats," a term coined by CBS radio station manager Harry Butcher due to FDR's conversational speaking style. Roosevelt sought to translate the specialized, complicated language of banking into words of one syllable that could be better understood by himself and the average citizen—by "a mason at work on a new building," he said, "a girl behind a counter, a farmer in his field." Seated at a desk before six radio microphones and a small assemblage of family and colleagues, he imagined the American people listening in their living rooms or kitchens. "My friends," he opened, striking an immediate, personal tone. As he spoke, Frances Perkins recalled, "his face would smile and light up." He was not merely "talking directly to the people of the nation," observed Sam Rosenman, but rather "to each person in the nation." And Roosevelt, like Lincoln, sought to communicate with and guide his audience by telling a story.

"When you deposit money in a bank," Roosevelt explained, "the bank does not put the money into a safe deposit vault." It invests your money in bonds, loans, and mortgages "to keep the wheels of industry and of agriculture turning around." In normal times, the cash on hand is enough to cover the needs of people who put their savings in the bank. "What, then, happened . . . ?" A number of banks had "used the money entrusted to them in speculations and unwise loans"—they'd made bad decisions on how to invest the money they got from depositors. When the stock market crashed and banks collapsed, confidence in the entire banking system was damaged. A general rush to withdraw funds took place—"a rush so great that the soundest banks could not get enough currency to meet the demand." Now, backed by a new pledge by the federal government to provide loans and additional currency if necessary, approved banks would safely begin to open their doors again. "I can assure you," the president reasoned, "that it is safer to keep your money in a reopened bank than under the mattress."

FDR identified the very questions the people asked themselves and urgently needed answered. "A question you will ask is this: Why are all the banks not to be reopened at the same time? The answer is simple." The process of determining which banks could open immediately and which needed help would take time. "A bank that opens on one of the subsequent days," he assured the public, "is in exactly the same status as the bank that opens tomorrow." Again, as in his inaugural address, FDR asked the citizenry for courage and faith. "Let us unite in banishing fear. We have provided the machinery to restore our financial system; it is up to you to make it work."

The man had met the moment. Roosevelt had grasped the revolutionary opportunity that radio presented, that "marvelous twentieth century invention which has all but annihilated time, distance, and space." An estimated sixty million people, nearly half the US population at the time, listened to the president's radio chat.

FDR's calm, relaxed speaking voice was naturally attuned to the conversational style of the new radio age. This fireside chat felt intimate, not distant like a speaker shouting from behind a podium or delivering a formal address. Most important, his voice projected empathy, confidence, and warmth that made one believe and trust in his words.

So how did the public react? Early reports from that Monday suggested long lines at teller windows, alarming FDR and his team. But as it turned out, "it was a run to make new deposits, not to take money out." Headlines in city after city told similar stories. CITY RECOVERS CONFIDENCE, the *Chicago Tribune* proclaimed. RUSH TO PUT MONEY BACK SHOWS RESTORED FAITH AS HOLIDAY ENDS, declared the *New York Times*. Many depositors cited the renewed confidence the president's radio chat had given them. A bank president in San Antonio noted that the customers seemed to be "an entirely different list of people" from those who had scrambled to withdraw their money weeks before. "Their names and signatures are the same, but their frame of mind is as different as day and night."

With simple, plain language, Roosevelt had accomplished his purpose of explanation and persuasion. The banking crisis that had gripped the country with fear and panic settled down, and the stock market once again rose. By the standard of its impact on events, this first fireside chat, one historian noted, ranks "as one of the most important speeches in US history." The patient had survived the emergency. Only now could the doctor propose a plan to treat the sources of that disease.

Roosevelt had at first planned for members of Congress to return to their home districts after the emergency banking legislation had passed. But he quickly realized that if Congress adjourned now, the momentum gained from this first victory would be lost. So he asked congressional leaders to remain in continuous session, a request that would produce the historic turnaround that would forever be known as "the hundred days"—the standard by which all presidents since have been measured and compared.

Roosevelt decided during these first hundred days to unveil his vision for systematic economic and social reform in a second fireside chat on May 7, 1933. He began his second radio conversation building upon his first fireside chat, which had taken place just eight weeks earlier. What he had in mind was a partnership among government, farming, industry, and transportation. At the center of this new collaboration stood a

A political cartoon depicting Roosevelt spurring Congress into speedy action.

revolutionary bond between the president and the people as his partners in the government. His purpose sprang from what Frances Perkins called "his general attitude that the people mattered."

So what would this mean in practice? Before Congress adjourned on its hundredth day, fifteen major pieces of legislation would be passed and signed into law. This was made possible by the overwhelming majority of Democrats and sympathetic Independents in the US Congress—controlling 64 percent of the Senate and 73 percent of the House. Billions of dollars were set aside for programs that would hire workers to build public projects like roads, bridges, and airports; provide money for the unemployed; help people pay for their home mortgages; regulate banks to protect the money of depositors and investors; support workers' rights and ensure fair wages; and generate electricity in places that had none. All these programs put the needs of people at the center, creating government action designed to bring comfort to those who were suffering, providing a vast safety net of protection and regulation that would eventually become the New Deal. FDR and his administration, with the support of the Congress, listened and learned, and developed multiple layers of New Deal programs that touched every aspect of people's lives—where and how they lived, worked, were educated, were cultured, and would hopefully prosper.

FDR could accomplish this because he had no choice, he believed, but to experiment, create new agencies that would be inventive and quick to attack the multitude of problems that Americans faced. "We have to do the best we know how to do at the moment," he assured his labor secretary, Perkins. "If it doesn't work out, we can modify it as we go along." In the course of his first eighteen months in office, Roosevelt would create twenty new agencies, all known by their initials so they would be easy to remember.

The Civilian Conservation Corps, popularly called the CCC, was close to Roosevelt's heart, as it brought young men from all over the country to labor together in a practical program to restore the nation's forests, parks, and fields. The CCC provided much-needed work and purpose for more than three million young men over the course of the program, which stretched from 1933 to 1942. Most of these young men lived in cities, had recently left school, and were seeking "an opportunity to make their own way" at a time when jobs were scarce and salaries low. They earned money to send back to their needy families and received three meals a day and housing together in camps. At the same time, dozens of national forests had fallen into "a sad state of neglect" over the years and needed new trees, firewalls, and paths cleared. Roosevelt's vision for this national service project saw billions of trees planted. Even more important, the CCC planted "a moral and spiritual value"

Who was Frances Perkins?

Born in 1880, Frances Perkins was the rare woman to attend college at that time. During her final semester at Mount Holyoke College, her economic history professor required students to visit one of the local mills. "From the time I was in college I was horrified at the work that many women and children had to do in factories. There were absolutely no effective laws that regulated the number of hours they were permitted to work. There were no provisions which guarded their health nor adequately looked after their compensation in case of injury. Those things seemed very wrong. I was young and was inspired with the idea of reforming, or at least doing what I could, to help change those abuses."

Frances worked in settlement houses in Chicago with people who were poor and unemployed, studied childhood malnutrition, and fought for improved sanitary conditions in bakeries, for better fire protections for factory workers, and to limit the number of hours a week women and children were forced to work. She advocated compellingly to have important bills passed in New York State and was asked by then governor Franklin Roosevelt to oversee the state's labor department because of her unparalleled expertise in workplace health and safety.

When President Roosevelt selected her to be his secretary

to uplift and sustain a generation of aimless young men. When FDR selected Robert Fechner to lead the CCC and coordinate the four departments that would be a part of it, Roosevelt asked him how long he needed to set up his first camp. Fechner replied, "a month." Roosevelt countered, "Too long"; at once, Fechner halved the estimate. "Good," Roosevelt said simply.

By early July 1933, Roosevelt proudly declared, more than 250,000 men were at work in 1,500 camps. The Labor Department had managed to enroll ten thousand men daily until the target was reached. The corps members, deeply engaged in a wide variety of conservation tasks, had found "a place in the world"—they were to make a lasting transformation of the infrastructure of public lands, improving timberland, securing flood and fire control, managing and conserving forestland for generations to come. Many of these men had never seen a forest before, let alone dwelled in a natural setting. Few had performed hard physical labor. But, as Roosevelt had hopefully foreseen, they developed a broad range of job skills they could take back home with them, while working alongside others from different parts of the country, although Black, Mexican American, and Native American men who were enrolled were segregated in the camps. "I weighed about 160 pounds when I went there, and when I left I was 190," said one boy, filled with a newfound sense of self-respect. "It made a man of me all right."

If the unprecedented conditions of the Great Depression demanded the creation of "new and untried" programs, Roosevelt, as chief administrator, had to figure out which of these programs were working and which were not—so he used all manner of unconventional sources of intelligence that allowed him to change, toss, or revamp programs on the fly. Roosevelt, who could not travel easily, repeatedly nudged his aides: "Go and see what's happening. See the end product of what we are doing. Talk to people; get the wind in your nose."

FDR read newspapers from around the country plus letters that reached the White House—somewhere between six and eight thousand letters arrived every day after Roosevelt let it be known that he wanted to hear directly from the people. Eleanor also asked citizens to write her, citing the danger that a public figure "may be set apart from the stream of life affecting the country." Her daily newspaper column—the first such effort by a First Lady—not only offered advice but was open to receiving opinions and suggestions from the people. She, like

of labor, the first woman ever appointed to a cabinet position, Frances hesitated at first, fearing that labor unions "had always had, and would expect to have, one of its own people as Secretary." Roosevelt replied that "it was time to consider all working people, organized and unorganized." So she became the first-ever female officer in a presidential cabinet, at a time when a record thirteen to eighteen million Americans were unemployed due to the Great Depression.

What should she be called? Was there a female title corresponding to Mr. Secretary? *Robert's Rules of Order* suggested Madam Secretary, which was fine with Frances. Within the cabinet, she happily recounted that she never experienced "any suggestion of a patronizing note," of sexism or chauvinism—though at one point when the secretary of the navy was about to tell a story, he held back, wondering if it was appropriate for a lady to hear. "Go on," said the president, "she's dying to hear it."

The work of Frances Perkins lives on today in unemployment insurance, the minimum wage, a shorter work week, and federal laws regulating child labor and workers' safety. She leaves behind an even greater legacy: having helped pave the way for women to enter the male-dominated political world—changing the course of women's history in America.

her husband, had opened a two-way communication with the public.

More than any other source, FDR counted on Eleanor to provide him with "the unvarnished truth." She traveled hundreds of thousands of miles around the country, spending weeks and months at a time talking with a great variety of people from every region, listening to complaints, examining New Deal programs, gathering stories. Each time she returned home, she arranged "an uninterrupted meal" with her husband so the anecdotes would be "fresh and not dulled by repetition." FDR had developed absolute trust in the dependability and accuracy of her observations. "She saw many things the president could never see," Frances Perkins said. "Much of what she learned and what she understood about the life of the people of this country rubbed off onto the president." Eleanor's reports motivated Roosevelt to simplify programs, sharpen their effectiveness, and sometimes create altogether new agencies. As one project after another took shape, so his success at helping Americans continued to flourish. His intuitive touch became more confident and refined just as the country's confidence and trust in him and in themselves grew stronger. In the long run, FDR's New Deal domestic programs set a precedent for the federal government to play a key role in the economic and social affairs of the nation.

When World War II came in September 1939, FDR had to transform himself from Doc Roosevelt of Warm Springs and Dr. New Deal lifting the country from the depths of the Great Depression to Dr. Win the War. He would have to persuade both an isolationist Congress that was unwilling to send Americans to fight abroad and the American people that the country needed to prepare for war. More than 90 percent of the US public was opposed to America's involvement in what would turn out to be the deadliest international conflict in world history.

There were months of quiet until spring 1940, when in the space of a single week that shocked the world, the German blitzkrieg into

Western Europe led to thousands of deaths and the surrender of Holland, Belgium, Denmark, and eventually France, leaving only Great Britain standing against Adolf Hitler and the Nazis. Although Americans were overwhelmingly in favor of helping Great Britain, they were still opposed to becoming involved in a foreign war. And in fact, America was not in a position to be much help at all. The military had deteriorated after World War I and through the Great Depression, leaving America ranked seventeenth in military power after Holland surrendered to Germany. The US had only four hundred fighter planes—a one-day supply—and more horses than tanks. But FDR was determined to send whatever he could to help England, against the stern advice of his generals and by creatively coming up with workarounds to current law.

After being elected to an unprecedented third term, FDR explained to the American people in a late December 1940 fireside chat that the United States "must be the great arsenal of democracy," putting every effort toward manufacturing planes, ships, guns, and ammunition for Great Britain. "The sole purpose" of supplying Great Britain, he reassured them, "is to keep war away from our country and our people." But by the time FDR began his third term in 1941, fewer Americans believed the United States would be able to keep out of war.

FDR had to change his relationship with the business community, which had been marked by hostility during the New Deal. Only the business community, FDR recognized, could build the ships, tanks, planes, and weapons needed to help England and our allies, to prepare America itself for the possibility of war. So FDR reached out to the business world to make peace with them and to collaborate. The government would pay for the costs involved in transforming factories from making cars to making tanks and planes and ships. Regulations against trusts and monopolies would be relaxed. And the business community responded magnificently. The heads of General Motors and Sears Roebuck came into the government to run the production process, stating that they were thrilled to give back to the country that had served them so well. The assembly lines for planes and tanks began to move.

Then on December 7, 1941, the Japanese Navy launched a surprise assault from the air on the US Pacific Fleet at Pearl Harbor, Hawaii, killing 2,400 Americans and destroying battleships, boats, and planes. The next day, the US declared war on Japan. Three days passed before Nazi Germany and Italy declared war on the US. FDR was able then to portray US entry into the war as a defensive measure. Less than a month later, FDR explained the conflict in spiritual terms: "Our enemies are guided by brutal cynicism, by unholy contempt for the human race. We are inspired by a faith that goes back through all the years to the first chapter of the Book of Genesis: 'God created man in his own image.' We on our side are striving to be true to that divine heritage. We are fighting, as our fathers have fought, to uphold the doctrine that all men are equal in the sight of God."

A massive mobilization effort followed with millions of US armed service men and women being shipped overseas. Women took jobs in manufacturing plants, and productivity went up and was so staggering that a plane was produced every four minutes, a tank every seven minutes, and a ship that had once taken 250 days to build only months before was launched every single day!

And of equal significance, FDR was able to inspire the people to change course as well—to accept the sacrifices involved in a nationwide system of rationing to ensure equitable distribution of limited supplies of gasoline, rubber, cloth, meat, bread, and coffee. The need to preserve cotton and wool for uniforms led to changes in fashion—shorter skirts, no more pleated skirts, no more silk stockings; trousers became cuffless, jacket lapels narrower. One-piece bathing suits were replaced by two-piece bathing suits requiring less cloth. If women accepted the loss of pleated skirts and silk stockings, the most passionate outcry came when the rubber shortage led to an announcement that women's rubber girdles would no longer be manufactured. America's rubber supply had been diminished 92 percent when Japan attacked Indonesia. Women argued that without proper support from foundation garments a woman could not keep her posture erect or do physical work without tiring. It would menace their work in the factories. Finally, FDR listened to their concerns. An exception was made. Rubber girdles were deemed an essential part of a woman's wardrobe and could continue to be manufactured despite the rubber shortage.

Limits on gasoline sent drivers into a tailspin. For ordinary Americans five gallons meant no leisure driving. Streets were empty. For many Americans for whom cars had become symbols of independence this was really hard, but people eventually learned to walk again, to take buses, to play cards and do puzzles with neighbors at home. Perhaps the greatest grumbling took place when a ruling came down that people could have only one cup of coffee a day. The cargo ships that had carried coffee beans from Latin America were needed to ferry soldiers and weapons abroad. But once again people settled down.

It was FDR's political genius that he made everyone on the home front feel a part of the war effort, not only by accepting rationing of goods but by mobilizing a national rubber drive so that everyone could participate by bringing to their village squares old rubber toys, rubber dog bones, rubber hoses, rubber bands. The stockpile was increased by four hundred tons.

FDR, the educator who had explained the complexity of the banking crisis in his first fireside chat, would later ask the nation to spread a global map of the theater of war upon their tables so he could define the overarching strategy of the war and rally the citizens in the drama of the war. Despite the bleakness of the present outlook, he assured them, victory was bound to come. For this generation of Americans, he said, there is something larger and more important than the life of any individual or any individual group. In times of crisis when the future is in balance, people will come to understand what it means to be a nation, to be a community.

FDR's tenure, however, was not without its stains. He supported policies that both openly targeted Japanese American citizens after the attack on Pearl Harbor by placing them in internment camps and turned away European Jewish refugees in their greatest hour of need.

On February 19, 1942—against the pleas from his wife, Eleanor— FDR signed Executive Order 9066, which led to the forced relocation of approximately 120,000 Japanese Americans living on the West Coast. More than two thirds of these people were native-born American citizens. They were forced to abandon or sell their homes and businesses and were confined in inland internment camps operated by the military.

Prior to FDR's presidency, the 1924 US Immigration and Nationality Act strictly limited immigration, which prevented most Jewish people from entering the United States not only as the Nazis started ramping up their reign of terror but even after the US entered World War II. FDR did not ask Congress to consider expanding the immigration quotas, even when presented with these unprecedented circumstances. And still the US turned away the refugee ship *St. Louis* with its 930 Jewish passengers fleeing Germany. The passengers were denied entry, and the ship eventually took them back to Europe, where more than 250 were believed to have been murdered. These failures of leadership were all the more jarring for FDR's extraordinary sensitivity to the plight of ordinary Americans.

Elected to the presidency for four terms, Roosevelt discovered his communication skills were vital to his success in creating a common mission, explaining problems, mobilizing action, and earning the people's trust. The novelist Saul Bellow remembered the exhilarating experience of listening to Roosevelt speak as Bellow walked along a street in Chicago on a summer evening: "drivers had pulled over, parking bumper to bumper, and turned on their radios to hear Roosevelt. They had rolled down the windows and opened the car doors. Everywhere the same voice, its odd Eastern accent, which in anyone else would have irritated Midwesterners. You could follow without missing a single word as you strolled by. You felt joined to these unknown drivers, men and women smoking their cigarettes in silence, not so much considering the President's words as affirming the rightness of his tone and taking assurance from it."

Roosevelt believed that if the people "were taken into the confidence of their government and received a full and truthful statement of what was happening, they would generally choose the right course." Often referencing religious concepts in his speeches, he emphasized the importance of the Bible, prayer, and Christian morality. He frequently encouraged Americans to pray, thanked others for praying for him, and included prayers in his addresses. He did not make decrees from on high, rather he was joined in a continuous conversation with the people, so that everything he did was infused by their desires and their dislikes, their struggles and their successes. This reciprocal connection between Roosevelt and the citizens he served lay at the heart of his leadership.

Indeed, if ever an argument can be made for the conclusive importance of the character and intelligence of the leader in tough times, at home and abroad, it will come to rest on the broad, developed shoulders of Franklin Delano Roosevelt.

Who was Fala?

There was one other important member of FDR's team who he would not meet until he was well into his presidency: Fala the puppy. The black Scottish terrier, who became his friend in a way no other pet had been, was given to him by his cousin Margaret Suckley in 1940. Fala accompanied FDR everywhere—the Secret Service nicknamed him "the Informer," because if Fala was there, the president was in close proximity—whether it was in the president's study, in a chair at the foot of the president's bed, or in the kitchen, where apparently Fala was being fed so much that he developed an intestinal problem that landed him in the hospital. When Fala came home, FDR issued a stern order to the entire White House staff: "Not even one crumb will be fed to Fala except by the President." From then on, Fala was in perfect health. Fala received so much fan mail that he had his own secretary assigned to him.

In 1944, during FDR's reelection campaign, Fala accompanied the president on a trip to the Aleutian Islands in Alaska. A rumor was started that the president had forgotten Fala and then sent back a navy destroyer to pick him up. The story was untrue. But during the campaign, the Republicans accused FDR of spending millions of taxpayers' dollars to get Fala back. The president answered the attack in his famous "Fala speech" while talking to the International Teamsters Union. "These Republican leaders have not been content with attacks on me, or my wife, or on my sons," Roosevelt said in a mock serious tone. "No, not content with that, they now include my little dog, Fala.

"Well, of course, I don't resent attacks, and my family doesn't resent attacks—but Fala does resent them. You know, Fala is Scotch, and being a Scottie, as soon as he learned that the Republican fiction writers, in Congress and out, had concocted a story that I had left him behind on the Aleutian Islands and had sent a destroyer back to find him—at a cost to the taxpayers of two or three, or eight or twenty million dollars—his Scotch soul was furious. He has not been the same dog since.

"I am accustomed to hearing malicious falsehoods about myself. . . . But I think I have a right to resent, to object to libelous statements about my dog." The audience went wild, laughing and cheering and calling for more. And the laughter carried beyond the banquet hall; it reverberated in living rooms and kitchens throughout the country, where people were listening to the speech on their radios.

Less than seven months later, FDR died, and Fala stayed close by the president's wife, Eleanor. In her autobiography, Eleanor told of the time General Dwight Eisenhower came to lay a wreath on FDR's grave. "The gates of the regular driveway were opened, and his automobile approached the house accompanied by the wailing of the sirens of a police escort. When Fala heard the sirens, his legs straightened out, his ears pricked up and I knew that he expected to see his master coming down the drive as he had come so many times."

Roosevelt with Fala, his constant companion.

Lyndon Johnson

Chapter Nineteen

"I'm ready to try and make it with my brain."

As a young boy, Lyndon Johnson loved listening to his grandfather tell stories about his cowboy days on the old frontier. There in the Hill Country of Texas, Samuel Ealy Johnson Sr. detailed how he drove a herd of fifteen hundred cattle from ranches in Texas across twelve hundred miles of dangerous country up the Chisholm Trail to Abilene, Kansas. "I sat beside the rocker on the floor of the porch," the younger Johnson remembered, "thinking all the while how lucky I was to have as a granddaddy this big man with the white beard who had lived the most exciting life imaginable."

Central to Sam Sr.'s stories was the iconic image of the heroic cowboy leading cattle through icy rivers, ever careful to avoid the ultimate horror of the stampede. "When the rivers that crossed the trails were cold, the cattle would often hesitate partway across, circling and jumping on top of one another instead of moving in a straight line. Then the lead cowboy would have to ride out in front of the herd and get the cattle moving." Young Lyndon would never forget his grandfather's image of men and cattle circling aimlessly in the cold, treacherous currents, their continued progress dependent upon the daring and skill of the lead cowboy. But taming a stampede was the most dangerous adventure of all. To soothe the cattle, cowboys sang lullabies. That failing, all

you could do was outrun the wild herd, knowing there were prairie dog holes all around, and if the horse stepped into one of these holes, you could be crushed to death by the oncoming stampede.

Lyndon's admiration for the bold cowboy in his beloved paternal grandfather's cattle-driving tales shaped his concept of manhood and stayed with him the rest of his life, although he never experienced the working day of the cowboy, nor the long and lonely nights on the plain, for by the time he was born in 1908, the world of the cattle drives had collapsed. In the 1880s and 1890s, as the railroads spread throughout the West, the long drives to market became increasingly unnecessary. The economic life of many in the West became more and more dependent on the decisions of the few in the East—the massive trusts and monopolies that kept prices up on essential goods like food and fuel, the railroads that imposed costly rates to transport goods, and the powerful politicians who didn't give much thought to the men and women who worked the land on the frontier.

During this period of economic distress, Johnson's grandfather, who was previously aligned with the Democratic Party, joined the newly formed Populist Party, often traveling hundreds of miles to attend large political camp meetings resembling religious festivals. The populists called for various reforms that would make government more responsive to the needs of working people. But the Populist Party had also faded by the time Lyndon was born. As a result, Sam Ealy Johnson Sr., and many of his generation, had fewer options for work—and to succeed. Accustomed to continual movement, the old man spent the last decades of his life in his small farmhouse on the Pedernales River in the hard and inhospitable Texas Hill Country, finding pleasure in the chance to relive his youthful days through the stories he told his grandson.

Lyndon and his grandfather would talk until the sun set. Even then, the boy did not want him to stop. But the talk always came to an end when Sam stood up. "You better go along now, son, your mama is waiting." Then, seeing the boy's disappointed face, he would invite Lyndon into the study, where there was a rolltop desk opened by a large gold key. Grandfather Johnson would take the key from his pocket and unlock the bottom drawer, filled with sticks of candy in all the colors of the rainbow. Every day the boy chose a different color; his grandfather locked the drawer, returned the key to his right pocket, and suddenly, from his other pocket, pulled another present—a big red apple. "I remember how I thought that deep pockets were wonderful things to have," Lyndon recalled. And then, feeling fulfilled and happy, he would promptly hurry down the road, mounting the steps of his own house quickly, anxious to avoid his mother's scolding.

One of the many joys of story time with his grandfather was that it offered young Lyndon the "perfect escape" from the battles within the Johnson family household—a place often filled with the severe tensions that contributed to Lyndon's excitable temperament. From an early age and continuing into young adulthood, Lyndon had to negotiate between his father and mother, each representing very different and clashing worlds of values, expectations, and emotions.

"My mother told me the first year of her marriage was the worst year of her life," Johnson remembered. Having grown up in "a two-story rock house, with a fruitful orchard of perfectly spaced trees, terraced flower beds, broad walks," and a white picket fence, Lyndon's mother was utterly unprepared for the disorder and isolation of the small cabin on a muddy stream with no modern conveniences that belonged to Lyndon's parents. His mother, Rebekah Baines, was the daughter of a college-educated lawyer, and herself a graduate of Baylor University at a time when few women attended college. She grew up Baptist, and her grandfather, George Washington Baines Sr., had been one of the best-known Baptist leaders in Texas. She was aspiring to be a writer when she interviewed the "dashing and dynamic" young politician Sam Johnson Jr. for her family newspaper during his first term in the state legislature. A "whirlwind courtship" followed, leading to marriage and "the problem of adjustment to a completely opposite personality," as well as "a strange and new way of life."

Accustomed to culture, books, and intellectual discussions about philosophy and literature, Rebekah found that the man she had fallen in love with enjoyed nothing more than sitting up half the night with his political buddies, drinking beer, sharing gossip, swapping stories. Sam's family also belonged to a different church, the Christadelphian Church, a lay community patterned after first-century Christianity. Rebekah had originally hoped that Sam would run for national office and carry her away to the nation's capital, where ideas and ideals would be discussed, but he soon made it clear that he had no interest in leaving the family homestead; and at that time, as a married woman, Rebekah felt she did not have the freedom to pursue her own dreams. Her days and nights were consumed with drawing water from the well, feeding chickens, boiling clothes, and scrubbing floors on her hands and knees, leaving little time for the unread books "piled high" in her bedroom, and no time at all for writing. She was miserable. "Then I came along," Lyndon recalled his mother describing, "and suddenly everything was all right again. I could do all the things she never did." Rebekah was over the moon with her firstborn baby son, later writing dramatically about the morning of his birth. "Now the light came in from the east, bringing a deep stillness, a stillness so profound and so pervasive that it seemed as if the earth itself were listening. And then there came a sharp compelling cry—the most awesome, happiest sound known to human ears—the cry of a newborn baby; the first child of Sam Ealy and Rebekah Johnson was 'discovering America.'"

Lyndon seemed at first the perfect instrument for Rebekah to realize her own ambitions. Relatives and friends claimed they had "never seen such a friendly baby," nor one as curious and intelligent. He learned the alphabet before he was two years old, learned to read and spell before he was four, and at three could recite long passages from the poets Longfellow and Tennyson. "I'll never forget how much my mother loved me when I recited those poems," Johnson said. "The minute I finished she'd take me in her arms and hug me so hard I sometimes thought I'd be strangled to death."

When Lyndon was five, his family left behind the cabin on the river and moved to a frame house in Johnson City—named for the family. Though Johnson City was hardly more than a village, it offered Rebekah some escape from her isolation. It had a high school at which she soon taught debating, a newspaper for which she wrote a weekly column, and an opera house in which local plays, directed by Rebekah, were performed.

Even after she gave birth to four other children, Lyndon remained Rebekah's favorite. "I remember playing games with her that only the two of us could play. And she would always let me win even if to do so we had to change the rules. I knew how much she needed me. . . . I liked that. It made me feel big and important. It made me believe I could do anything in the world."

But opposite the bright and beaming side of the moon was an equally dark side—a deep insecurity that would plague Lyndon Johnson for the rest of his life. When he failed to fulfill his mother's ambitions for him—when he became a sluggish student or resisted continuing violin and dancing lessons—she withdrew her love and affection. "For days after I quit those lessons she walked around the house pretending I was dead," Johnson glumly said. "And then . . . ," he added, "I had to watch her being especially warm and nice to my father and sisters." Love was alternately lavished and snatched away, a transactional arrangement for obedience and achievement. In later years, Johnson would exhibit a similar pattern in dealing with friends, colleagues, and members of his staff. He would blanket someone with generosity, care, and affection but, in return, expect total loyalty and perfect achievement. Failing this standard was viewed by him as a betrayal. His affection would be withdrawn, a pattern of behavior so pronounced, it earned the nickname the Johnson "freeze-out."

While Johnson's mother was also instrumental in fostering his aspirations and fueling the cultural and educational side of his personality, his father would teach him the rules of engagement when it came to politics—and the roller coaster of emotions that went along with it. From the time Lyndon was a small boy, he identified with his father Sam Johnson's political ambitions—Sam served in the Texas legislature on and off over the course of nearly twenty years. In the evenings, when Sam sat in the brown rocker on his own porch swapping tales and jokes with three or four political buddies, the boy stood in the half darkness of the doorway, straining to overhear the comings and goings of people in the legislature. He liked the animated, crude way the men spoke, the deep knowledge they had of the different families in their region.

When the legislature was in session, Sam would sometimes take young Lyndon along. "I loved going with my father to the legislature," Johnson remembered. "I would sit in the gallery for hours watching all the activity on the floor and then would wander around the halls trying to figure out what was going on." Sam Johnson was a popular figure in the statehouse—friendly, down-to-earth, "who attracted people and knew how to deal with people." He told his son, "If you can't come into a room full of people and tell right away who is for you and who is against you, you have no business in politics." He was known to have an "explosive" temper, "but it was like a sunshine thing," a neighbor recalled. "It was gone in a minute and then he was always going about doing something nice."

A progressive Democrat, Sam Jr. took a stand against bigotry and the violent racism of the Ku Klux Klan. He championed the underdog, using his office to help poor farmers, army veterans, and soldiers' widows. "We've got to look after these people," Sam told a friend, "that's what we're here for." He advocated for folks being squeezed by the interests of big business, supporting bills to establish an eight-hour workday, regulate public utility companies—water, gas, electric power—and tax corporations.

When Lyndon was nine years old in the spring of 1918, a loyalty bill was passed in the Texas legislature that said that any person using disloyal language at any time or place in the presence of another could be imprisoned. "My father stood right up against that situation," Johnson later said. "He got up on the floor of the House of Representatives and made a wonderful speech pleading for tolerance and common sense."

Lyndon was both his father's shadow and replica. They looked alike and shared the physical attributes of long arms and legs, prominent nose and ears, and hard squint. Lyndon learned to envelop people in the same fashion as his father did—often intruding on another's personal space. "They walked the same, had the same nervous mannerisms," recalled Wright Patman, who served with Sam in the state legislature and later became a congressman, "and Lyndon clutched you like his daddy did when he talked to you." And like his father, outgoing young Lyndon struck up conversations with everyone he met. He became a favorite of the older women in his new hometown of Johnson City, asking how they were feeling, how things were going. In this tight-knit community, if he heard a group of men talking politics on the street, he would stand on the sidelines, hanging on their words. At the age of only ten, he became an after-school entrepreneur, opening a shoe-shine business in Cecil Maddox's barbershop, the place where politics and the latest items of news were discussed.

The only thing Lyndon loved more than accompanying his father to the statehouse was traveling along with him on the campaign trail. "We drove in the Model T Ford from farm to farm, up and down the valley, stopping at every door. My father would do most of the talking. He would bring the neighbors up to date on local gossip, talk about the crops and about the bills he'd introduced in the legislature, and always he'd bring along an enormous crust of homemade bread and a large jar of homemade jam. When we got tired or hungry, we'd stop by the side of the road. He sliced the bread, smeared it with jam, and split the slices with me. I'd never seen him happier. Families all along the way opened up their homes to us. If it was hot outside, we were invited in for big servings of homemade ice cream. If it was cold, we were given hot tea . . . sometimes I wished it could go on forever."

At home, as Lyndon grew older, the strain of being at the center of a tug-of-war between his parents grew unbearable. "I remember one Thanksgiving," he said, his mother "had gotten out the wedding china and roasted a huge turkey. Everything was set just right. She sat at the head of the table with her fancy lace dress and big wide sleeves. She was saying the prayers when a knock came on the door. My daddy answered and found a Mexican family with five children. They lived nearby. My father had done a lot to help them over the years. Now they were returning his favor. They had brought him a green cake, the biggest cake I'd ever seen. Well, the minute he saw them out there, cold and hungry, he invited them to dinner. He was always doing things like that. The dinner was loud. There was a lot of laughing and yelling. I liked it. But then I looked at my mother. Her face was bent toward her plate and she said nothing. I had a feeling that something was wrong, but I was having such a good time I didn't pay attention. After the meal, she stood up and went to her room. I followed a little behind her and heard her crying in there. I guess she was really counting on it being a private occasion. I looked at her sad face and I felt guilty. I went in and tried to make her feel better."

In school, Lyndon became something of a troublemaker—too restless to sit still or concentrate in class, and avoiding completing his homework. But still his classmates recognized the superiority of his intelligence. He was "very brilliant," one schoolmate recalled. The boys his age were simply not in "his class mentally." Even the older boys "saw that he talked—and thought—faster than they did." His mother tried to remedy his lack of preparation by reading his assignments out loud while he ate breakfast. If it took longer to read the lesson than to finish breakfast, Rebekah would walk him to school, reciting from the text all the way. Still, Lyndon never came to experience the joy of reading, and he felt "smothered" by his mother's "force feedings" of his lessons. As he got older, he could sit still only if the stories were real histories and real biographies, that is, if they spoke mostly of the actions of other men. "Is it true?" he repeatedly asked of a story. "Did it actually happen, Mama?" He agreed to open a book only if it was about history or government. Through adulthood, Lyndon Johnson remained insecure about his academic record.

While Lyndon admired his father, he also fretted about meeting his father's expectations about his own manliness—the traditional idea of bravery and strength. "In the fall and the spring, I spent every moment when I wasn't in school out in the open. With the other boys, I went hunting squirrels and rabbits. I carried a gun and every now and then I pointed it at the animals but I never wanted to kill any of them. I wanted only to know that I could kill if I had to. Then one day my daddy asked me how did it happen that I was the only boy in the neighborhood who had never shot an animal. Was I a coward? The next day I went back into the hills and killed a rabbit. It jumped out at me from behind a bush and I shot it in between the eyes. Then I went to the bathroom and threw up."

Lyndon was deeply humiliated by his father's questioning of his manhood, but his tests were easier to endure than his mother's gloomy silence, prompted, now in his teen years, by his unwillingness to entertain the notion of attending college. He knew by his mother's withdrawal that he had not lived up to the splendid vision she had held of him. He was becoming his own person, and was baptized in 1923 as a member of the Disciples of Christ. Finally, he made up his mind that it was time to leave home.

The summer after he graduated high school in 1924, a few friends decided to travel from Texas to California for adventure and to seek work. To Lyndon, the trip was a form of reliving his grandfather's life on the frontier. But the old frontier had promised economic and spiritual independence, and in California, in 1924, that independence was not easy to secure. Indeed, Johnson was barely able to survive on the grapes he picked, the dishes he washed, and the cars he fixed. Just the same, he remembered living happily for a time in different places, free of the emotional whims of both his mother and his father. He was immensely curious about the different kinds of people he worked with—the field hands in the Imperial Valley, the cooks in the all-night cafés, the garage mechanics in the big cities. He constantly entertained his fellow workers with stories and jokes. People seemed to like him; they admired his quickness.

Johnson lived here and there for nearly a year; then, when his money dried up completely, he took a job in Los Angeles as a clerk to a criminal lawyer, a cousin of his mother's. There Lyndon stayed for another year, until one August day in 1926 when, suddenly faced with an offer of a ride to Texas, he realized that after two years away he was ready to return home. He decided to go to college after all and "become a political figure." Despite his resolution, Lyndon stayed away from the study of books for another six months, taking, instead, a job repairing roads. Finally, one hot afternoon in February 1927, he went to his mother and said, "All right, I'm sick of working just with my hands and I'm ready to try and make it with my brain." He borrowed seventy-five dollars and enrolled in Southwest Texas State Teachers College.

A portrait of Lyndon at about nineteen years old.

Chapter Twenty

"A steam engine in pants."

"THE WAY YOU GET AHEAD IN THE WORLD, you get close to those that are the heads of things," Lyndon told his roommate when he finally arrived at college in San Marcos, Texas. "Like President Evans, for example."

Cecil Evans had served as the president of Southwest Texas State Teachers College for fifteen years and was well respected by faculty and students alike. Aware of the demands on the president's time, Johnson concluded "there was only one way to get to know Evans, and that was to work for him directly." It was school policy to give students part-time jobs in the library, cafeteria, bookstore, administrative offices, or maintenance department, and for Lyndon this helped to cover the costs of college. His first job was on the outdoor janitorial crew, picking up papers and trash. Most students did the minimum work necessary to keep their jobs, but Lyndon labored with extravagant enthusiasm, making a game of collecting the largest trash pile in the shortest time. His eagerness earned him a promotion to the janitorial crew that worked inside the administration building. Assigned to mop floors, Lyndon focused on the hallway outside the president's office, allowing him to strike up conversations as President Evans passed by. Like Lyndon, Evans had loved politics from his earliest days. In fact, Evans hoped that someday he might run for office. With Lyndon, as with no other student or even most faculty members, Evans could enjoy conversations about business in the legislature or stories about various political figures. When Lyndon asked if he could work in his office running errands and delivering messages, Evans promptly agreed.

What began as a lowly position soon became, in Lyndon's hands, a generator of actual power as he expanded the limited function of messenger by encouraging people to communicate with President Evans through him. Occupying a desk in the president's foyer, he would announce the arrival of visitors as if he were the appointments secretary rather than the office messenger. In time, faculty members and college officials, whose names Lyndon always remembered, came to think of the skinny young Texan with curly black hair as a direct channel to the president.

Increasingly impressed by Lyndon's sharp observations about state politics, Evans brought him to the state legislature in Austin when committee hearings were held on funding for state colleges and other educational matters. Soon, Evans began relying on his new messenger to write up reports on the hearings, which Lyndon did with flair, analyzing the positions of individual legislators as well as the mood and atmosphere of the legislature as a whole. Before long, Lyndon was handling the president's political correspondence, drafting reports for various state agencies, and taking up residence in a room above the garage in the president's house. In time, he almost seemed the son President Evans never had—a son who not only provided affection and companionship but whose organizational skills and attention to detail allowed him to assume burdensome tasks and responsibilities belonging to his mentor.

"Kissing up" to his superiors, however, did nothing for his standing with peers. Several of Lyndon's classmates regarded him as "ruthless," prepared "to cut your throat to get what [he] wanted." They "didn't just dislike Lyndon Johnson," one said, "they despised him." While Lyndon understood that ambition "creates a discontent with present surroundings and achievements," a bottomless hole to fill, he failed to understand when to ease up and was often unaware of the human cost of his own compulsive energies.

Lyndon's unbridled ambition was harnessed in the service of a larger purpose for the first time when he was forced to take a yearlong break from college to make enough money to be able to afford to finish school. At twenty years old, he was hired to teach math and history at the Welhausen School and was quickly promoted to principal of the six-teacher Mexican American school in Cotulla, Texas, a dusty, impoverished town not too far from the border with Mexico. Most of the families lived in dirt hovels, engaged in a continual struggle to wring a living from the dry and treeless land.

As principal, Lyndon occupied his first true position of authority and used every leadership trait he already possessed—ability to persuade, willingness to fight for what he wanted, intuition, creativity, initiative, and boundless energy—to expand opportunities for his students and to improve their lives. The students adored him, teachers came to admire him, and he left an enduring impression upon the little community as a whole. At last, biographer Robert Caro observes, Lyndon was "the somebody he had always wanted to be." He was neither trying to absorb power from an older mentor nor savagely competing with peers. He was simply trying to elevate the hopes and conditions of the needy in this South Texas town.

The critical leadership trait of empathy fired Lyndon's efforts at Cotulla. "My students were poor and they often came to class without breakfast, hungry," Johnson later recalled. "And they knew, even in their youth, the pain of prejudice." Because there was no school funding for extracurricular activities, he used half his first month's salary to buy sports equipment and then badgered the school board to include track-and-field events, baseball games, and volleyball matches in the school budget. In addition to his administrative responsibilities as principal, he took on extra duties teaching fifth-, sixth-, and seventh-grade classes, coaching debate, and serving as the softball coach, the drama coach, and the choir leader. At first he had the children practice and compete against one another. Soon, however, he arranged field days with a dozen other regional schools.

Johnson (center) with his fifth-, sixth-, and seventh-grade classes
at the Welhausen School in Cotulla in 1928.

"I was determined to spark something inside them," Johnson said, "to fill their souls with ambition and interest and belief in the future. I was determined to give them what they needed to make it in this world, to help them finish their education. Then the rest would take care of itself."

A chorus of voices decades later testifies to the enormous impact Lyndon left on the school. "He respected the kids more than any other teacher we ever had," said former student Juan Gonzalez. "He put us to work," another student remembered. "But he was the kind of teacher you wanted to work for. You felt an obligation to him and to yourself to do your work." He was strict, they all agreed; he made them stay after school if they hadn't done their homework. But he was "down-to-earth and friendly," and years later they were grateful so much had been demanded of them.

Despite his good intentions, Johnson was convinced, rightly so for Texas in the 1920s, that his students needed to know English to break through from poverty. So he made a rule that no Spanish could be spoken on school property, including the playground. Students caught speaking Spanish were brought to his office and punished. His inflexibility on the issue demonstrated his ignorance that his pupils' own cultural traditions and language might be an independent source of strength and fulfillment for them.

Even so, the year Johnson spent as principal and teaching in Cotulla was a pivotal experience, one to which Johnson returned again and again. "I can still see the faces of the children who sat in my class," he said years later. This was the display of a different kind of leadership, one based on empathy, generosity, and an ambition for a greater good that he had never exercised before.

When Johnson returned to college, he excelled on the debate team, edited the school newspaper, and immersed himself in student politics. In his senior year, Johnson delivered his first political speech at an annual picnic outside the small community of Henly. This was an important event in South Central Texas and one Lyndon had attended with his father since he was ten years old. Now he was there to rally support for Pat Neff, a former governor who was up for election as railroad commissioner. Neff had recently helped Lyndon's father secure a job as a railway inspector, so Lyndon was proud to throw his support behind Neff. When Lyndon rose to make his remarks, his style of speaking was "so wrapped up in youthful enthusiasm and sincerity of purpose," state representative Welly Hopkins recalled, "that his audience came along with him." While "it wasn't a rich oratorical style," there was "a timber in his voice that was pleasantly received." Indeed, his speech was considered "the hit of the Henly picnic."

On the spur of the moment that day, Hopkins, who was about to launch a campaign of his own for the state senate, invited Lyndon to take a leading position in his campaign—a chance encounter that would have a far-reaching impact on Lyndon's future. "Even in that day," Hopkins recalled of Lyndon, "politics was in his blood." Not only was he "steeped in political lore," but he was "gifted with a very unusual ability to meet and greet the public," and to organize. Within days, Lyndon had mobilized a half dozen of his college friends into a small, tightly knit political machine.

"We worked Blanco County in and out," Hopkins recalled of his travels with Lyndon. No matter how tired they were, Lyndon scoured the countryside for votes, even if the car had to travel to a single farm at the end of an unpaved road. "On one occasion," Hopkins laughingly recalled, Lyndon had him stand in a dry creek bed to deliver a ten-minute speech to a group of three—a man, his wife, and their relative. Such attention to detail paid off. Hopkins secured a surprising victory. "I always felt he was the real balance of the difference as to whether I'd be elected," a grateful Hopkins said. Word spread that there was a "wonder kid in San Marcos who knew more about politics than anyone in the area."

Lyndon was poised for and excited about entry into a political career, but the times dictated otherwise. When Johnson graduated in 1930, America was just entering the Great Depression, meaning there was no opportunity for a government job. Fortunately, his uncle George Johnson, longtime head of the history department at Sam Houston High, helped him land a position as a teacher of public speaking and debate. The moment Lyndon arrived at Sam Houston High, he set a dramatic goal for the debate team: though they had never "won anything" in competition with neighboring schools, Lyndon told them that for the first time in the history of the school, the team not only would win the city and district competitions but would go on to the state championship. Straightaway, he had set a psychological—and lofty—target to elevate the team's ambitions before the debating season even got underway.

At Houston High, as at Cotulla, Lyndon channeled his drive for success to benefit others, using his bold leadership style to raise money for the debate club. Luther Jones, one of the club members, recalled overhearing a "rather vigorous argument Johnson had with the principal," who told him that funds for the debate team had never been part of the school budget. "Yes, but you've never had a teacher like me!" Johnson countered. He "could get people to do things they would under ordinary circumstances never think of doing," Jones observed.

Johnson appeared to his students "a human dynamo," "a steam engine in pants," driven by a work ethic and an unlimited enthusiasm that proved contagious. His first day on the job, he had students stand before their teammates and make animal noises, a comical way to brush off nervousness and self-consciousness. Debate team member Gene Latimer came to refer to Johnson as "the Chief" and remembered that Johnson had already decided "he will make state champions of us." And he worked the students as hard as he himself worked. Despite all the practice, there was plenty of singing and joking, and "he quickly becomes a favorite of students, teachers, the principal," Latimer recalled. Johnson went on to teach his students that storytelling was the key to successful debating. In contrast to the previous public speaking teacher, who came from the "old school" and trained his debaters to "be bombastic and loud," he urged a conversational style that illustrated points with concrete stories. "Act like you're talking to those folks," he counseled his students. "Look one of them in the eye and then move on and look another one in the eye." During competitions, he used gestures and facial expressions to cue and prompt—frowning, narrowing his eyes, creasing his brow, and shaking his head in wonder—creating a silent movie to steer and guide his students to victory.

From the start, Johnson sought to create an aura around the debate club that had previously been reserved for the football team. At the first competition, only seven people came to watch, but as the team's undefeated victory tally mounted, so did excitement for their successes. By the time the team clinched the city championship and began competing at the district level, every seat in the auditorium was filled. Johnson had transformed the sport of debate into a community-wide campaign—complete with pep rallies, cheerleaders, and team sweaters. When the team won the district-level championship, pictures of the two star debaters, Latimer and Luther Jones, were splashed across city newspapers. Though the state championship was lost in the final competition by a single vote, by the time the school year ended, Latimer proudly noted "we were more important than the football team."

Johnson's services to Welly Hopkins's campaign were remembered and repaid with Hopkins's recommendation to the new Texas congressman Richard Kleberg that Lyndon Johnson was just the man he needed as his legislative secretary in his Washington, DC, office—in essence, his chief of staff, the man who would run every aspect of the congressional office. Responsibilities would include hiring and supervising a staff and making sure that constituents back home in Texas's Fourteenth Congressional District received answers to their letters and requests for help. After meeting Johnson, Kleberg promptly offered him the job. A few days later the two men set off on a Pullman train for the two-day trip to Washington, DC. "All that day I'd gone about feeling excited, nervous, and sad," Johnson recalled. "I was about to leave home to meet the adventure of my future. I felt grown-up, but my mind kept ranging backward in time. I saw myself as a boy skipping down the road to my granddaddy's house. I remembered the many nights I had stood in the doorway listening to my father's political talk. I remembered the evenings with my mother when my daddy was away. Now all that was behind me."

If ever a destination seemed a destiny for Johnson, it was Washington, DC—a city whose peculiar intricacies he would master and, for a while, command as completely as he had commanded his college days in San Marcos, and his work in Cotulla and at Houston High. Upon seeing the Capitol dome for the first time, Johnson vowed that someday he would become a congressman in his own right. "I would not say I was without ambition ever," he recalled. "It was very exciting to me to realize that the people, many of them that you were passing, were probably congressmen at least, maybe senators, members of the cabinet. And there was the smell of power. It's got an odor you know. Power I mean."

Such was the nature of Johnson's driven temperament that he had no sooner settled into the Dodge Hotel, where the majority of congressional secretaries lived, than he began his quest to determine the sources and relationships of power in the nation's capital. There was no time to waste—DC was a big, competitive town, and he had a lot to learn—so he got right to work, coming up with completely inventive ways to get ahead. He decided he needed to take four separate showers in the shared bathroom his first night so he could talk to as many people as possible. The next morning he brushed his teeth every ten minutes— all to come into contact with as many people as he could to figure out who had the most information to share. "This skinny boy was as green as anybody could be," an older congressional secretary said, "but within

a few months he knew how to operate in Washington better than some who had been here twenty years."

Managing a staff for the first time, Johnson filled his two positions with young men whose work ethic he had already helped form and tested—his star debaters from Houston High, Gene Latimer and Luther Jones. Johnson was "a hard man to work for because he insisted on perfection," Jones recalled. The Chief, as they still called him, "wanted to answer every day's mail every day." And every letter "had to be just right," which meant typing and retyping the same letter over and over again on the typewriter until it was exactly "the way he wanted it." One Saturday evening, Johnson came back to work after dinner to find Latimer and Jones gone. A note on the desk said they had gone to a movie and would be back at nine. Shuffling through the mail stack, he spied what he was searching for: an unanswered letter. Seizing it, he raced to the local theater, found the two men, and brought them outside to scold them—only to learn that the constituent's letter in question had been put aside based on his very order from earlier in the day. Feeling bad and anxious to make it up to them, Johnson invited Latimer and Jones to dinner at a local restaurant—even though he had already eaten dinner. So no sooner had the first drink arrived than up he jumped and proclaimed, "We've been relaxing long enough. There's still three more good working hours until we fold."

When critics wrote about Johnson's harsh manner in dealing with the members of his staff, Latimer insisted that his boss was "extremely sentimental about the people close to him." And yet, increasingly, the price of admission into his select extended family had grown from dedication and unquestioned loyalty to devouring all of his staff member's personal time and space. "If he caught you reading a letter from your mother," Jones said, or using the bathroom, "he'd say, 'Son, can't you please try a little harder to do that on your own time?'"

Lyndon Johnson could not unwind. Jones never remembered him

reading a novel or, indeed, reading anything other than the newspapers and current magazines he obsessively consumed. He rarely went to movies or plays, for he disliked sitting in the dark for three hours—unable to talk. At baseball games, he would insist on talking politics between innings and even between pitches. At social events, he danced with the wives of congressmen and government officials rather than with single girls, discussing the latest news and political gossip as they twirled across the floor. All his life, he would continue to work at this same compulsive pace.

Within a matter of months, Congressman Kleberg's office had developed a reputation as one of the most efficient on Capitol Hill. And for Kleberg, "a bluff and good natured, multi-millionaire," the situation was ideal. Preferring to spend his time playing golf, poker, or polo, he was happy to let Johnson run the show. From the start, Johnson gave top priority to meeting the needs of Kleberg's constituents at home. Through prompt and helpful answers to the hundreds of letters they sent each month—veterans with claim of injuries sustained during World War I, desperate farmers hoping for aid from the federal government, unemployed men and women in need of a government job—word of Kleberg's reflected passion began to spread across the district; on the inside, Johnson's reputation as a doer was established. With stunning audacity, ingenuity, hard work, and speed, Johnson had made himself a congressman in all but name.

By the age of twenty-five, Lyndon Johnson was on the path to a political career. He had laid out a plan for a different kind of leadership, an ability to direct people and run things and a distinctive, grinding pattern of behavior that would mark his management style the rest of his days. Already he had become a political animal. The instinctive ability to locate the gears and levers of power in any institution, to secure wise and faithful mentors, to identify and nurture dedicated staffers, and to transform minor positions into substantial sources of influence would accompany every stage of his upward climb.

Chapter Twenty-One

"I see something I know I want—
I immediately exert efforts to get it."

THE SAME QUALITIES LYNDON JOHNSON BROUGHT to every stage of his climb—single-minded determination, contagious enthusiasm, flattery mingled with threats, unstoppable energy, a forceful personality, and an overwhelming desire to win—were obvious in his successful effort to win the hand of Claudia "Lady Bird" Taylor in marriage.

The daughter of a wealthy businessman, Lady Bird had recently graduated from the University of Texas with a degree in journalism. After a single, day-long date in Austin, Johnson, to his credit and good fortune, decided not to let this intelligent, reserved, sensitive, and shrewd woman go. During their first conversation, she later remembered, he told her all manner of "extraordinarily direct" things about himself—"his salary as a chief of staff to a congressman, his ambitions, even about all the members of his family, and how much insurance he carried. It was as if he wanted to give a complete picture of his life and of his capabilities." She found him "very, very good-looking, with lots of black, wavy hair," but "I thought he was just out of his mind" when "before the day was over" he asked her to marry him.

"I'm ambitious, proud, energetic and madly in love with you," Johnson declared to Lady Bird. "I see something I know I want—I immediately exert efforts to get it." They sent dozens of letters back and forth, and on his next visit about two months later, he issued an ultimatum: "We either get married now or we never will." When she agreed, he let out a "Texas yip" and then drove straight to San Antonio, where they were married in a simple ceremony the next day without any of their family present. "I don't think Lady Bird ever had a chance once he set eyes on her," Latimer observed three decades later. She was his "balancing wheel," Jones said. He was impatient; she was calm. He was gruff and foul-mouthed; she was gentle and gracious. Without such patience and devotion, without a love steadily given and never withdrawn, Johnson's rise is hard to imagine.

Lady Bird moved to Washington as Johnson's wife, and the home she established for them there proved crucial not only to Lyndon's stability but to his growing ambitions. Lady Bird offered a welcoming hospitality to Lyndon's guests at any time of day or night. He might call her as late as six or seven to say he was bringing home a half dozen people, and by the time they arrived, she would have the table set, drinks ready, and supper cooking.

Among the many guests, none came to play a larger role in the Johnsons' life than Sam Rayburn, the Democratic congressman from Bonham, Texas, who had served with Lyndon's father in the state legislature and would go on to become Speaker of the House for seventeen years, the most powerful position in the US House of Representatives. Without a wife or family of his own, Mr. Sam, as he was affectionately nicknamed by the folks in his hometown, was often lonely in the hours when the House was not in session. Sensing this, Lyndon more and more frequently began inviting him for dinner, invitations that soon extended to breakfasts on weekends so the two men could read the Sunday papers together. The warmth and informality of being at home created the basis for a genuine companionship and deep friendship to evolve, providing Lyndon with a wise, trusted, and most useful mentor and Mr. Sam with

the affectionate and loyal son he never had. And soon Mr. Sam's exercise of brute political force would push Johnson to the next way station of his political rise—with a little help from President Franklin Roosevelt.

Johnson and Lady Bird in Washington, DC, in 1934 or 1935.

It was a Tuesday morning in June 1935, when, by executive order, President Roosevelt created the National Youth Administration, another in a long list of his New Deal programs. The NYA was designed to save "a lost generation" of young people during the Great Depression by providing part-time work for students from needy families who could not otherwise afford to stay in school, as well as full-time jobs for thousands of unemployed youths between the ages of sixteen and twenty-one who had already finished school. Within hours, Johnson approached Mr. Sam and proposed himself as the perfect candidate for director of the NYA in Texas. Straightaway, Rayburn worked his own political channels to ask the White House to appoint Johnson to the post, despite the fact that the twenty-six-year-old did not have the experience to run a statewide agency; the largest staff he had ever managed consisted of three people. But thanks to Rayburn's advocacy, Johnson got the job as Texas director of the National Youth Administration and became the youngest of the forty-eight state NYA directors. He and Lady Bird happily returned to their home state.

For Johnson, the mission of the NYA—to provide education, training, and jobs for young people—was personal; it wasn't too long ago that he had been poor and struggled to find work. "Sure, I guess I know a little bit about youth's hard lot in life," he said at the time. However, the enormity of the statewide undertaking—adapting rigid federal guidelines to sprawling and diverse Texas—overwhelmed Johnson until he came up with a plan to "start the ball rolling" with an all-important first project. He would put thousands of out-of-school youth to work building roadside parks along state highways where travelers could stop to rest, have something to eat, and use the bathroom. Within a matter of weeks, the paperwork was approved in Washington, DC, and Johnson's plan was put into operation. While the NYA paid the young people for their labor, the Texas Highway Department provided the supervision, trucks, and materials. State engineers trained the young men to mix concrete, build driveways off the roads into the parks, lay bricks for barbecue pits, construct picnic tables and benches, and plant shade trees and curbside shrubs. Johnson was "beside himself with happiness" when the first of the projects was up and running, for he knew that it would create an atmosphere of success. When the roadside parks project proved triumphant, he made sure it was publicized throughout Texas, and in a short time it actually became "a model for the nation." When First Lady Eleanor Roosevelt came to Texas in 1936, she asked to meet the state's NYA director, who she had already heard so much about.

As the pressure on Johnson for continued accomplishments increased, however, accounts of his frantic, harsh, even abusive behavior toward his staff escalated. "Everything had to be done NOW," one staffer recalled. The team worked six days a week, from eight a.m. to midnight. Sundays were reserved for staff meetings to go over what had been completed and outline plans for the week ahead. The lights and the elevators in the government building were supposed to be turned off at ten p.m., but Johnson persuaded the building manager to leave them on until midnight, and sometimes one a.m., until the building owner intervened.

He instilled fear, which kept everyone on edge. Staffers never knew what might trigger an outburst. It could be a cluttered desk, which Johnson took as a sign of disorganization, or a clean desk, which for him signified inactivity. More often than not, though, Johnson's tantrums were followed by indulgent affection, glowing praise, or apologies. Despite this chaos, a majority of his staff members stayed on—and remained loyally dedicated to him.

Why? The answer requires an understanding and appreciation of Johnson's own unsurpassed work ethic, the sense among staff members that they were learning important skills from him, and the shared commitment of being engaged in an important mission. No matter how late they stayed, nearly all the staff members agreed, Johnson stayed later. No matter how early they arrived, he was already there. Here, as in Washington, Lady Bird proved a crucial partner. By making her home an extension of the workplace, she softened the often inconsiderate harshness of Johnson's compulsive pace.

Various staff members even lived with the Johnsons in a room on the second floor. "We weren't like boarders," one recalled, "we had the run of the house and I felt like a member of the family." Mind-numbing meetings going over NYA rules and regulations, "paragraph by paragraph, page by page," were often held on the Johnsons' porch. "This was usually pretty late at night," another staffer recalled. "Lady Bird always had coffee and cake for us."

More than anything else, however, what allowed the staff to endure Johnson's overbearing behavior was the sense they were joined together in an incredibly exciting new organization that promised to change the lives of thousands of young people who had lost hope during the early years of the Depression, providing them with jobs, keeping them in school, teaching them marketable skills, renewing their faith in the future. By hitching their lives to that of Lyndon Johnson, his staffers knew they were riding the momentum, breadth, and meaning of a much larger story.

The swiftness with which Lyndon Johnson made seemingly life-altering decisions was clear when an opportunity suddenly arose for him to run for the House of Representatives. On February 23, 1937, not eighteen months into his directorship of the Texas NYA, Lyndon spied a headline on a newspaper left on a park bench announcing the death of longtime Congressman James Buchanan from his home district. Johnson decided immediately to run for the seat in a special election called to fill the sudden vacancy—despite being considered too young, little known in Central Texas, and likely facing stiff competition. Lady Bird asked her father for ten thousand dollars to fund the campaign. And, Johnson remembered, "I was at the bank at 9 a.m. the next morning and there it was."

Johnson read his official campaign announcement from the porch of the Johnson City home. After Lyndon spoke, Sam Johnson, stricken the year before by a massive heart attack, rose to embrace his son. "My father became a young man again," Johnson recalled. "He looked out into all those faces he knew so well and then he looked at me and I saw tears in his eyes as he told the crowd how terribly proud he was of me and how much hope he had for our country if only his son could be up there in the nation's capital with [President] Roosevelt and [Sam] Rayburn and all those good Democrats. When he finally sat down, they began applauding and they kept applauding for almost ten minutes. I looked over at my mother and saw that she, too, was clapping and smiling. It was a proud moment for the Johnson family." Lyndon Johnson had finally found a path to merge the passions and values of both of his parents through the engine of his driving ambition.

From the start of the campaign, Johnson employed his tireless work ethic, believing he could win so long as "he could get up earlier and meet more people and stay up later than anybody else." The youngest man in the contest, Johnson would simply out-campaign his rivals. He would stop "in every store, every fire station, every place of business," a campaign worker recalled, and he would personally meet every person in there all the way to the back door where the janitor was sitting. He would "press the flesh" and "look them in the eye," as his father had advised him so long ago, and as he had taught the members of the debate team and his staff at the NYA. While his competitors focused on population centers in large cities and towns, Johnson ventured to every small village and crossroads, searching out far-flung homes and farms. If he spotted the glow of a kerosene lamp in the distance, he would head for it. With his long legs, he could climb over barbed-wire fences to talk with farmers plowing their fields. He kept his speeches short. "A five minute speech," he pointed out, "with fifteen minutes spent afterward is much more effective than a fifteen minute speech, no matter how inspiring, that leaves only five minutes for handshaking."

So great was Johnson's anxiety two days before the special election that sweat poured down his face as he walked door-to-door asking for votes in Austin. Severe pains knotted his stomach, and he felt nauseous. After delivering a speech at a big rally that evening, he collapsed. Rushed to the hospital, doctors found that his appendix was on the verge of bursting. An emergency operation was necessary. His campaign came to a dead and agonizing halt. But his long days of relentless effort had paid off. From his hospital bed he learned that he had won the election, beating his nearest opponent by more than three thousand votes.

To stand out from the better-known pack, Johnson had campaigned as a "total Roosevelt man," supporting every aspect of President Roosevelt's New Deal. Soon after the election, he had the opportunity to meet President Roosevelt. Returning to the port of Galveston, Texas, after a fishing cruise in the Gulf of Mexico, FDR greeted the young congressman-elect at the dock and invited him to join his special train as it traveled through Texas. "I've just met the most remarkable young man," Roosevelt later told White House aide Tommy Corcoran. "Now I like this boy, and you're going to help him with anything you can."

When Franklin Roosevelt took office four years earlier, nine out of ten American farms had no electricity. "The lack of electric power divided the United States into two nations," one historian noted, "the city dwellers and the country folk." Farm wives enjoyed none of the conveniences of twentieth-century life—refrigerators, washing machines, irons, vacuum cleaners. Farmers had to rely on hand labor to draw water from a well or milk the cows. For decades, private energy companies had refused to install power lines in remote rural areas; it cost too much to be profitable to electrify an area that was sparsely populated. With the creation of the Tennessee Valley Authority in 1933 and the Rural Electrification Administration in 1935, the New Deal brought electricity to millions of farm families, but the needs of the people of the Hill Country in Johnson's home district had been left out. During the campaign, Johnson had promised the people that if elected, he would bring electricity to them; that if he had to convince the president personally to make it happen, he would do just that. Now he intended to keep that pledge.

Johnson landed himself a meeting at the White House with President Roosevelt, the latest, and most prestigious, of a long line of powerful men who he had looked up to and who had mentored him. Roosevelt chitchatted and joked around to avoid the ask he knew was coming from Johnson. "Before I knew it," Johnson lamented, "my fifteen minutes was gone . . . and I found myself in the West Lobby without ever having made my proposition. So I had to go back and make that damn appointment all over again." For the second meeting he was able to secure with FDR, Johnson came prepared with an exhibition of large, three-foot-tall pictures of two recently constructed dams and a map of the power lines that showed the energy flowing to the "city big shots" while neglecting the poor folk in the countryside—represented by pictures of old tenant farmer shacks. "Lyndon, now what in the hell do you want?" President Roosevelt demanded. "Just why are you showing me all these?"

Johnson then painted "a mental picture of all those women out there, old before their time, bending over the wash pot, and all those men getting up on a cold winter morning to milk those cows, where there could have been electric washing machines and milking machines." For Johnson, lack of electricity was not confined to facts and figures; it was grounded in emotional memories of his mother hauling water from a well, washing clothes on a corrugated washboard, heating the iron on a red-hot woodstove even at the height of summer, scrubbing floors on her hands and knees—consumed by backbreaking chores that left her too exhausted to read the books piled high beside her bed.

Roosevelt was enchanted by the gifts of this fellow storyteller. In the end, FDR surrendered to the conviction of the young man and agreed to approve a loan to bring electricity to the Hill Country. Johnson was thrilled, savoring the successful meeting as "one of the happiest moments of my life." Strange poles were erected, and wiring began appearing on Hill Country farms. When the power was finally turned on, life would never be the same for its residents. One night when the project was completed, the Hill Country was finally linked to the rest of America. Historian Robert Caro tells the story of a family coming home that night and seeing a bright light emanating from inside their home.

"Oh my God," the mother said. "The house is on fire."

"No, Momma," her daughter said. "The lights are on." All over the Hill Country! "People began to name their kids for Lyndon Johnson," Caro writes.

To Johnson's lasting regret, his father did not live long enough to witness and share in his son's achievements. The summer after Johnson took his seat in the House, Sam suffered another heart attack. For two months he remained in the hospital, kept inside an oxygen tent. When Johnson returned home that fall, Sam pleaded with his son to bring him "home to that little house in the hills where people know when you're sick and care when you die." Johnson resisted at first; the doctors had told him that his father needed oxygen and that no oxygen tent was available in their town. "You have to help me, son," Sam pleaded. Johnson understood. "I brought him his clothes, helped him dress, and I carried him home." Nestled in his own room, surrounded by family and friends, his father seemed to improve. But just two weeks later, shortly after his sixtieth birthday, Sam Johnson died. His body was laid to rest beside that of his own father in the small family graveyard.

The spirit of his father and grandfather inspired Johnson's agenda and manner in Congress going forward. "When I thought about the kind of Congressman I wanted to be," Johnson said much later in life, "I thought about my Populist grandfather and promised myself that I'd always be the people's Congressman, representing all the people, not just the ones with money and power. My grandfather taught me early in life that neither misery nor squalor is inevitable so long as the government and the people are one . . . so long as the government assumes the positive role of eliminating the special interests that cause most of our problems in America. . . ." And years earlier, as he was leaving Texas to work for Congressman Kleberg, his father's parting words were "Now you get up there, support FDR all the way, never shimmy and give 'em hell."

Lyndon took that charge and ran with it. When he first took his seat in the House "a consensus about the boy" and his bright future soon developed among the inner circle of FDR's young New Dealers who served in the president's administration. Johnson became not simply a member of this group but, as he so intensely craved, the central pin around which the group wheeled. President Roosevelt's "special interest" in the young congressman also sharpened. There was something Roosevelt saw in Lyndon Johnson that made him think that "if he [Franklin] hadn't gone to Harvard, that's the kind of uninhibited young pro he'd like to be." Roosevelt went so far as to predict that "in the next generation the balance of power would shift south and west, and this boy could well be the first Southern president."

Chapter Twenty-Two

"The most miserable in my life . . ."

FROM HIS EARLY TWENTIES, LYNDON JOHNSON had operated upon the premise that if "he could get up earlier and meet more people and stay up later than anybody else," success would be his. For a decade he had worked nonstop. He had no hobbies and had developed no ways to relax. He had now set his sights on winning a seat in the United States Senate in 1941, running in a special election that arose after the sudden death of Texas's senior senator Morris Sheppard, which he could do without forfeiting his seat in the House. Could Johnson apply his signature style that took him from congressional staffer to NYA director to congressman, where instead of one congressional district, he would represent the whole state, made up of twenty districts in which he was virtually unknown?

The enormous scale of the state of Texas, larger than all the New England states combined, proved challenging for Johnson, whose gifts of persuasion hinged upon making connections on a personal, handshake level. Now necessity demanded that in each district he reach the largest audiences possible, speaking from a stage, separating him from the people. In such formal settings, Johnson had a hard time communicating naturally. Inevitably, the crowds began drifting away before his long speeches drew to a close. The same man whose "tremendously commanding presence" could dominate any room he entered seemed uneasy when up on a distant stage, frozen in place, delivering a prepared speech.

Johnson's confidence was further rattled when a series of early polls showed him badly trailing his four main opponents, all better known than Johnson, including Texas governor W. Lee "Pappy" O'Daniel. Concern that he might lose began to take a physical toll upon Johnson's body. "My throat got bad on me, and I had to spend a few days in the hospital," he explained. Those two days grew into two weeks, then worsened into "nervous exhaustion," a condition that his campaign team sought to conceal. "He was depressed and it was bad," Lady Bird recalled. While he had collapsed during his first congressional campaign because of appendicitis, the stress and anxiety of this new campaign set off a series of physical ailments—rashes, ulcers, colitis, and inflamed bowels—that would impact his body for years to come.

His spirits began to lift when he and his team came up with a strategy to draw more people to his rallies and reduce the effect of his speaking weaknesses. During his time as debate coach, he had created a carnival aura around the tournaments, providing pep rallies, songs, and cheerleading normally associated with sports. What if they could turn traditional political rallies into circuslike entertainment, as if the Henly picnic of his youth had exploded into a full-blown variety show? The campaign moved quickly, hiring a charismatic radio personality and successful advertising executive to produce and market theatrical and musical events, write scripts, hire talent, and transport a twenty-four-piece jazz band and a cast of singers and dancers from rally to rally. The evenings, advertised in the local newspapers as patriotic pageants, began with selections from the jazz band, wearing white dinner jackets, followed by dressed-up soloists performing "America the Beautiful" and other patriotic songs.

With the audience appropriately warmed up, and as "God Bless America" played, Johnson ran out onto the stage. Standing in front of a towering backdrop of himself shaking hands with President Roosevelt, Johnson "shed his coat, rolled up his sleeves and launched into" an informal talk with the audience. He promised to be a senator who could get things done; he pledged to do the job President Roosevelt wanted him to do—had indeed asked him to do—to continue pushing forward the New Deal agenda. The well-advertised climax followed, the main reason no one left their seats: upon entry, every person had been given a raffle ticket; the numbers drawn from a giant bowl on the stage corresponded to prizes, worth anything from one to one hundred dollars for the lucky winners.

As Johnson's crowds swelled in size and enthusiasm, his poll numbers rose too. By Election Day, Johnson was confident of victory. Early returns gave him such a healthy lead that a photograph appeared in the press showing him being carried in the air by campaign workers. The *Dallas Morning News* stated, "The voters of Texas Saturday will more than likely send Congressman Lyndon B. Johnson to Washington as their junior Senator."

But they didn't. Johnson surprisingly lost. When all the ballots were counted, he was defeated by a margin of 1,311 votes.

Johnson was crushed. As he prepared to return to his seat in the House, he feared a dwindling of the respect and affection he had gained over the years in Washington. He felt he had disappointed, even embarrassed, President Roosevelt, whose backing he had campaigned upon and who had gone out of his way to support his candidacy. "We gave him everything we could, everything," Roosevelt adviser Tommy Corcoran recalled, but "he didn't win." So worried was Johnson, feeling he had lost favor with the White House, that he avoided calling on the president.

Eventually, Roosevelt reached out to Johnson and tried to lift his spirits. Despite FDR's continued support, Johnson remained downhearted. He was no longer the boy wonder; he no longer saw a limitless future before him. He was simply one of 435 congressmen stuck in a place where everyone, including his overburdened staff, knew he had failed. This defeat, which should have been merely an obstacle in a promising political career, became, for Johnson, a life-altering ordeal, changing the nature of his ambition and setting in motion a long and deep period of depression he later described as "the most miserable in my life."

On top of his traumatic sense of humiliation, Johnson's future prospects in the House of Representatives were murky. The House was no place for a young man in a hurry. Sam Rayburn had been in the House for a quarter of a century before becoming speaker at the age of fifty-eight. Fear of dying young heightened Johnson's characteristic sense of urgency. Johnson men shared a history of fatal heart disease. If family history held true, he could not afford to spend decades moving upward at a snail's pace.

The size of the House also played against Johnson's strengths. The membership, which continually changed after elections every two years, made it difficult for Johnson to build the network of personal relationships that had always been the heart of his power and success. His ability to understand people's individual needs and motivations depended upon repeated, informal exchanges that were not the norm in a body of 435 representatives, separated into different office buildings, protected by ever-growing staffs. Johnson did, of course, continue to serve his constituents, but these routine duties no longer gratified his swelling ambition. "I always had the feeling he was a little restless," fellow Democratic Texas congressman O. C. Fisher recalled, "looking for bigger worlds to conquer." Indeed, Johnson viewed the seven years spent in the House between 1941 and 1948 as a kind of torment.

Five months after Johnson returned to his seat in Congress, the United States entered World War II following the Japanese attack on the Pearl Harbor naval base in Hawaii on December 7, 1941. The next day Lyndon Johnson, the first US congressman to enlist in the armed forces, requested and received a leave of absence and reported for active duty in the navy, where he had been a reservist. After finishing training in Washington, DC, Johnson headed to San Francisco and then for inspection duty in the Pacific. While stationed in New Zealand and Australia, he was an observer of bomber missions in the South Pacific. He was later awarded a Silver Star Medal for "gallantry in action," which he considered among the high moments of his life. Twelve months later, however, his military service abruptly ended, when President Roosevelt issued a special order that required all senators and congressmen to choose between serving in uniform or in Congress. Nevertheless, Johnson's memory of this brief service never faded.

Johnson in his World War II naval uniform, 1942.

Thrust back into his job in the House after his brief war service, Johnson began to devote more and more of his time and energy to making money. Financial insecurity had marked his childhood years. Now, as he was able to rely largely on his staff for constituent matters, he could turn his attention to pursuing the accumulation of what would, before a decade had passed, become a massive fortune, which started with Lady Bird's 1943 purchase of a small radio station and was followed by investments in bank stocks, real estate, and cattle. While it was never proven that Johnson explicitly used his power in

Congress to benefit his businesses, it is indisputable that the rising fortunes of the little radio station in Texas paralleled Johnson's rising political career in Washington.

Not surprisingly, Johnson's fading interest in his congressional job hurt his relationship with his staff. His unpredictable and abusive behavior worsened. "One day I didn't get a telephone number fast enough for Mr. Johnson and he threw a book at me," recalled a female staffer, who said she was "a little afraid of him after that." Even before his Senate run, Johnson's two longest-serving aides, Luther Jones and Gene Latimer, had quit. Jones knew after less than a year on the House staff that he simply "had to get away" or be "devoured" by Johnson. Latimer lasted exactly a year to the day of his arrival on Capitol Hill. "I was literally working myself to death," he recalled. "I never took a breath." Johnson quickly replaced Jones and Latimer with able men, but without the inspiration of Johnson's intensely focused energy, without the thrill of shared engagement in important, beneficial projects, the new team never achieved the camaraderie that had bound the initial team together despite their unstable and sometimes oppressive "Chief."

The Lyndon Johnson who had been the principal of the elementary school at Cotulla, spending his meager salary on athletic equipment for his underprivileged students, was very different from the congressman whose politics became more conservative, more focused on protecting business interests than working people, as his own wealth increased. The ambition to better the lives of others that had given his life direction and meaning during his early years in politics—his work with the NYA, his fight to bring electricity to the Hill Country—was now focused solely on himself. He had lost the worthy sense of purpose that had accompanied his drive for power, that ambition for a greater good, larger than for self, to improve the lives of others, so central to genuine leadership.

Lyndon Johnson's loss of bearings grew more stark upon the 1945 death of his greatest political mentor, President Franklin Roosevelt. When another Texas US Senate seat opened in 1948, he resolved to make one last try to reach the upper house. As he prepared for the statewide run in an increasingly conservative Texas, he shifted still further to the right, even rejecting his former loyalty to FDR's New Deal. While he still believed in some of the programs President Roosevelt had initiated, Johnson completely changed his tune on the role of government to regulate business and help people: "I believe in free enterprise and I don't believe in the government doing anything that the people can do privately. Wherever it's possible, the government should get out of business."

As the campaign opened, the forty-year-old Johnson was filled with fear, as he usually was before any election, but this time it was all or nothing. A loss would forfeit his congressional seat and lock him out of official Washington for the first time since his twenties. "I just could not bear the thought of losing everything," he confessed, as if his identity depended upon his position and standing. Once again, the elevated stress that elections invariably brought Johnson bubbled to the surface in an array of physical ailments—fevers, chills, stomach pains, headaches, depression, even kidney stones. He described the pull of politicking itself as a compulsion, a sickness that "gets better until the next election comes around."

Out on the campaign trail, he worked twenty hours a day—shaking hands, making short speeches, giving radio interviews. He "even worked in the bathtub," his secretary Dorothy Nichols recalled. "You'd be in a little hotel in this little town, and you'd get a summons to come into the bathroom to talk to the Congressman. You'd go in and he'd be in the tub, and he would talk to you and two or three secretaries would come in and take letters. He never stopped."

Maintaining the importance of flamboyantly seizing the attention of voters, Johnson crisscrossed the state in a helicopter, something no candidate had previously done. The helicopter—dubbed the *Johnson City Windmill*—was a gimmick to draw astonished voters from far-flung corners of Texas. Circling the town square or the local football field, Johnson would blast his arrival over the helicopter's loudspeaker. "This is Lyndon Johnson, your next United States senator, and I'll land in just a minute. I want to shake hands with all of you." If the town lacked a proper landing site, he would consult a list of voters from the different small towns and villages who had written him over the years. "Hello there, Mr. Jones," his voice would boom overhead. "This is your friend Lyndon Johnson. I'm sorry we can't land today, but I want you to know that I'm up here thinking of you and appreciate your kind letter and comments. I just want you to be sure and tell your friends to vote for me at election time."

On Election Day, the results were so close that neither Johnson nor his opponent, then governor Coke Stevenson, was able to declare victory immediately. "They were stealin' votes in east Texas," Johnson supporter and Austin mayor Tom Miller recalled, "we were stealin' votes in south Texas. Only Jesus Christ could say who actually won it." But Jesus wasn't counting the votes, and, by an eighty-seven-vote margin, Johnson finally won the Senate seat he had sought for so long.

Chapter Twenty-Three

*"Time is the most valuable thing you have;
be sure you spend it well."*

BY THAT MERE EIGHTY-SEVEN VOTES, Lyndon Johnson had gained entry to a wholly different institution with different dynamics of power from the House, one far better suited to his temperament and leadership gifts. Smaller, more intimate, less rule bound, and more stable (given the six-year terms in the Senate rather than the two-year turnover in the House), the Senate was ideally constructed for a leader whose ability to persuade, charm, tame, and overwhelm depended upon personal encounters, engaging people face-to-face or in small groups.

No sooner had Johnson arrived than he set about figuring out how the Senate operated—the same approach he took to get ahead in Washington as a young staffer for Congressman Kleberg. He quickly learned that the center of power was an informal coalition, an inner club of Southern Democrats and conservative Republicans. A bargain had been struck whereby the conservative Republicans would vote with the white senators from the South against civil rights legislation, and, in return, the Southern Democrats would oppose liberal social and economic measures—like the sorts that had passed during the New Deal. The undisputed leader of this club, commanding the respect of almost every member of the Senate, was Richard Russell, a Democrat from

What is the civil rights movement?

After the Civil War, America entered the Reconstruction era, implemented by Congress to provide the conditions under which the Southern states would be readmitted to the Union. A flurry of pro–civil rights amendments to the Constitution were passed, offering great hope for Black people, in large part because formerly enslaved and other Black people fought for change, registered to vote, and elected to office leaders who sought equal rights and equal protection for Black Americans so they could become educated, acquire land, seek employment, and use public accommodations.

• Slavery was officially abolished by the Thirteenth Amendment to the Constitution (pushed through Congress by Lincoln and ratified after his death).

• The Fourteenth Amendment (ratified 1868) established that anyone born in the United States, including formerly enslaved people, were citizens.

• The Fifteenth Amendment (ratified 1870) secured the right to vote for Black men.

But it didn't take long before federal troops were withdrawn from the South and Jim Crow laws and "black codes" were passed—and at times violently enforced—to restrict and roll back the hard-won rights that Black people had gained during

Georgia, who used his power to stop civil rights and voting rights for Black Americans.

From the beginning, Johnson recognized that Russell's mentorship would be the key to his hopes of gaining influence in the Senate, and he set in motion a strategy to court the senior senator. Though the two men were wildly different in temperament and style, they shared a consuming devotion to work. Russell was a bachelor, and the Senate was his entire existence, not unlike Sam Rayburn, Johnson's previous mentor, who was wholly dedicated to his work in the House of Representatives.

Johnson respected, loved, dutifully served, and thoroughly took advantage of both mentors. He understood the anxiety and loneliness both men experienced when they were away from work. At the time, most men did no housework at all—no cleaning, no grocery shopping, no cooking—so without a wife, Russell was on his own. "He would arrive early enough in the morning to eat breakfast at the Capitol and stay late enough at night to eat dinner across the street. And in these early mornings and late evenings I made sure there was always one companion, one senator, who worked as hard and as long as he, and that was me, Lyndon Johnson. On Sundays the

House and Senate were empty, quiet, and still; the streets were bare. It's a tough day for a politician, especially if, like Russell, he's all alone. I knew how he felt for I, too, counted the hours till Monday would come again, and knowing that, I made sure to invite Russell over for breakfast, lunch, or brunch or just to read the Sunday papers. He was my mentor, and I wanted to take care of him."

Johnson decided that the role he wanted to play in the Senate was to be on the leadership team for the Democratic Party, even though the Democrats were in the minority because there were fewer elected Democrats than Republicans in the Senate. Most Senate activity was determined by the majority party, like decisions about what bills were voted on, but each party still needed leaders to round up senators to support or oppose bills as they came up for a vote. Johnson sought the position of party whip, so called for tracking and gathering votes from other senators in his party, a role similar to that of the cowboys of his grandfather's time, who had to herd cattle to get them moving in one direction. Johnson begged Russell for the job he called "one of the most urgently desired goals of his life." In 1951, with Russell's support, Johnson became the youngest party

Reconstruction and to terrorize, punish, and exclude them from fully participating as citizens. Racism was a toxic presence in the North and West, too, where Black people suffered from widespread discrimination and from segregation in neighborhoods and schools.

Over the next decades, Black men and women, including young people, and their white allies, strategized and stood up to the discrimination and oppression Black Americans faced. President Harry Truman was the first president since Reconstruction to commit the US government to the realization of civil rights when he ordered the desegregation of the armed forces and called for federal laws to advance civil rights. Congress rejected his appeals for legislation, but Truman pushed for many of the proposals on his own.

In the 1950s and 1960s, civil rights leaders and activists used nonviolent means—marches and sit-ins, voter registration drives, election campaigns, attempts at passing civil rights laws, and court battles—to continue the fight to secure the rights Black people and other marginalized groups deserved. They found an empathetic supporter in Senator and then President Lyndon Johnson, and together they accomplished more for civil rights than the country had seen since the 1860s. But still—the struggle for equal rights and opportunities and against racism and discrimination continues to this day.

whip in history. Two years later, the post of minority leader opened, a level up from the position of whip, and he launched a characteristically intense campaign for the position. He was unanimously elected by his fellow Democratic senators.

In the months following his election as party leader, Johnson quickly and greatly expanded his ability to convert seemingly ordinary operating and technical tasks into sources of genuine power, just as he had back when he became a messenger for his college president. For example, the party leader was responsible for scheduling bills for debate on the Senate floor, so if a senator required prompt action on a bill or wanted to delay a controversial vote, he would seek Johnson's assistance. Johnson also had the power to assign office space, and his allies ended up with the best offices. At the core of Johnson's success in the Senate, however, was his celebrated ability to read character, to assess the needs, hopes, and ambitions of almost every individual with whom he interacted. In short order, Johnson was able to memorize the entirety of the institution—its people, rules, and traditions. "When you're dealing with all those senators," he explained, "the good ones and the crazies, the hard workers and the lazies, the smart ones and the mediocres—you've got to know two things right away. You've got to understand the beliefs and values common to all of them as politicians, the desire for fame and the thirst for honor, and then you've got to understand *the* emotion most controlling that particular senator."

And whatever Johnson learned of his colleagues, he never forgot. Over time, he was able to create a mental portrait of every Democratic senator—all white men at that time, with the exception of Hispanic American senator Dennis Chávez, from New Mexico, who served from 1935 to 1962. The first female senator, Rebecca Felton, a Democrat from Georgia, was appointed in 1922, but from 1949 to 1955 there was not a single female Democrat in the Senate. So Johnson set his sights on knowing his male colleagues' strengths and vulnerabilities, their aspirations in the Senate and perhaps beyond, how far they could be pressured and by what means, how they liked their liquor, how they felt about their wives and families, and, most important, how they felt about themselves—what kind of senator they wanted to be. As Johnson's mental profiles of his colleagues became more intimate and expansive, his political instincts became nearly perfect. He then used his knowledge and power to get colleagues the perks and opportunities they desired, so that when the time came, senators owed debts large and small to Johnson, debts that would be collected in the future.

When Democrats, by a single vote, gained a majority in the Senate in 1955, the forty-six-year-old Lyndon Johnson was elected the youngest majority leader in the history of the Senate. He suggested that he would work with his political opponents in the Republican White House by referencing his favorite quote from Isaiah 1:18: "Come now, and let us reason together"; Johnson was well versed in the Bible and frequently quoted it in public speeches and private conversations, often in a "ministerial tone." With his boundless energy, clever ways, single-minded determination, executive drive, entrepreneurial flare, storytelling gifts, and political savvy, he had reached the most powerful position in the Senate.

If at last Johnson was "sitting on the top of the world," even being considered a possible candidate for the presidency in 1956, the road to get there had taken a drastic toll on his body. Plagued with exhaustion, indigestion, and constant stress, Johnson finally decided to take a rare break from work to spend the Fourth of July weekend at the Middleburg, Virginia, country estate of friend and supporter George Brown. On the two-hour ride, "my chest really began to hurt," Johnson recalled, like a "truck had crushed my chest in." Fortunately, another guest, who himself had suffered a heart attack, recognized the symptoms: "My God, man, you're having a heart attack." An ambulance transported Johnson to Bethesda Naval Hospital just outside Washington, the nearest major cardiac unit. "It was a very hectic ride, it hurt him desperately," recalled Frank "Posh" Oltorf, an old friend who rode along in the ambulance. "I think he definitely felt there was a possibility that he'd die before we got there."

Lady Bird was waiting for her husband when he arrived at the hospital, where he went into shock, hovering between life and death. As the days turned into weeks, his odds for survival greatly increased, but the doctors told the press that the majority leader could not "undertake any business whatsoever for a period of months." Political chatter speculated that he might not be able to continue the burdensome role of majority leader. The upward trajectory of his career was interrupted, and perhaps brought to an end.

Johnson fell into a depression so consuming that it appeared he was grieving over his own death—at only age forty-seven. This compelled him to reassess his life as everything he held dear was at risk—his present power, his future ambitions. "He'd just sort of lie there," his aide George Reedy recalled. "You'd feel that he wasn't there at all, that there was some representation of Johnson alongside of you, something mechanical.

"Then one day he got up and he hollered to have somebody come up and give him a shave," Reedy recounted, "and just in a matter of minutes the whole damned hospital started to click. He took over the corridor, installed a couple of typewriters there, he was dictating letters, he was just going full speed." What had reanimated him from his corpselike state? It was not something the doctors and the nurses or even the round-the-clock care from Lady Bird had given him. What animated him was more than four thousand letters of concern, condolence, and love he'd received from ordinary Americans. "He'd read them over and over and over again," Reedy remembered, "oh, he was just basking in those letters." Finally, it "got to the point where we couldn't let them all in his room: there wouldn't have been enough room for him." The letters, Johnson exulted, showed that "everybody loves Lyndon," and they lit in him a fierce need to give back that love. Just as he always wanted constituents' letters answered immediately, so he rose to action now to reply to every single get-well letter. He needed reconnection to these people. Stenographers were installed in the physicians' station in the hospital corridor; the typewriters were going nonstop; the seventeenth floor became a hive of activity. The letters did not merely occupy his time, entertain, or distract him. They invigorated him as would life-giving transfusions.

"Time is the most valuable thing you have; be sure you spend it well" had been a favorite, oft-repeated saying of Johnson's. Now, however, it took on a sharper urgency, and it applied directly to him. He had been a most excessive, immoderate man. Ceaseless striving and immense stress, an unhealthy diet, no exercise—this could now be deadly. It was necessary that he restrain a lifetime of bad habits. In his six-month period of recuperation at his Texas ranch, healthy food replaced breakfasts of cigarettes and black coffee, dinners of fried steaks and fried potatoes. He exercised daily in a newly built swimming pool, drank less bourbon, lost forty pounds, and took regular naps. He tried to walk more slowly and somewhat soften the excitable speed of his speech. He spent more time with his wife and daughters, Lynda Bird and Luci Baines, and even behaved in a gentler, or at least less demanding, fashion toward his staff.

A real transformation was taking place within Johnson. Death had brushed up hard against him, and he was struggling mightily within himself. But he seemed to be remembering the deep moral strains of his faith, as he would later say, "From our Jewish and Christian heritage, we

draw the image of the God of all mankind, who will judge his children not by their prayers and by their pretensions, but by their mercy to the poor and their understanding of the weak. We cannot cancel that strain and then claim to speak as a Christian society." His New Deal friend Jim Rowe had sent him a recently published biography on Abraham Lincoln, which detailed the profound change Lincoln had undergone during a waiting time when he was out of politics. This was Johnson's waiting time, a time of gathering strength and direction. When Lincoln had suffered his deep depression, he had asked himself, *What if I die now? What would I be remembered for?* Coming back from "the brink of death," Johnson asked himself a similar set of questions. He had learned to manipulate the legislative machine of the Senate with a precision and technical expertise without parallel in American history. But what good was he doing with all that power? Power without purpose and without vision was not the same thing as leadership.

As the January 1957 opening of the new eighty-fifth congressional session drew near—the date doctors gave as safe for the patient to return to Washington—Johnson made plans to deliver a major public speech that would display his physical and mental readiness to resume full command of the Senate.

Leading up to it, all through November, with George Reedy's help, Johnson nervously worked on the speech. Though delivering formal speeches was not his strong suit, he had decided to use the speech as an occasion to rededicate himself to the values that had originally drawn him into public service: the idea that government should be used to help those in need—the poor, the undereducated, the ill-housed, the elderly, the sick. "We've got to look after these people," his father had repeatedly told him, "that's what we're here for." Johnson had returned to work from this crucible of a massive heart attack, which tested his very will to live, with a renewed commitment to his father's plainspoken advice, determined to act upon it while he had the time—and if he had the chance.

In the speech, the man who had abandoned the New Deal and played down his views on civil rights in order to remain politically electable in an increasingly conservative Texas introduced a powerful "Program with a Heart," in which he demanded more financial support for impoverished senior citizens, lower taxes for people with low incomes, more federal money for education and housing, a constitutional amendment to eliminate the poll tax (which forced people, usually targeting Black people, to pay money in order to vote), increased opportunities for immigrants to enter the country, and public roads and water conservation.

On several occasions during his speech, the audience "leapt to their feet, clapped their hands, stamped their feet, beat on the tables and whistled to show their approval." The compassion he truly felt—and was able to find within himself once more—for the marginalized, the undereducated, and the poorly housed fueled his delivery. "People walked out of that speech dazed," Reedy said, stunned by "the amount of emotion that he put into it and the fire." Johnson had not only demonstrated his physical readiness to lead through the impassioned conviction of his speech; he had shown a deep resolve to move both his state and the country forward on a more progressive and just path.

With clear purpose, the wayward son of the New Deal had returned.

What is the filibuster?

The Senate tradition of unlimited debate has allowed for the use of the filibuster, a loosely defined term for action designed to prolong debate and delay or prevent a vote on a bill, resolution, amendment, or other debatable question. Derived from a Dutch word for "pirate," it is a way for a small minority in the Senate to thwart the will of the majority, just like a single pirate or small band of plunderers could take over an entire ship.

Prior to 1917 the Senate rules did not provide for a way to end debate and force a vote on a measure. That year, the Senate adopted a rule to allow a two-thirds majority to end a filibuster, a procedure known as cloture.

The way a filibuster works is that the filibustering senators must speak on the floor of the Senate nonstop. It does not matter what they speak about—they can recite poetry or sing songs, read aloud from books and newspapers—the idea is that

Johnson immediately committed himself to the passage of a civil rights bill. For eighty-two years, since the passage of the 1875 Enforcement Act, though various civil rights measures had been passed by the House of Representatives, the Southern bloc in the Senate had used the filibuster to keep the door to the passage of any civil rights bill firmly shut.

But Black people in America still faced racism and discrimination in education, housing, jobs, and access to public places; and in many parts of the country they were terrorized and ruled by fear. When Black soldiers returned from Europe after fighting in World War II, white officials denied them access to programs that supported veterans with loans to buy homes and money to pay for college. Additionally, many Black veterans returned to communities in the South where they and their families faced Jim Crow laws that treated them like second-class citizens at best, barring them from "whites only" places like restaurants, swimming pools, and public schools.

they are engaging in an endless debate. No other bills can be debated or voted on during a filibuster. In 1975 the Senate reduced the number of votes required for cloture to stop a filibuster from two thirds of senators voting to three fifths of all senators duly chosen and sworn in, or sixty of the one-hundred-member Senate. What this means in practicality is that to get any bills through a filibuster or a threatened filibuster, supporters of those bills must have the backing of a supermajority of sixty senators.

Case in point: the Civil Rights Act of 1875 outlawed various forms of segregation and protected the rights of Black men to vote. It was overturned by the Supreme Court in 1883, and for decades thereafter, the white Southern bloc used the filibuster to keep civil rights and anti-lynching bills off the floor of the Senate.

For decades, Black activists had been pushing for expanded civil rights using a variety of peaceful means. In the late 1940s and 1950s civil rights leaders began to bring lawsuits to fight segregation and discrimination. One of the most impactful was *Brown v. Board of Education* to desegregate public schools. In 1954, the US Supreme Court decided in that case to ban and make illegal racial segregation in public schools. But still in several Southern states where young Black children tried to enter what had been white-only schools, they faced a barrage of harassment, violent attacks, and cruelty by white supporters of segregation. In some cases the Black children had to be escorted into the buildings by federal troops.

The following year in Montgomery, Alabama, the Black civil rights activist Rosa Parks refused to sit in the back of a bus, where Black people were required to sit, and she was arrested—sparking a 382-day bus boycott by the Black residents of Montgomery. The Reverend Dr. Martin Luther King Jr., an eloquent minister and a member of the executive committee of the National Association for the Advancement of Colored People (NAACP), was one of the leaders of the boycott, and he inspired and motivated activists and insisted that protesters keep their demonstrations peaceful. During these days of the boycott, King was arrested, his home was bombed, he was subjected to harassment and abuse, but he never gave up. On December 20, 1956, King called for the end of the boycott after the Supreme Court of the United States declared unconstitutional the laws requiring segregation on buses, allowing Black and white people to ride buses as equals.

Johnson's own views were in line with a shifting mood in the country toward true civil rights for Black Americans, and he was in the right place at the right time to respond to it and even help move public sentiment forward. White anger and violence in the face of a peaceful civil rights movement prompted President Dwight Eisenhower to send a bill to Congress expanding federal authority to protect Black citizens in a wide range of activities, including voting rights. Passed by the House the previous year, the bill landed on Johnson's Senate desk for consideration in early January 1957. Despite the long historical track record of failure on civil rights progress for Black Americans, he told friends that before summer's end, he would carry a civil rights bill through the Senate for the first time in more than three quarters of a century.

As Johnson studied the bill passed by the House, he understood at once that as written—like every other civil rights bill sent to the Senate over the past decades—it was dead on arrival. The Southern Democrats would filibuster it to death. So Johnson proposed changes to it, alterations he felt were the only way to get the bill passed. He promised his mentor and head of the Southern bloc, Richard Russell, that the bill would be limited to the protection of voting rights for Black Americans. It would not force communities to integrate socially or economically, so owners of restaurants and stores and sports facilities could continue to bar Black people from entering white-only establishments and using white-only doorways and water fountains. Based on those restrictions, Russell agreed not to unleash the filibuster. Johnson then worked different coalitions in the Senate to make the needed amendments to weaken the bill as promised. Finally, while he understood that the bill was inadequate, he persuaded Northern senators that an admittedly watered-down bill was preferable to no bill at all.

On September 9, 1957, the Civil Rights Act of 1957, in almost exactly the form Johnson had envisioned seven months earlier, became the law of the land. Although critics spoke of how toothless the bill was, Johnson felt that the fact of its passage was more important than its content. "We've shown we can do it," he said. "We'll do it again in a couple of years." The brand burned into that bill was Johnson's—for better and for worse. It was LBJ, newspapers noted, who had stitched together an improbable coalition of Westerners, Easterners, liberal Democrats, and conservative Republicans. It was LBJ who had prevented fellow Southern Democrats from killing the bill through filibuster. But it was also LBJ who, through wheeling and dealing and compromise, pushed through a bill that did not deal with the fundamental problem of segregation.

As a first step, though, this civil rights bill was an important one because it was designed to ensure and protect Black Americans' right to vote. Speaking on the floor of the Senate, Johnson said, "A man with a vote has his destiny in his own hands." Even Martin Luther King Jr. wrote a letter to then vice president Richard Nixon that a weak bill "is much better than no bill at all." But King vowed to keep the struggle for civil rights alive, using this new law as a weapon in the long and grueling battle. He wrote: "History has demonstrated that inadequate legislation supported by mass action can accomplish more than adequate legislation which remains unenforced for the lack of a determined mass movement. This is why I am initiating in the south a crusade for citizenship in which we will seek to get at least two million Negroes registered in the south for the 1960 elections."

It was that upcoming presidential race that captured the attention of national political figures, the press, and the people. "The Democratic Party owed Johnson the [presidential] nomination," Massachusetts senator John F. Kennedy declared a year after the bill's passage in 1958. "He's earned it. He wants the same things for the country that I do. But it's too close to Appomattox," Kennedy said, referring to the end of the Civil War. The wounds of the Civil War still had not healed in the country, and most Northern voters could not imagine trusting a Southerner with the presidency. Former presidential nominee Adlai Stevenson agreed and, putting it more bluntly, judged Johnson "the best qualified Democrat for the presidency from the standpoint of performance and ability, but plagued with a great weakness: he was a Southerner."

Twenty years earlier, when President Franklin Roosevelt first laid eyes on Lyndon Johnson, he foresaw in the talkative and hardworking congressman the makings of a future president. But with his political intuition, Roosevelt also understood that first "the balance of power" would have to "shift south and west." That shift had not occurred by the time the Democratic Party convened in mid-July of 1960. The Democrats chose John F. Kennedy as their nominee for president.

As a shrewd act of political calculation, Kennedy offered the second spot on the ticket to Johnson. To the surprise of many, LBJ accepted, giving up his commanding position as majority leader to accept the historically insignificant position of vice president. Immediately after Kennedy's victory, made possible in large part by the Democratic win in Texas that LBJ helped deliver, Johnson devised a radical plan to enlarge the power of the vice presidency itself. But that effort failed.

The Kennedy White House crackled with the dynamism and flair of the dashing, eloquent young senator turned president who was bursting with policy innovations and ideas—like landing astro-

A Kennedy/Johnson campaign poster for the 1960 election.

nauts on the moon and rebuilding impoverished communities around the world through the Peace Corps. By his side was his elegant, glamorous, intelligent wife, Jacqueline. Johnson couldn't figure out quite how to fit in. With insufficient outlet for his overflowing energies, deprived of center stage, he plunged into a profound depression, finding fleeting fulfillment only in his work as chairman of the President's Committee on Equal Employment Opportunity, created to eliminate racial discrimination in hiring by the federal government and by companies with federal contracts. In meetings on civil rights issues, Johnson came to life. By contrast, in meetings on other subjects, Johnson was quiet and withdrawn.

Like Theodore Roosevelt, Johnson found he simply wasn't "made to be Vice President." Also like Theodore Roosevelt, he felt lost and diminished without the kind of meaningful work and a spotlight that provided justification for his existence. The ceremonial aspects of the office of vice president—"trips around the world, chauffeurs, men saluting, people clapping"—meant "nothing" to Johnson. He "detested every minute of it" and felt, one friend recalled, "he had come to the end of the political road."

Then, as it did for Theodore Roosevelt, Johnson's job as vice president came to a sudden, violent end. On November 22, 1963, President Kennedy was on a campaign trip to Dallas to seek support for his policies, with his sights on reelection. As his motorcade, with its open-top black limousine, rounded the corner past the Texas School Book Depository Building into Dealey Plaza, an assassin's bullets shot him dead.

Chapter Twenty-Four

"It is all of us, who must overcome the
crippling legacy of bigotry and injustice."

"EVERYTHING WAS IN CHAOS," Lyndon Johnson recalled of the hours and days following President Kennedy's assassination. One shocking event cascaded into the next as the country learned in real time, aghast and traumatized, that shots had been fired at Kennedy's motorcade and that the president had been killed. Lyndon and Lady Bird Johnson had also traveled in the motorcade, two cars behind the president's car. Although early reports had the vice president wounded too, he and Lady Bird had escaped unharmed. Within two hours following the president being pronounced dead, Vice President Lyndon Johnson boarded Air Force One at Love Field in Dallas. Flanked by his wife, Lady Bird, on his right and President Kennedy's widow, Jacqueline, on his left, Lyndon Johnson placed his hand on Kennedy's copy of the Catholic missal and was sworn in as the thirty-sixth president of the United States of America by Dallas federal district judge Sarah T. Hughes.

"I went in to see Mrs. Kennedy and though it was a very hard thing to do, she made it as easy as possible. She said things like, 'Oh, Lady Bird, we've liked you two so much,'" Lady Bird described in her audio diary of that very day. "I tried to express something of how we felt. I said, 'Oh, Mrs. Kennedy, you know we never even wanted to be Vice President and now, dear God, it's come to this.' I would have done anything to help her."

Upon arriving at Andrews Air Force Base outside Washington, DC, with President Kennedy's casket aboard the plane, the new president gave a brief statement: "This is a sad time for all people. We have suffered a loss that cannot be weighed. For me, it is a deep personal tragedy. I know that the world shares the sorrow that Mrs. Kennedy and her family bear. I will do my best. That is all I can do. I ask for your help—and God's."

Johnson believed in the power of prayer. He worshipped at National City Christian Church in Washington, DC, and at the First Christian Church in Johnson City when he was in Texas. He also frequently attended services at churches of different denominations. He would accompany Lady Bird Johnson to St. Mark's Episcopal Church in DC. He would also attend mass at Catholic churches with his daughter Luci. While his practice in the years before the presidency had been inconsistent, once in the White House, he and Lady Bird began regularly praying before their private meals. In this harrowing time, he would need all the prayers he could get.

For four days, from Kennedy's assassination to his funeral, Americans remained transfixed before television screens as the three networks canceled all regular programming to cover the news. In fact, an entire generation, including President Johnson's younger daughter, Luci, remembers where they were or what they were doing when they heard the news that President Kennedy had been shot and killed. Sixteen-year-old Luci Johnson was in Spanish class at the National Cathedral School in Washington, DC, but "no one ever said a word about my father or mother," she recalled many years after. She was later informed that her parents were not injured, but their lives were changed forever—as was the country.

The new First Family, which included Luci's older sister, Lynda, who was nineteen, would not move into the White House for two weeks in order to give Mrs. Kennedy and her two young children—five-year-old Caroline and two-year-old John Jr.—the opportunity to move out.

"We were all spinning around and around, trying to come to grips with what had happened," recalled President Johnson. "We were like a bunch of cattle caught in the swamp, unable to move in either direction, simply circling round and round." With this imagery, Johnson harkened back to his childhood in the Texas Hill Country, to the stories his grandfather had told. "I knew what had to be done," he continued. "There

during his time in office, and escalated as the Vietnam War did. During the war protests, Luci remembered, "Many times we awakened to the voices of picketers screaming, 'Hey, hey, LBJ, how many boys did you kill today?' Often these were the last words we heard on the nightly news before going to bed." And sometimes, the stress on the First Parents was so great that Luci and Lynda had to take care of *them*. Luci recalled that late one night during the Vietnam War, her father asked her to take him to church so he could pray for guidance and strength.

It's no wonder, then, that White House kids grow up differently. Luci remembered campaigning around the country for her father's 1964 presidential election. "This taught me how to get out of myself—a very useful gift for every teenager."

Lynda and Luci departed the White House as married women—Luci's wedding reception was at the White House in 1966, celebrated with an eight-foot-tall wedding cake, and the following year Lynda's ceremony took place at the White House.

President Gerald Ford's daughter, Susan, was the first—and only to date—First Kid to host a high school prom at the White House. Her class of 1975 covered the cost of the evening with funds they had been raising since seventh grade.

is but one way to get the cattle out of the swamp. And that is for the man on the horse to take the lead, to assume command, to provide direction. In the period of confusion after the assassination, I was that man."

President Johnson chanced to hold the power, and he intended to use it. He set his sights on the unfinished policy agenda of President Kennedy, which included tax cuts to boost the economy, support from the federal government for education from kindergarten through college, laws to expand access to medical insurance, and, most pressing, a stronger civil rights bill than the one passed in 1957. "And I'm going to pass it without changing a single comma or a word," he told his aides.

The pressure to pass a meaningful civil rights bill had been mounting for years, thanks to the men, women, and children who risked their lives to desegregate their communities. In the early 1960s, Black and white Freedom Riders traveled on buses through the South and were met by arrests, beatings, and mobs threatening to "burn them alive." In Alabama, Martin Luther King Jr. organized what became known as the Children's Crusade. On May 2, 1963, six months before Kennedy's assassination, children from local high schools began a peaceful march through Birmingham, and by the end of the day, one thousand children had been arrested. The next day, one thousand more children showed up. With no room left in the jails, the white commissioner of public safety, T. Eugene "Bull" Connor, commanded his police to hit the children with high-pressure water hoses intended to knock them down and to sic vicious attack dogs on the kids. The images on the news shocked and sickened the nation and prompted President Kennedy to introduce his civil rights bill to end segregation in the South, which, Kennedy said in a nationally televised address, "denied equal rights, denied the opportunity to eat at a restaurant or lunch counter or go to a movie theater. . . . It seems to me that these are matters which concern us all, not merely Presidents or Congressmen or Governors, but every citizen of the United States." But still the bill went nowhere in Congress.

A few months later, civil rights activists held the March on Washington for Jobs and Freedom, timed to commemorate the hundredth anniversary of the Emancipation Proclamation. The march was a huge success, as more than a quarter of a million people gathered around the Reflecting Pool on the National Mall to peacefully protest, and Martin Luther King Jr. declared, "I have a dream." Still there was no movement in Congress on Kennedy's civil rights bill.

Three days after Kennedy's assassination, Johnson called on Dr. King. The two men would have a consequential and complicated relationship over the course of Johnson's presidency, with King always nudging Johnson on civil rights, voting rights, and human rights from his position as an activist. On this particular call, King told the new president that "one of the great tributes we can pay in memory of President Kennedy is to enact" some of the progressive legislation that the slain president had championed. Chief among these was the civil rights act.

Who was Bayard Rustin?

Born in 1912, Bayard Rustin started agitating against segregation in the late 1930s and organized the 1947 Journey of Reconciliation, which became the model for the Freedom Rides of the 1960s; these were interracial bus rides through the South that were orchestrated to challenge Southern segregation laws. Rustin and other Black and white bus riders left Washington, DC, to travel through the Jim Crow South, testing the 1946 US Supreme Court decision in *Morgan v. Virginia* that found that segregated travel was indeed unconstitutional. The FBI secretly investigated Rustin because he was a leading civil rights activist and voice for nonviolence, focused on sharing with Martin Luther King Jr. what he learned about peaceful protests during a seven-week trip to India to study the philosophy and practice of nonviolence developed by Mohandas Gandhi.

Rustin became the lead organizer of the March on Washington, but he stayed out of the spotlight because after being arrested and publicly outed as a gay man, he did not want the criticism and discrimination he endured to have a negative effect on the movement. In the 1980s, he became a part of the LGBTQ+ movement and an advocate for education on the AIDS virus. In his 1986 testimony on behalf of New York State's gay rights bill, Rustin stated that "gay people are the new barometer for social change." He believed that discrimination and injustice in any form should not be tolerated and must be protested. In 2013, a quarter century after his death, President Barack Obama posthumously awarded him the nation's highest civilian honor, the Presidential Medal of Freedom.

The vision Johnson traced in those early days had been incubating in his mind and his heart for many decades, and ultimately would become core elements of his Great Society agenda, an expansion of and follow-up to FDR's New Deal programs. Believing that Kennedy's death had created "a sympathetic atmosphere" for the passage of his stalled agenda, Johnson planned to turn the "dead man's program into a martyr's cause." But Johnson understood the window of opportunity was very narrow. If he had any chance of succeeding, he had to move ahead at warp speed before the supportive mood began to decline.

From the outset, Johnson decided his number one priority would be civil rights. But Johnson's advisers were hesitant and skeptical. "The presidency has only a certain amount of coinage to expend," one of them told Johnson, "and you oughtn't to expend it on this. It will never get through," he said about the civil rights bill. "Well," Johnson replied with an unambiguous answer, "what the hell is the presidency for?"

Five days after Kennedy's assassination, Johnson delivered an address to a joint session of Congress that is considered one of the most important in his political career. "All that I have," he began, "I would have given gladly not to be standing here today." With simple eloquence, he urged Congress to honor Kennedy's memory by enacting the slain president's civil rights bill. But the applause that followed Johnson's speech was not going to be enough to get the bill through. Even if it could get past the committees headed by Southerners in the House, it would be stopped in the Senate, where Southern leaders were fully prepared to mount a filibuster, shutting down all other business until either the bill was withdrawn or its proponents managed to secure a two-thirds cloture vote to bring debate to an end. As long as the filibuster endured, no other piece of legislation could reach the floor. Such prolonged deadlock would only deepen the national crisis and severely wound the new administration's prospects.

Johnson was unwavering. Like Abraham Lincoln, Theodore Roosevelt, and Franklin Roosevelt, Johnson knew that people were "more easily influenced" by stories "than any other way," that stories were remembered far longer than facts and figures. So now, when talking with civil rights leaders and die-hard Southern segregationists, Johnson told variations of the same personal story to underscore his conviction that the oppressive system of segregation that had governed daily life in the South for three quarters of a century must stand no longer. He told of his longtime Black employees—his maid and butler, Helen and Gene Williams, and his college-educated cook Zephyr Wright—and how when they would drive his extra car from Washington back to Texas each year, there was no place on the road they could stop and go in and eat on the difficult three-day trip. "It gets pretty hot. We want to wash up. But the only bathroom we're allowed in is usually miles off the main highway," Gene Williams related to Johnson, who then in turn shared the story. And Zephyr Wright had to "go squat in the middle of the field to pee." It was humiliating. Something had to be done.

Johnson concluded that now, thanks to years of strategic battles waged by civil rights activists, the country was finally primed to put into law a real solution for all Black Americans. If the civil rights bill currently stonewalled in Congress could become the law of the land, Gene, Helen, Zephyr, and all Black Americans would no longer have to suffer the indignities of a cruelly unjust system of segregation.

The proposed bill contained the most flammable social, political, and moral issues—and the most deeply personal ones—Johnson had ever taken on. The chances of failure were large. "My strength as President was then tenuous—I had no strong mandate from the people. I had not been elected to that office." The next presidential election was only eleven months away. Nor did he make the decision without a tremendous sense of personal loss: "It was destined to set me apart forever from the South, where I had been born and reared. It seemed likely to alienate me from some of the Southerners in Congress who had been my loyal friends for years."

And yet, as a consequence of the civil rights movement, the country was changing, and so was Johnson. He intended to use "every ounce of strength" he possessed to achieve passage of the civil rights bill. Civil rights leader Roy Wilkins, executive director of the National Association for the Advancement of Colored People, was immediately "struck by the enormous difference between Kennedy and Johnson." While Kennedy was personally sympathetic to the plight of Black Americans, he was "dry-eyed, realistic," whereas Johnson was passionate. Civil rights leaders Martin Luther King Jr. and Whitney Young also came away from their first meetings with the new president profoundly impressed by his "deep convictions" and "the depth of his concern" for civil rights. Indeed, King told friends that "it just might be that he's going to go where John Kennedy couldn't."

After the House passed the bill on February 10, 1964, as a result of determined strategizing and fierce advocacy from civil rights leaders, Johnson prepared for the Senate fight, and he made it absolutely clear that this time, unlike 1957, he would allow no significant compromises. "I knew that the slightest wavering on my part would give hope to the opposition's strategy of amending the bill to death." Uncharacteristically, the master wheeler-dealer had drawn a line in the sand. And upon that outcome Johnson's relationship to his heritage, to his political career, and most of all to his vision for the country's future, hung in the balance.

To make his position transparent, he invited his close friend and mentor Richard Russell, leader of the Southern opposition, to join him in the White House for a Sunday-morning breakfast. "Dick, I love you and I owe you," Johnson began. "I wouldn't have been leader without you. I wouldn't have been vice-president, and I wouldn't have been president. So everything I am, I owe to you, and that's why I wanted to tell you face to face, because I love you: Don't get in my way on this civil rights bill, or I'm going to run you down."

"Well, Mr. President," Russell responded, "you may very well do that. But if you do, I promise, you'll not only lose the election, but you'll lose the South forever."

Johnson retorted: "Dick, you may be right. But if that's the price I've got to pay, I'm going to gladly do it."

It would prove a fight to the end. Russell would do everything in his power to stop desegregation, to stop progress. For his part, Johnson envisioned a time when the old South could be freed from "old hostilities" and "old hatreds," when a new South would rise, "growing every hour," joined "in single purpose" with "every section of this country."

Even before the House bill reached the Senate, Russell had begun mobilizing his troops for what would become the longest filibuster in American history. He prepared a tag team of senators to talk for four or five hours at a time, reading the Constitution, reciting poetry, slamming sections of the bill. While Russell feared Johnson's mastery of the process, he knew that history was on his side. Never had advocates for a civil rights bill been able to achieve the two-thirds vote necessary to invoke cloture and bring debate to a close.

From the outset, Johnson knew that Russell's objective was "to talk the bill to death." Johnson also feared that the longer the bill was kept from coming to a vote, the greater the frustrations of the civil rights movement, the more likely the chance that any flaring violence in the cities might provoke white backlash against civil rights. The battle thereby became a tug-of-war over a ticking clock. Civil rights supporters aimed to shrink time, opponents to extend it.

A master political strategist, Johnson was certain "that without Republican support"—given the split in the Democratic Party between Southerners and Northerners—"we'd have absolutely no chance of securing the two-thirds vote to defeat the filibuster. And I knew there was but one man who could secure us that support, the Republican senator from Illinois, Everett Dirksen," the Republican minority leader. For Johnson, this issue went beyond party politics. Bipartisan unity was essential: "Unless we have the Republicans joining us," unless we "make this an American bill and not just a Democratic bill," there will be "mutiny in this goddamn country."

Like a tailor stitching a custom suit, Johnson took measure of Dirksen. A decade of working together had taught Johnson that Dirksen had no hesitation asking for "a laundry list" of favors in return for his support on legislation. But this time, Johnson offered Dirksen something far more important than perks and favors; he appealed to Dirksen's hunger to be remembered, honored. "I saw your exhibit at the World's Fair, and it said, 'The Land of Lincoln,'" Johnson pointed out. "And the man from Lincoln is going to pass this bill and I'm going to see that he gets proper credit." With a gift for flattery equal to Dirksen's vanity, he assured the senator "if you come with me on this bill, two hundred years from now there'll be only two people they'll remember from the state of Illinois: Abraham Lincoln and Everett Dirksen!"

How could Dirksen resist? Still, the civil rights forces appeared a half dozen votes short as the filibuster dragged on. The time had come for both the president and the civil rights coalition to shift into overdrive. Johnson personally recruited several Western senators, while religious leaders of all denominations reached out to their congregations to put pressure on wavering senators. On June 9, 1964, after more than five hundred hours of filibustering stretched over seventy-five days, the pro–civil rights forces believed they finally had secured the necessary sixty-seven votes to invoke cloture.

The next day, the filibuster was broken, and finally the majority could register its vote. There was nothing now to stop the passage of the sweeping bill that would end legal segregation in the United States—at last. On July 2, after the House accepted the Senate's version, Johnson signed into law the Civil Rights Act of 1964 at a memorable ceremony in the East Room of the White House before members of Congress and civil rights leaders, including Dr. King, who looked over Johnson's shoulder as he signed the bill. During the reception, Johnson reminded Lady Bird that this was the ninth anniversary of his heart attack, the profound experience that had altered his outlook on power and purpose. "Happy anniversary," she told him with a laugh.

And a joyous day it was—one built on the blood and toil of activists over the course of decades. After the signing, Johnson talked about the dawning of his commitment to civil rights: "the sad truth that to the extent Negroes were imprisoned, so was I. On this day, July 2, 1964, I knew the positive side of that same truth: that to the extent Negroes were free, really free, so was I. And so was my country."

Johnson next set his sights on a vastly strengthened voting rights bill. But he felt that the dust had to settle first before he could press on for this next item on the agenda of the civil rights coalition. Congress, he believed, needed time to heal the wounds of division. On a practical level, federal agencies needed time to develop and implement plans to desegregate public places—restaurants, bathrooms, theaters. And having just won the 1964 presidential election by a landslide, Johnson also believed the American people needed a period of calm without renewed division in order to get used to the vast social impacts of the civil rights bill.

His commitment to the objective of voting rights was never in question, but he sought to pass other aspects of his Great Society agenda first, including establishing health insurance coverage for senior citizens through Medicare, a public works bill for impoverished communities, a nationwide job training act, a revitalization of inner cities, expanded poverty relief, and much more. Let this agenda get through to help all Americans, Johnson promised Dr. King, and voting rights would be the absolute number one priority in 1966.

To King, the prospect of waiting any longer was unacceptable. A discriminatory system of sham tests to deny Black citizens the right to register to vote all over the South had worked precisely as white Southern officials had planned: for example, of fifteen thousand voting-age Black Americans in Selma, Alabama, only 335 were registered to vote. Years of trying to register Black citizens to vote had been met by threats, intimidation, crushing violence, and even murder from white opponents. King and other civil rights leaders devised a strategy to push Johnson to prioritize voting rights.

On March 7, 1965, around six hundred civil rights activists gathered at Brown Chapel African Methodist Episcopal Church in Selma, Alabama, to begin a peaceful fifty-four-mile march to Montgomery, the state's capital, led by John Lewis, chairman of the Student Nonviolent Coordinating Committee, and the Reverend Hosea Williams of the Southern Christian Leadership Conference. When they reached the narrow Edmund Pettus Bridge, they walked side by side, singing "We Shall Overcome," the anthem of the civil rights movement. At the top of the bridge, however, the protesters were met by state troopers and Sheriff James "Jim" Clark Jr.'s mounted posse, armed with pistols, nightsticks, bullwhips, tear gas, and billy clubs. As television cameras recorded the scene, "the mounted men charged. In minutes it was over, and more than sixty marchers lay injured, old women and young children among them. More than a score were taken to the hospital." Lewis, the twenty-five-year-old head of the SNCC, sustained a skull fracture. As the marchers retreated, the mounted posse pursued them. Ever after, the day was known as Bloody Sunday. The violence against innocent civilians, which millions of television viewers witnessed, mobilized the conscience of the nation.

On Bloody Sunday, Johnson had directed Attorney General Nicholas Katzenbach to work nonstop to draft the strongest possible voting rights bill. Through seven crisis-filled days, the horrific events

Who was John Lewis?

In 1961, John Lewis, then a twenty-one-year-old theology student, was one of the original thirteen Freedom Riders, joining because he said "at this time, human dignity is the most important thing in my life." Lewis was badly beaten by a mob at a South Carolina Greyhound bus terminal on his way to New Orleans, along with the group of Black and white civil rights activists who protested segregated bus terminals. The rides drew national attention, ultimately changed the way Black people could travel, and set the stage for the Civil Rights Act of 1964 and the Voting Rights Act of 1965.

Even after the beating, Lewis, considered one of the civil rights movement's most courageous young leaders, continued his activism and went on to lead the Student Nonviolent Coordinating Committee (SNCC), which organized student rallies and sit-ins. At the March on Washington in 1963, for which Bayard Rustin was deputy director, Lewis spoke along with his mentor Martin Luther King Jr. and asked the crowd of 250,000, "How long can we be patient? We want our freedom and we want it now. . . . We must say: 'Wake up America! Wake up!' For we cannot stop, and we will not and cannot be patient."

in Selma echoed throughout the American people. By the following Sunday morning, the draft bill was completed, and the time to push for a voting rights bill had come. Johnson decided to transmit the bill to Congress in person, to use the bully pulpit to appeal directly to the people.

"I speak tonight for the dignity of man and the destiny of democracy," Johnson began, speaking with determination. "I urge every member of both parties, Americans of all religions and of all colors, from every section of this country, to join me in that cause.

"At times history and fate meet at a single time in a single place to shape a turning point in man's unending search for freedom. So it was at Lexington and Concord. So it was a century ago at Appomattox. So it was last week in Selma, Alabama. . . .

"There is no Negro problem. There is no Southern problem. There is no Northern problem. There is only an American problem. And we are met here tonight as Americans—not as Democrats or Republicans—we are met here as Americans to solve that problem. . . .

"There is no issue of States rights or national rights. There is only the struggle for human rights. . . .

"But even if we pass this bill, the battle will not be over. What happened in Selma is part of a far larger movement which reaches into every section and State of America. It is the effort of American Negroes to secure for themselves the full blessings of American life.

"Their cause must be our cause too. Because it is not just Negroes, but really it is all of us, who must overcome the crippling legacy of bigotry and injustice."

Here Johnson stopped briefly. He raised his arms and repeated the words of the old Baptist hymn. "And we ... shall ... overcome."

"There was an instant of silence," one White House staffer recalled, "the gradually apprehended realization that the president had proclaimed, adopted as his own rallying cry, the anthem of Black protest, the hymn of a hundred embattled Black marches." Then, in a matter of seconds, "almost the entire chamber— floor and gallery together—was standing, applauding, shouting, some stamping their feet."

Johnson then continued. "The real hero of this struggle is the American Negro. His actions and protests, his courage to risk safety and even to risk his life, have awakened the conscience of this Nation. His demonstrations have been designed to call attention to injustice, designed to provoke change, designed to stir reform.

"He has called upon us to make good the promise of America. And who among us can say that we would have made the same progress were it not for his persistent bravery, and his faith in American democracy."

And then, as Johnson neared the close of his speech, he returned to his own experience as a teacher in the poor Mexican American community of Cotulla, Texas—the place where his ambitions were first joined with a deep sense of purpose.

> After Bloody Sunday, John Lewis continued his work in support of civil rights and voting rights. The Georgia Democrat was later elected to Congress, where he served for thirty-three years. The son of Alabama sharecroppers, Lewis said Martin Luther King Jr. was "the person who, more than any other, continued to influence my life, who made me who I was." Since Lewis's death in 2020 at the age of eighty, Democrats in Congress have been pushing to pass the John Lewis Voting Rights Act to protect the rights of voters from continuing abuses that keep mainly people of color from freely exercising their right to vote.

"Somehow you never forget what poverty and hatred can do when you see its scars on the hopeful face of a young child.

"I never thought then, in 1928, that I would be standing here in 1965. It never even occurred to me in my fondest dreams that I might have the chance to help the sons and daughters of those students and to help people like them all over this country.

"But now I do have that chance—and I'll let you in on a secret—I mean to use it. And I hope that you will use it with me."

The applause swelled to a crescendo, ignited by the emotional conviction of this moment. "What convinces is conviction," Johnson liked to say. "You simply have to believe in the argument you are advancing." In this instance, Johnson spoke directly from the heart.

Listening to the speech from Selma, John Lewis and Dr. King were overcome: "tears came down his face. Dr. King started crying and we all cried," Lewis remembered years later. "And Dr. King said to me, 'John, we will make it to Montgomery and the Voting Rights Act will be passed.'"

And it was. For the signing of the Voting Rights Act on August 6, 1965, Johnson chose the President's Room in the US Capitol, where Abraham Lincoln, on that same August day a little more than a century earlier, had signed a bill that freed enslaved people forced into service by the

What was Johnson's relationship with Mexican Americans?

In 1968, President Lyndon Johnson signed a bill authorizing the week of September 15 as annual National Hispanic Heritage Week, expressing his long-standing support for Mexican Americans born from his experience in Cotulla, Texas, where he worked as a teacher and principal and witnessed the "pain of prejudice" on the faces of his students. The week was expanded to a month by President Ronald Reagan in 1988 and is observed to this day. Johnson's own commitment to Mexican Americans continued long after his formative experience in 1928.

As a newly elected senator in 1949, Johnson learned that a Mexican American World War II soldier who had died was refused burial in a Texas "white" cemetery. So he arranged for the man to be buried at Arlington National Cemetery with full military honors. According to transcripts of the Lyndon Johnson presidential recordings at the University of Virginia's Miller Center, Johnson

Confederates. "Today is a triumph for freedom as huge as any victory that has ever been won on any battlefield," Johnson told the gathering of civil rights leaders, cabinet officials, White House staff, senators, congressmen and -women, and his eighteen-year-old daughter Luci, who recalled asking her father why he selected to sign the bill at the Capitol and not the White House. "We are going to Congress because there are going to be some courageous men and women who may not be returning to Congress because of the stand they have taken on voting rights," Luci remembered her father saying. "And there are going to be some extraordinary men and women who will be able to come to the Congress because of this great day." The president told the assembled group: In just four months' time, "this good Congress" worked together to pass "one of the most monumental laws in the entire

told Martin Luther King Jr. of his desire for "equality for all" well before the first Selma march, which took place March 7, 1965. In the mid-1960s, Johnson's Great Society programs were designed to alleviate poverty in the Mexican American community and provide opportunities for many Mexican American leaders to rise.

As part of that effort, Johnson signed into law the Immigration and Nationality Act of 1965, an effort to eliminate race discrimination in immigration and open the doors to Latinx people and others "who can contribute most to this country—to its growth, to its strength, to its spirit." Speaking at the Mexican American Conference in El Paso, Texas, in October 1967, Johnson said, "I am talking about people I have known all my life and people that I care about deeply," and he noted that "for too many years, your government paid too little heed to both the status and the hopes of the Mexican American community."

history of American freedom." Yet, even as he proclaimed the collapse of "the last of the legal barriers" to oppression, Johnson insisted that the fight for freedom had only just begun.

Johnson knew—and our study of history affirms—that without the civil rights movement, he would not have been able to achieve the milestones he did to combat racial discrimination and exclusion: to secure for Black people equal access to restaurants, transportation, and other public facilities; to break down barriers in the workplace, provide equal opportunities for education, and expand access to voting for Black people and others who were marginalized. These successes provided a blueprint and inspiration for other groups seeking equality—women, LGBTQ+ communities, senior citizens, people with disabilities, and others.

The change Johnson ushered in was possible because aroused citizens, inspired by activist leaders, lobbied, litigated, and protested. The outside movement had reached the corridors of power within the White House, and together they worked for systemic reform. Johnson's Southern roots, legislative wizardry, and ambition for a greater good ideally fitted him for the great civil rights struggle that altered the face of the country.

Johnson signing the Voting Rights Act while others, including Dr. Martin Luther King Jr., look on.

EPILOGUE

"Let us strive on to finish the work we are in;
to bind up the nation's wounds. . . ."
—**Abraham Lincoln**

I AM OFTEN ASKED: If you could have dinner with one of the presidents you've studied, who would it be? My answer is always the same: Do I have to choose just one? Now that you, too, have come to know "my guys," let's imagine a dinner party to which you and I and the four of them are invited. Who sits where? What will be served? What do I ask first? All those questions—and many more—race through my mind before we enter an elegant private dining room. There are place cards at the round table for six, and going clockwise are Theodore Roosevelt, me, you, Lyndon Johnson, Franklin Roosevelt, and Abraham Lincoln. Theodore and Lyndon are seated across from each other and immediately launch into a lively battle of manliness, chests puffed, ribbing each other in a good-natured manner, each trying to dominate, neither letting the other get the last word. It's certainly entertaining, but hard for anyone else to get in a word. Franklin sits back amused, interjecting lighthearted banter as the evening unfolds. Franklin is a source of pride and envy for Theodore: pride because Franklin so clearly followed in his footsteps as a young reformer, and envy because Franklin held office for so much longer and achieved more than Theodore. For Lyndon, Franklin is the ultimate mentor upon whose New Deal legacy his own

Great Society rests. And then there is Abraham. He sits quietly at first, his long legs stretched out and crossed at the ankle, the slight curl of a half grin on his lips, taking in the proceedings until he hears talk beginning of what advice our guys would have for today. He has a few stories—and wisdom—to share. When he speaks, in his gentle, folksy, intelligent, and reasoned way, he gets straight to the heart of the debate about which era had it the hardest. Somehow, he is able to bridge all the time periods represented at the table and find our commonalities. You can hear a pin drop as we all listen intently to his words, for he is someone we all look up to, the head of this family of presidents.

These four presidents—Lincoln, the two Roosevelts, and Johnson—form a family tree of sorts, a lineage of leadership that spans the entirety of our country's history. They were very different men, from different backgrounds, born with different gifts, faced with different hardships, but they shared a family resemblance of leadership traits. They shared a fierce ambition and a compulsion for hard work, though each expressed it differently. Theodore Roosevelt's inexhaustible energy saw him doing a deep dive to learn everything he could about each issue he confronted. He wielded power with dramatic flair, learning some humility along the way. Johnson outworked everyone—first to arrive at the office, last to leave—and had a knack for sniffing out the sources of power and mining them to reach his goals. FDR's work ethic was put into overdrive when he contracted polio, whether it was to relearn how to wiggle his big toe or, later, to put that conscientiousness into action to save the American economy during his first week in the presidency or to lead the country through a world war. Lincoln's work ethic was ingrained from his earliest days—the physical labor on the farm, the miles he walked to find a book to read, the mental wrestling that kept him up countless late nights to learn whatever subject was at hand and then to communicate it in a debate, in a courtroom, in his speeches, or through the written word.

Each of the four faced—both personally and professionally—dramatic tests, failures, and reversals in the forms of health challenges, deaths of loved ones, political heartbreak, and broken promises. The way each overcame these hardships was to strip away ego and face their lowest moments with an honest reckoning of their strengths and weaknesses. Once on the other side of their despair, they all discovered they could assuredly rely on their abilities to fuel their resilience. They relayed and shared this confidence with the American people to get the country through its collective hardships.

Each used the communication tools of his time to the fullest. The power of Lincoln's logic and his storytelling skills shone through in his printed speeches and debate performances. He could captivate audiences of thousands through narratives that wove together down-home wisdom, humor, and well-constructed arguments. Theodore Roosevelt understood how to engage and influence the press just as a new form of reporting—investigative journalism—was beginning to rise. FDR spoke intimately, personally, and directly to the people through the radios that populated most living rooms during his era. And LBJ, who began his career excelling in one-on-one communication, learned how to effectively reach large audiences through his televised speeches, understanding the power that televised images of the civil rights struggle had to move public sentiment—and influence prospects for passing legislation.

In their presidencies, all four were driven by the ideal that to serve meant listening to the needs of the people and doing everything in their power to help them—even if it had never been done before, and even if it was not explicitly written into the Constitution. They were masters of timing, finding the sweet spot between resistance to change and a wave of public sentiment that can usher it in. Even so, all of them had areas where they fell short, too, for there is just so much progress that a leader can achieve based on the times in which they live and work.

While we can and should be clear-eyed about their deficiencies, policy failures, and mistakes, we also must temper our critiques with the understanding that in a country that is as diverse and dynamic, free and forward-looking as ours, even our present moment too will someday be the subject of skeptical examination by a future generation.

Most important, though, I hope you take away from this book that while there was no single path that these four young men of different backgrounds, abilities, and temperaments followed to reach the pinnacle of leadership in the United States, what they shared once in office was their capacity to look beyond their own needs and lives, with the goal of enriching the nation, a desire to propel America forward on the ideals of the founders' vision of equality and liberty. Two of the four men—Lincoln and Franklin Roosevelt—died in office. Theodore Roosevelt and Lyndon Johnson both survived beyond their presidencies to experience the problematic aftermath of leadership. While their personal stories came to different ends, these leaders all hoped that their achievements would shape and enlarge the future for Americans, and that their successes would endure, securing them a place in our shared memory.

And so, as we assess how each of these leaders left the country they served and loved, we should consider: Which qualities did they possess that helped them bring their visions for the nation to life? Did characteristics or actions taint their legacies? How far did they push progress, and where did they fall short? How did they inspire others? What is left to be done in our time, and how can it be accomplished? How did they judge themselves and wish to be remembered?

For Lyndon Johnson, the achievement he held in highest regard was his work on civil rights and voting rights. His Great Society waged a war on poverty, provided economic aid for both blighted inner-city communities and distressed rural areas, made medical care available for the elderly and the poor, conserved natural resources, expanded educational opportunities for all young people, and much more. Johnson explained that the programs were "an extension of the Bill of Rights," an expanded definition of freedom requiring that every American have "the opportunity to develop to the best of his talents." He was enormously proud of this progress. But ultimately his

presidency ended as sadly as it had begun, mired in the horrors of the Vietnam War, about which he concealed the full extent and nature from the American people.

No statesman can successfully pursue a war policy unless he has instilled a sense of shared direction and purpose. In war, more than any other time, when great sacrifices fall on ordinary men and women, the people must be sufficiently informed to understand the choices being made by their government. As the terrain shifted from domestic politics to the war in Vietnam, Johnson demonstrated a failure of leadership that would compromise his credibility and trust, scar his legacy, and nearly tear the country apart. By the war's conclusion in 1973, as many as two million people had died, including more than fifty-eight thousand Americans and over one and a half million Vietnamese. By the standards of honesty and collaboration between a leader and the people, Johnson realized he had failed, and he declined to run for a second full term. His presidential career was over.

Nearly four years after leaving the White House, and having passed the baton to President Richard Nixon, Johnson addressed leaders from the civil rights movement who had come to his new presidential library in Austin, Texas, to mark the social justice progress made during his tenure and "to take a hard look at the racial injustice that continued to plague America" in 1972. Johnson was ill and attended against the advice of his doctors, focused keenly on the future—knowing full well his legacy had been cut in two by the Vietnam War. "Our objective must be to assure that all Americans play by the same rules and all Americans play against the same odds. . . . We know there is injustice. We know there is intolerance. We know there is discrimination and hate and suspicion, and we know there is division among us. But there is a larger truth. We have proved that great progress is possible. We know how much still remains to be done.

"And if our efforts continue, and if our will is strong, and if our hearts are right, and if courage remains our constant companion, then, my fellow Americans, I am confident we shall overcome." That was the last public speech Johnson would make. He died six weeks later from a heart attack at the age of sixty-four. Honoring a request Johnson made when he was still in office, the Reverend Billy Graham officiated at his burial.

Theodore Roosevelt died in his sleep at age sixty from what doctors believed was a coronary embolism, a clot that blocked an important blood vessel to the heart. "Death had to take him sleeping," Vice President Thomas Marshall cabled from Washington, "for if Roosevelt had been awake, there would have been a fight." Roosevelt had savored "every hour" of being president, "the greatest office in the world," he said. He left office with the pride in knowing, as one writer said, that he had given himself to the duties that confronted him "without stint or limit." Through his Square Deal legislation, he had softened some of the worst aspects of industrialism, protecting women and children from exploitation, enforcing rules for workmen's compensation, ending outrageous pricing by railroad companies, and opening corporate books to public inspection. His antitrust activities had broken up monopolies that were not playing by the rules of the game, and he had forced meatpacking plants to clean up their act. He was the guiding spirit behind the conservation movement, saving millions of square miles of forests, national parks, bird reservations, and wildlife preserves as part of our common heritage. His nearly ten post-presidential years, however, were filled with frustration and the  reality that his star had dimmed. His refusal to make way for new leaders had eventually foiled his ambitions for reform, at least from within the Republican Party. After he turned on the party and ran as a third-party candidate against his hand-selected successor, William Howard Taft, Democrat Woodrow Wilson won the presidential election of 1912. Progressivism would thereafter find its new home with a different party, the Democrats, and this time through a different Roosevelt.

President Franklin Roosevelt rescued the American people from the Great Depression and the world from Nazis and fascists during World War II, and left behind landmark programs that altered our social and economic landscape. But he also supported policies that openly targeted Japanese American citizens after the attack on Pearl Harbor by placing them in internment camps. He allowed anti-Semites in his administration to turn away European Jewish refugees desperately fleeing the Nazis and refused to destroy the Nazi death camps. Roosevelt never apologized for these decisions, disregarding intense pressure from his wife Eleanor. But despite these failures, FDR was beloved.

On the afternoon of April 12, 1945, FDR was having his portrait painted, and as they were about to break for lunch, he said, "I have a terrific pain in my head." He had suffered a cerebral hemorrhage—

bleeding in his brain—and died two hours later. The *New York Times* reported, "in the streets of every American town, strangers stopped to commiserate with one another. Over and over again one heard the same lament: 'We have lost our friend.'" One citizen wrote, "The greatest human tribute is that because one man died 130 million feel lonely."

Of the four presidents we have studied together, no one thought more about his legacy than Abraham Lincoln. The ambition to accomplish something worthy of recognition that helped rescue him from a profound depression at age thirty-one also fueled Lincoln's entire life as he sought to educate himself, overcome hardship and disappointment, evolve his views on race, save the Union, win the war, and free the enslaved. Kindness, empathy, humor, humility, passion, and ambition all marked him from the start. But he grew, and continued to grow, into a leader who became so powerfully fused with the problems tearing his country apart that his desire to lead and his need to serve merged into a single unstoppable force. That force has not only enriched subsequent leaders but provided our people with a moral compass to guide us.

Even so, abolitionist leader Frederick Douglass saw Lincoln as the complex man that he was, as well as a product of his times: not nearly as forward-thinking as radical abolitionists but, compared to the majority opinion in the country, a true reformer. "Viewed from the genuine abolition ground," Douglass said, "Mr. Lincoln seemed tardy, cold, dull, and indifferent; but measuring him by the sentiment of his country, a sentiment he was bound as a statesman to consult, he was swift, zealous, radical, and determined."

Less than six weeks after his second inauguration on Good Friday, April 14, 1865, Lincoln awakened with great and unaccustomed cheer. At long last, the punishing Civil War was coming to an end. The Republic had been saved. The streets were filled with people "drunk with joy," strolling arm in arm, talking, laughing, singing. Ten days earlier, the Confederate capital at Richmond had been evacuated. The following week, Confederate general Robert E. Lee had surrendered his army to Union general Ulysses S. Grant at Appomattox.

Lincoln had breakfast that morning with his wife, Mary, and their oldest son, Robert, a captain in the army and a member of General Grant's staff, who had just returned from the front. Lincoln then headed for his regularly scheduled Friday cabinet meeting. The forbidding war room of maps, battle planning, and military paraphernalia that had characterized cabinet meetings for longer than four years had on this day acquired a brighter mood and a serious new subject—how best to proceed with reconciliation with the South and reconstruction of the Union. "Enough lives have been sacrificed," Lincoln said. "We must extinguish our resent ments if we expect harmony and union." To the question of what to do with the rebel leaders, Lincoln made clear that "none need expect he would take any part in hanging or killing those men, even the worst of them." He understood that their continued presence might hobble the process of healing, but he preferred to simply "frighten them out of the country, open the gates, let down the bars, scare them off," emphasizing his intentions with a gesture of uplifted palms as if shooing sheep from the paddock. Lincoln said they should be informed, however, that "no attempt will be made to hinder them" if they voluntarily chose to leave the US. But "if they stay, they will be punished for their crimes."

For three hours and more, the cabinet members hashed out the nuts and bolts needed to begin the re-creation of a unified country. Lincoln

did not want to impose federal power on the South. "Let 'em up easy," Lincoln repeated on several occasions, "let 'em up easy." The process of reconstruction must be built step-by-step and remain sensitive to unfolding events. Of utmost importance, he believed, the process must be flexible.

There was general agreement among the members of the cabinet that Lincoln had never seemed "more glad, more serene." In the afternoon, Lincoln and Mary took a leisurely carriage drive. "You almost startle me by your great cheerfulness," Mary told her husband. He replied, "I have never felt better in my life." The couple discussed their future plans. Lincoln was fifty-six, Mary forty-six. They hoped to travel with their sons—to journey through Europe, visit the Holy Land, cross the Rocky Mountains and see California and the West Coast for the first time.

After dinner that evening, Lincoln entertained a small group of friends. He and Mary were scheduled to attend the theater that night. Lincoln loved the theater. When the gaslights dimmed, and the actors took the stage, Lincoln was able to surrender his mind "into other channels of thought." As the hour reached eight o'clock, Lincoln stood up. "I suppose it's time to go, though I would rather stay," he said, enjoying the evening with friends. "It had been advertised that we will be there and I cannot disappoint the people."

Lincoln's assassin, the actor John Wilkes Booth, was a familiar figure in the theater world. Having learned by midday of the president's plans, Booth had decided that this night would provide the perfect chance to kill the man he considered an "even greater tyrant" than the ancient Roman ruler Julius Caesar. He believed history would honor him for the deed, and he would thereby achieve immortality. Thus was set in motion one of the most tragic moments in the history of the country.

Booth was already inside Ford's Theatre when the Lincolns took their seats in the private state box high above the stage. Booth moved silently forward to within two feet of Lincoln, raised his gun, pointed it behind Lincoln's left ear, and fired. In a white fog of smoke, Lincoln slumped forward. Leaping from the box down to the stage, Booth caught the spur of his riding boot on one of the flags decorating the box. His awkward fall broke his leg, but before hobbling off the stage and escaping into the alley, Booth raised his dagger and shouted the words "Sic semper tyrannis" (Thus always to tyrants).

There was a savage irony in these words. Lincoln had warned decades earlier that lawlessness, murder, and mob rule would create fertile ground for a tyrant, men of towering egos who would seek distinction by "pulling down" rather than "building up." The dying president, who had worked much of his life to oppose extremism, hate, and cruelty—who, that very afternoon, had advised his colleagues against forcing their will on the defeated Southern states—was himself the victim of a racist extremist who would be remembered in infamy only for the man he killed.

"Mr. Lincoln had so much vitality," doctors reported, that for nine hours after sustaining the wound that "would have killed most men instantly," he continued to struggle. At 7:22 the following morning, that struggle came to an end. Abraham Lincoln was pronounced dead. "Now," Lincoln's secretary of war Edwin Stanton said, "he belongs to the ages." Stanton's tribute proved a not merely poetic but accurate description of the living values he passed on to Theodore Roosevelt, Franklin Roosevelt, Lyndon Johnson, and all of us and the succeeding generations. These four presidents sought justice and equality that would endure long past their terms in office.

Now, as we six continue our meal around our imaginary dinner table, "my guys" and I go quiet, and the spotlight turns to you: What do these values look like in today's world? What kinds of leaders do we need now to meet the founding call to create a "more perfect Union"? As a nation, we have yet to "bind up" our collective wounds. We still have much to overcome. What lessons can you take from these men and from so many other figures from history to help shape tomorrow? These are questions that we now look to your generation to wrestle with. It is your turn to agitate and to compromise, to vote and to organize, to learn from the past and to forge new connections, to mold a new crop of leaders who offer us humanity, purpose, and wisdom, not in turbulent times alone, but also in our everyday lives.

$\star$　$\star$　$\star$　$\star$　$\star$

ACKNOWLEDGMENTS

$\star$　$\star$　$\star$　$\star$　$\star$

IT WAS BETH LASKI'S VISION, ENTHUSIASM, AND PERSEVERANCE that were the catalysts for this book to come into being. Having worked with me for more than twenty years, Beth had long hoped I could bring my passion for history and storytelling to young people, for she herself had been one of those middle schoolers she wanted me to reach. There were other signs, too, along this book's journey: I became a grandmother of four loving, bright, fun, and curious grandchildren—Willa, Lena, Sasha, and Lucas. I was invited to portray myself as Lisa Simpson's teacher on the wildly popular television show *The Simpsons*. And I have met scores of young people all over the country who are interested in and excited about history.

But where to start in writing a book for young readers? The idea was frankly overwhelming as I am always moving from one book for adult readers to the next, traveling for lectures, and in more recent years, working on documentary projects. So about six years ago now, I discussed this interest with my longtime agent Amanda "Binky" Urban and longtime publisher Simon & Schuster, specifically president and CEO Jonathan Karp, whose wisdom and cherished counsel set me on a course with S&S Books for Young Readers senior vice president and publisher Justin Chanda and editorial director Kendra Levin. It was their inspired idea to start my journey of writing for and reaching young people by adapting my *Leadership: In Turbulent Times* for middle school–age readers. I was all in!

My *Leadership* book was born from my own time in graduate school when my classmates and I debated fundamental questions of leadership. I brought that inquisitiveness to my examination of the leadership of Abraham Lincoln, Theodore Roosevelt, Franklin Roosevelt, and Lyndon Johnson—"my guys," as I like to call them, because believe it or not, I have spent the last five decades studying presidential history. I sought to unpack the special qualities that helped propel their rise to the presidency—traits they may have been born with, acquired as young people, or developed over time.

But I was also in the midst of writing *An Unfinished Love Story: A Personal History of the 1960s* and could not imagine how this project could take form until Kendra matched me so perfectly with the wonderfully gifted writer Ruby Shamir to adapt my *Leadership* book, as she had a wealth of experience working on superb books for young readers. Not only did Ruby do a fantastic job but she was a fabulous, enterprising, and cheerful collaborator. She worked ever so closely with me and with Beth to expand and contract *Leadership* so that this book could become a work of its own. The creative energy expended in reimagining this book for Generation Alpha was terrifically exciting and inspiring.

When the manuscript was almost complete, Laurent Linn, our art director at Simon & Schuster, thoughtfully engaged the immensely talented artist Amy June Bates to bring the presidents and their stories to life by capturing their essence in lively and moving illustrations. The cover alone is a stunning work that I hope we'll turn into a poster to hang in libraries and classrooms throughout the country.

Working with collaborators in this way was new to me, and I loved being part of a team, which also included managing editor Amanda Brenner, copy editor Brian Luster, proofreader Stephanie Evans, editorial assistant Alma Gomez Martinez, and researcher Juan Carcamo. To help bring this book into the hands of young readers, I put my absolute trust in the publicity and marketing team at Simon & Schuster, led by Julia Prosser and Stephen Bedford along with, on the children's side, Nicole Russo, Anna Elling, Cassandra Fernandez, Brian Murray, and many others. I've had the great privilege of working with Simon & Schuster for four decades now.

I am so thrilled about this new young readers book, and it would never have come to be if I had not written *Leadership: In Turbulent Times* with the support of the late, great Alice Mayhew and of Jonathan Karp, whose keen instincts helped me think about the structure of the book in a different way.

Linda Vandegrift, as always, was by my side. All my books have been informed by her extraordinary talent and incomparable research skills. Together, we have grown as storytellers.

Lastly, this book was a labor of love to begin with, as I could not bear to leave my guys behind after writing biographies about them. So I brought them all together with help and support from my late husband, Richard Goodwin, and our best friend, Michael Rothschild.

☆ ☆ ☆ ☆ ☆

SELECTED BIBLIOGRAPHY

☆ ☆ ☆ ☆ ☆

I FIRST FELL IN LOVE WITH THE STUDY OF HISTORY IN HIGH SCHOOL. I came to treasure the small details that made an event or a figure from the distant past come alive. Those details come from a variety of primary and secondary sources, including the work of other historians who uncovered and interpreted them. For this book, I relied on the sources from my other books, along with some new sources listed below.

Most of the sources used for this book can be found in my adult books and in articles I wrote:

"Lincoln and the Art of Transformative Leadership." *Harvard Business Review.* September–October 2018. https://hbr.org/2018/09/lincoln-and-the-art-of -transformative-leadership.

"The Divided Legacy of Lyndon B. Johnson." *The Atlantic.* September 7, 2018. https://www.theatlantic.com/ideas/archive/2018/09/the-complicated-legacy -of-lyndon-johnson/569068.

Leadership: In Turbulent Times. New York: Simon & Schuster, 2018.

The Bully Pulpit: Theodore Roosevelt, William Howard Taft, and the Golden Age of Journalism. New York: Simon & Schuster, 2013.

Team of Rivals: The Political Genius of Abraham Lincoln. New York: Simon & Schuster, 2005.

Wait Till Next Year: A Memoir. New York: Simon & Schuster, 1997.

No Ordinary Time: Franklin and Eleanor Roosevelt: The Home Front in World War II. New York: Simon & Schuster, 1994.

Lyndon Johnson and the American Dream. New York: Harper & Row, 1976.

Presidential libraries, the US National Archives, and university research centers are great resources for material on US presidents and other major American political figures. I relied on material from the following institutions:

Abraham Lincoln Presidential Library and Museum

Eleanor Roosevelt College at the University of California, San Diego

Franklin D. Roosevelt Presidential Library and Museum

John F. Kennedy Presidential Library and Museum

Lyndon B. Johnson Presidential Library and Museum

Martin Luther King, Jr. Research and Education Institute at Stanford University

Theodore Roosevelt Center at Dickinson State University

While *Leadership: In Turbulent Times* was the initial inspiration for this book, I also mined other sources, including my other previous books and the following:

✳ ✳ ✳ ABRAHAM LINCOLN ✳ ✳ ✳

Chapter One

Barrett, Joseph Hartwell. *Life of Abraham Lincoln, Presenting His Early History, Political Career, and Speeches in and out of Congress; Also, a General View of His Policy as President of the United States; with His Messages, Proclamations, Letters, Etc., and a History of His Eventful Administration, and of the Scenes Attendant Upon His Tragic and Lamented Demise.* Cincinnati: Moore, Wilstach & Baldwin, 1865.

Bartlett, David W. *The Life and Public Services of Hon. Abraham Lincoln, with a Portrait on Steel. To Which Is Added a Biographical Sketch of Hon. Hannibal Hamlin.* New York: H. Dayton, 1860.

Black, Robert. *A Memoir of Abraham Lincoln, President Elect of the United States of America, His Opinion on Secession, Extracts from the United States Constitution, &c. To Which Is Appended an Historical Sketch on Slavery, Reprinted by Permission from "The Times."* London: Sampson Low, Son, 1861.

Burlingame, Michael. *Abraham Lincoln: A Life.* Vol. 1. Baltimore: Johns Hopkins University Press, 2008.

Lamon, Ward H. *The Life of Abraham Lincoln: From His Birth to His Inauguration as President.* Boston: James R. Osgood, 1872. https://www.loc.gov/item/ltf96017987.

Shenk, Joshua Wolf. *Lincoln's Melancholy: How Depression Challenged a President and Fueled His Greatness.* New York: Houghton Mifflin Harcourt, 2005.

Victor, Orville James. *The Private and Public Life of Abraham Lincoln: Comprising a Full Account of His Early Years, and a Succinct Record of His Career as Statesman and President.* New York: Beadle, 1864.

Wilson, Douglas L., and Rodney O. Davis, eds. *Herndon's Informants: Letters, Interviews, and Statements about Abraham Lincoln.* Urbana and Chicago: University of Illinois Press, 1998.

Chapter Two

The 1619 Project. New York Times Magazine. https://www.nytimes.com/interactive/2019/08/14/magazine/1619-america-slavery.html.

Arnold, Isaac N. *The Life of Abraham Lincoln.* 4th ed. Chicago: A. C. McClurg, 1887.

Berlin, Ira. "The Origins of Slavery." Gilder Lehrman Institute of American History. https://ap.gilderlehrman.org/essay/origins-slavery-0.

Browne, Francis Fisher. *The Every-Day Life of Abraham Lincoln: A Narrative and Descriptive Biography.* Chicago: Browne & Howell, 1914.

Cochran, Luci. "The 1619 Landing—Virginia's First Africans Report & FAQs." Hampton History Museum. https://hampton.gov/3580/The-1619-Landing-Report-FAQs.

Feller, Daniel. "Andrew Jackson: The American Franchise." Miller Center, University of Virginia. https://millercenter.org/president/jackson/the-american-franchise.

Guy-Sheftall, Beverly, ed. *Words of Fire: An Anthology of African-American Feminist Thought.* New York: The New Press, 1995.

Holland, J. G. *The Life of Abraham Lincoln.* Springfield, MA: Gurdon Bill, 1866.

Howells, William Dean. "Life of Abraham Lincoln," in *Lives and Speeches of Abraham Lincoln and Hannibal Hamlin.* New York: W. A. Townsend, and Columbus, OH: Follett, Foster, 1860.

Leidner, Gordon. *Lincoln's Gift: How Humor Shaped Lincoln's Life and Legacy.* Naperville, IL: Cumberland House, 2015.

Stewart, Maria W. *Maria W. Stewart, America's First Black Woman Political Writer: Essays and Speeches.* Edited and introduced by Marilyn Richardson. Bloomington, IN: Indiana University Press, 1987.

———. "An Address: African Rights and Liberty." Speech delivered at the African

Masonic Hall, Boston, February 27, 1833. https://awpc.cattcenter.iastate.edu
/2020/11/20/an-address-african-rights-and-liberty-feb-27-1833.

Tarbell, Ida M. *The Life of Abraham Lincoln*. 4 vols. New York: Lincoln Historical
Society, 1903.

Chapter Three

Agrawal, Alka. "All the President's Pills: Mercury-Laden Depression Drug May
Have Poisoned Lincoln." *Science*. July 20, 2001. https://www.science.org
/content/article/all-presidents-pills.

Basler, Roy P., ed. *The Collected Works of Abraham Lincoln*. 8 vols. New
Brunswick, NJ: Rutgers University Press, 1953.

Donald, David Herbert. *Lincoln*. New York: Simon & Schuster, 1996.

Hansen, Daniel R. "Do We Need the Bar Examination? A Critical Evaluation of the
Justifications for the Bar Examination and Proposed Alternatives." *Case
Western Reserve Law Review* 45, no. 4 (1995): 1191–1235.

Herndon, William H., and Jesse W. Weik. *Herndon's Lincoln: The True Story of a
Great Life*. 3 vols. Springfield, IL: Herndon's Lincoln Publishing, 1888.

Lamon, Ward H. *The Life of Abraham Lincoln: From His Birth to His
Inauguration as President*. Boston: James R. Osgood, 1872.
https://www.loc.gov/item/ltf96017987.

Tarbell, Ida M. Assisted by J. McCan Davis. *The Early Life of Abraham Lincoln*.
New York: S. S. McClure, 1896.

Chapter Four

"The 1858 Midterm Election." US Senate. https://www.senate.gov/about/origins
-foundations/electing-appointing-senators/1858-midterm.htm.

Baker, Jean H. *Mary Todd Lincoln: A Biography*. New York: W. W. Norton, 1989.

Basler, Roy P., ed. *The Collected Works of Abraham Lincoln*. 8 vols. New
Brunswick, NJ: Rutgers University Press, 1953.

Fling, Sarah. "Frederick Douglass and Abraham Lincoln." White House Historical
Association. December 4, 2019. https://www.whitehousehistory.org
/frederick-douglass-and-abraham-lincoln.

Holland, J. G. *The Life of Abraham Lincoln*. Springfield, MA: Gurdon Bill, 1866.

Lapsley, Arthur Brooks, ed. *The Writings of Abraham Lincoln*. Vol. 5. New York:
Lamb Publishing, 1906.

Meacham, Jon. *And There Was Light: Abraham Lincoln and the American
Struggle*. New York: Random House, 2022.

Nicolay, John G., and John Hay, eds. *Abraham Lincoln: Complete Works*. Vol 1.
New York: Century, 1907.

Chapter Five

Gormly, Kellie B. "How Kate Warne, America's First Woman Detective, Foiled a Plot to Assassinate Abraham Lincoln." *Smithsonian Magazine*. March 29, 2022. https://www.smithsonianmag.com/history/how-kate-warne-americas-first -woman-detective-foiled-a-plot-to-assassinate-abraham-lincoln-180979829.

Jordan, Hill, James I. Robertson, and J. H. Segars, eds. *The Bell Irvin Wiley Reader*. Baton Rouge, LA: Louisiana State University Press, 2001.

Miller, Connie A., Sr. *Frederick Douglass American Hero: And International Icon of the Nineteenth Century*. Bloomington, IN: Xlibris, 2009.

Nicolay, John G., and John Hay, eds. *Abraham Lincoln: Complete Works*. Vol 1. New York: Century, 1907.

Oldroyd, Osborn H., comp. *The Lincoln Memorial: Album-Immortelles*. New York: G. W. Carleton, 1882.

Rubenstein, David M. *The American Story: Conversations with Master Historians*. New York: Simon & Schuster, 2019.

Chapter Six

Douglass, Frederick. "The Colonization Scheme." *Frederick Douglass' Paper*. January 22, 1852.

Herndon, William H., and Jesse W. Weik. *Herndon's Lincoln: The True Story of a Great Life*. 3 vols. Springfield, IL: Herndon's Lincoln Publishing, 1888.

Nicolay, John G., and John Hay, eds. *Abraham Lincoln: Complete Works*. Vol 1. New York: Century, 1907.

Oldroyd, Osborn H., comp. *The Lincoln Memorial: Album-Immortelles*. New York: G. W. Carleton, 1882.

Seward, Frederick William. *Reminiscences of a War-Time Statesman and Diplomat: 1830–1915*. New York: G. P. Putnam's Sons [Knickerbocker Press], 1916.

———. *Seward at Washington as Senator and Secretary of State: A Memoir of His Life, with Selections from His Letters, 1861–1872*. New York: Derby and Miller, 1891.

US Emigration Office. *Report on Colonization and Emigration, Made to the Secretary of the Interior*. Washington, DC: Government Printing Office, 1862.

★ ★ ★ THEODORE ROOSEVELT ★ ★ ★

Chapter Seven

Amponsah, Ata D., Matthew Moore, and Janae Strickland. "Welcome to the Harvard Black Community." *Harvard Crimson*. September 11, 2017. https://www.thecrimson.com/article/2017/9/11/welcome-black-harvard.

Appleby, Joyce. "National Expansion and Reform, 1815–1860." Gilder Lehrman Institute of American History. https://ap.gilderlehrman.org/node/292.

Boffey, Philip M. "Theodore Roosevelt at Harvard." *Harvard Crimson*. December 12, 1957. https://www.thecrimson.com/article/1957/12/12/theodore-roosevelt-at-harvard-pthe-crimson.

Cohen, Miriam. "Women and the Progressive Movement." Gilder Lehrman Institute of American History. https://ap.gilderlehrman.org/essays/women-and-progressive-movement.

Dalton, Kathleen. *Theodore Roosevelt: A Strenuous Life*. New York: Vintage Books, 2004.

Morris, Edmund. *The Rise of Theodore Roosevelt*. New York: Modern Library, 2001.

Chapter Eight

Cordery, Stacy A. *Alice: Alice Roosevelt Longworth, from White House Princess to Washington Power Broker*. New York: Viking, 2007.

Putnam, Carleton. *Theodore Roosevelt: The Formative Years, 1858–1886*. New York: Charles Scribner's Sons, 1958.

Sewall, William Wingate. *Bill Sewall's Story of T. R.* New York: Harper & Brothers, 1919.

Chapter Nine

Morris, Edmund. *The Rise of Theodore Roosevelt*. New York: Modern Library, 2001.

Chapter Ten

Glass, Andrew. "Pendleton Act Inaugurates U.S. Civil Service System, Jan. 16, 1883." *Politico*. January 16, 2018. https://www.politico.com/story/2018/01/16/pendleton-act-inaugurates-us-civil-service-system-jan-16-1883-340488.

Roosevelt, Theodore. *An Autobiography*. New York: Charles Scribner's Sons, 1920.

———. *Fear God and Take Your Own Part*. New York: George H. Doran, 1916.

Theriault, Sean M. "Patronage, the Pendleton Act, and the Power of the People." *Journal of Politics* 65, no. 1 (February 2003).

Chapter Eleven

Castor, Henry. *Teddy Roosevelt and the Rough Riders*. Toronto: Random House of Canada, 1963.

Long, John Davis. *The Journal of John Davis Long*. Edited by Margaret Long. Rindge, NH: Richard R. Smith, 1956.

Office of the Historian. "The Spanish–American War, 1898." US Department of State. https://history.state.gov/milestones/1866-1898/spanish-american-war.

Roosevelt, Theodore. *The Works of Theodore Roosevelt*. 24 vols. Edited by Hermann Hagedorn. New York: Charles Scribner's Sons, 1923–1926.

"World of 1898: International Perspectives on the Spanish American War." Library of Congress. https://guides.loc.gov/world-of-1898.

Chapter Twelve

A Compilation of the Messages and Papers of the Presidents. 11 vols. New York: Bureau of National Literature, 1897.

Davis, Deborah. *Guest of Honor: Booker T. Washington, Theodore Roosevelt, and the White House Dinner That Shocked a Nation*. New York: Atria Paperback, 2013.

Dayen, David. "How Teddy Roosevelt Saved Football." *Politico Magazine*. September 20, 2014. https://www.politico.com/magazine/story/2014/09/teddy-roosevelt-saved-football-111146.

Dyer, Thomas G. *Theodore Roosevelt and the Idea of Race*. Baton Rouge, LA: Louisiana State University Press, 1980.

"Football." Theodore Roosevelt Center at Dickinson State University. https://www.theodorerooseveltcenter.org/Learn-About-TR/TR-Encyclopedia/Culture%20and%20Society/Football.

Lodge, Henry Cabot. *Selections from the Correspondence of Theodore Roosevelt and Henry Cabot Lodge, 1884–1918*. Vol. 1. New York: Charles Scribner's Sons, 1925.

⋆   ⋆   ⋆   **FRANKLIN DELANO ROOSEVELT**   ⋆   ⋆   ⋆

Chapter Thirteen

Black, Conrad. *Franklin Delano Roosevelt: Champion of Freedom*. New York: PublicAffairs, 2003.

Boffey, Philip M. "Franklin Delano Roosevelt at Harvard: F.D.R. Was a Fair Student, an Extracurricular Demon, and a Gentleman-Democrat." *Harvard Crimson*. December 13, 1957. https://www.thecrimson.com/article/1957/12/13/franklin-delano-roosevelt-at-harvard-phistorians.

Burns, James MacGregor. *Roosevelt: The Lion and the Fox (1882–1940)*. New York: Open Road Media, 2012.

Dallek, Robert. *Franklin D. Roosevelt: A Political Life*. New York: Viking, 2017.

Freidel, Frank. *Franklin D. Roosevelt: The Apprenticeship*. Boston: Little, Brown, 1952.

———. *Franklin D. Roosevelt: A Rendezvous with Destiny*. Boston: Little, Brown, 1990.

Lash, Joseph P. *Eleanor and Franklin: The Story of Their Relationship*. New York: W. W. Norton, 1971.

Simon, James F. *FDR and Chief Justice Hughes: The President, the Supreme Court, and the Epic Battle over the New Deal*. New York: Simon & Schuster, 2012.

Ward, Geoffrey C. *Before the Trumpet: Young Franklin Roosevelt, 1882–1905*. New York: Vintage Books, 2014.

———. *A First-Class Temperament: The Emergence of Franklin Roosevelt, 1905–1928*. New York: Vintage Books, 2014.

Chapter Fourteen

Boffey, Philip M. "Franklin Delano Roosevelt at Harvard: F.D.R. Was a Fair Student, an Extracurricular Demon, and a Gentleman-Democrat." *Harvard Crimson*. December 13, 1957. https://www.thecrimson.com/article/1957/12/13/franklin-delano-roosevelt-at-harvard-phistorians.

Cook, Blanche Wiesen. *Eleanor Roosevelt, Volume 1: The Early Years, 1884–1933*. New York: Penguin Books, 1993.

Dallek, Robert. *Franklin D. Roosevelt and American Foreign Policy, 1932–1945*. New York: Oxford University Press, 1979.

Rowley, Hazel. *Franklin and Eleanor: An Extraordinary Marriage*. New York: Farrar, Straus & Giroux, 2010.

Tobin, James. *Master of His Fate: Roosevelt's Rise from Polio to the Presidency*. New York: Christy Ottaviano Books, 2021.

Chapter Fifteen

Gallagher, Hugh Gregory. *FDR's Splendid Deception: The Moving Story of Roosevelt's Massive Disability—and the Intense Efforts to Conceal It from the Public*. New York: Dodd, Mead, 1985.

Leuchtenburg, William E. *Franklin D. Roosevelt: A Profile*. New York: Hill & Wang, 1967.

Roosevelt, Eleanor. *This I Remember*. New York: Harper & Brothers. 1949.

Roosevelt, Franklin Delano. Letter to Henry Waring Chadeayne. October 5, 1921. https://www.manhattanrarebooks.com/pages/books/1605/franklin-delano-roosevelt/typed-letter-signed.

Tobin, James. *The Man He Became: How FDR Defied Polio to Win the Presidency*. New York: Simon & Schuster, 2013.

———. *Master of His Fate: Roosevelt's Rise from Polio to the Presidency*. New York: Christy Ottaviano Books, 2021.

Wilson, Daniel J. "A Crippling Fear: Experiencing Polio in the Era of FDR." *Bulletin of the History of Medicine* 72, no. 3 (Fall 1998): 464–95.

——. *Living with Polio: The Epidemic and Its Survivors*. Chicago: University of Chicago Press, 2005.

Chapter Sixteen

Rogers, Naomi. "Race and the Politics of Polio: Warm Springs, Tuskegee, and the March of Dimes." *American Journal of Public Health* 97, no. 5 (May 1, 2007): 784–95.

Wilson, Daniel J. "A Crippling Fear: Experiencing Polio in the Era of FDR." *Bulletin of the History of Medicine* 72, no. 3 (Fall 1998): 464–95.

Chapter Seventeen

Perkins, Frances. *The Roosevelt I Knew*. New York: Viking Press, 1946.

Richardson, Gary, Alejandro Komai, Michael Gou, and Daniel Park. "Stock Market Crash of 1929." Federal Reserve History. Federal Reserve Bank of St. Louis. November 22, 2013. https://www.federalreservehistory.org/essays/stock-market-crash-of-1929.

Rosenman, Samuel I. *Working with Roosevelt*. New York: Harper & Brothers, 1952.

Tobin, James. *Master of His Fate: Roosevelt's Rise from Polio to the Presidency*. New York: Christy Ottaviano Books, 2021.

Chapter Eighteen

"Action, and Action Now": FDR's First 100 Days*. Hyde Park, NY: Franklin D. Roosevelt Presidential Library and Museum, 2008. Exhibition guide. https://www.fdrlibrary.org/documents/356632/390886/actionguide.pdf/07370301-a5c1-4a08-aa63-e611f9d12c34.

National Park Service. "Company 818 and Segregation in the Civilian Conservation Corps." US Department of the Interior. Last updated February 22, 2022. https://www.nps.gov/articles/000/company-818-and-segregation-in-the-civilian-conservation-corps.htm.

Perkins, Frances. *The Roosevelt I Knew*. New York: Penguin, 2011.

Roosevelt, Franklin Delano. *The Public Papers and Addresses of Franklin D. Roosevelt*. Vol. 2: *The Year of Crisis, 1933*. New York: Random House, 1938.

Silver, Nate. "Obama's No F.D.R.—Nor Does He Have F.D.R.'s Majority." *FiveThirtyEight*. March 1, 2010. https://fivethirtyeight.com/features/obamas-no-fdr-nor-does-he-have-fdrs.

White, Cody. "The CCC Indian Division." *Prologue* 48, no. 2 (2016). https://www.archives.gov/publications/prologue/2016/summer/ccc-id.html.

"The Woman Behind the New Deal." Frances Perkins Center. https://francesperkinscenter.org/learn/her-life.

LYNDON JOHNSON

Chapter Nineteen

Johnson, Rebekah Baines. *A Family Album*. New York: McGraw-Hill, 1965.

Sidey, Hugh. "The Presidency: A Reminder of Rebekah Baines." *Life*. December 16, 1966.

Chapter Twenty

"Teaching in Cotulla." *Lyndon B. Johnson: Alumnus*. San Marcos, TX: Texas State University. Digital exhibit. https://exhibits.library.txstate.edu/s/univarchives /page/cotulla.

Updegrove, Mark. "Lyndon B. Johnson: Power." Interview by Lillian Cunningham. *Presidential*. Produced by the *Washington Post*. September 4, 2016. Podcast transcript. https://www.washingtonpost.com/graphics/business/podcasts /presidential/pdfs/lyndon-b-johnson-transcript.pdf.

Chapter Twenty-One

Caro, Robert A. *The Years of Lyndon Johnson: The Path to Power*. New York: Vintage Books, 1990.

Herzog, Madelyn. "Discovering LBJ's Austin." *Texas Monthly*. May 6, 2013. https://www.texasmonthly.com/news-politics/discovering-lbjs-austin.

Johnson, Claudia "Lady Bird." "Oral History Interview IV." Interview by Michael L. Gillette. Lyndon B. Johnson Presidential Library. February 4, 1978. Transcript. http://www.lbjlibrary.net/assets/documents/archives/oral_histories /johnson_c/CTJ%204.pdf.

National Park Service. Lyndon B. Johnson National Historic Site brochure. US Department of the Interior. 1972. http://npshistory.com/brochures /lyjo/1972-2.pdf.

Chapter Twenty-Two

Caro, Robert A. *The Years of Lyndon Johnson: Master of the Senate*. New York: Vintage Books, 2003.

Guinn, Jack. "Screwball Election in Texas." *American Mercury* 53 (September 1941): 275.

McKay, Seth Shepard. *W. Lee O'Daniel and Texas Politics, 1938–1942*. Lubbock, TX: Texas Tech Press, 1944.

Chapter Twenty-Three

"The Congress: The 84th's Temper." *Time*. November 15, 1954. https://content.time.com/time/subscriber/article/0,33009,820381-1,00.html.

Lau, Tim. "The Filibuster Explained." Brennan Center for Justice. April 26, 2021. https://www.brennancenter.org/our-work/research-reports/filibuster -explained.

Lepore, Jill. *These Truths: A History of the United States*. New York: W. W. Norton, 2018.

Mohr, Melissa. "What Does the 'Filibuster' Have to Do with Pirates?" *Christian Science Monitor*. March 4, 2021. https://www.csmonitor.com/The-Culture /In-a-Word/2021/0304/What-does-the-filibuster-have-to-do-with-pirates.

"RN, MLK, and the Civil Rights Act of 1957." Richard Nixon Foundation. January 15, 2017. https://www.nixonfoundation.org/2017/01/rn-mlk-and-the-civil -rights-act-of-1957.

US House of Representatives. "Proceedings and Debates of the 88th Congress." *Congressional Record* 110: January 7–October 3, 1964.

Chapter Twenty-Four

Anthony, Carl Sferrazza. *America's First Families: An Inside View of 200 Years of Private Life in the White House*. New York: Touchstone, 2000.

Boeri, David. "The Making Of LBJ's Historic 'We Shall Overcome' Speech." WBUR. March 14, 2014. https://www.wbur.org/news/2014/03/14/johnson-goodwin -civil-rights-speech.

Fields, Gary. "LBJ's Daughter Luci Watched Him Sign Voting Rights Bill, Then Cried When Supreme Court Weakened It." Associated Press. June 8, 2023. https://apnews.com/article/lyndon-johnson-daughter-voting-rights -supreme-court-cf792bdb6228ba20f257a73f055eddb9.

Hockenberry, John. "How LBJ Celebrated Mexican-Americans." *The Takeaway*. Produced by PRI and WNYC Studios. October 5, 2015. Podcast. https://www.wnycstudios.org/podcasts/takeaway/segments/how-lbj -celebrated-mexican-americans.

Killion, Nikole. "Lyndon Johnson's Daughter Takes Up Her Father's Cause on 56th Anniversary of Voting Rights Act." CBS News. August 8, 2021. https://www.cbsnews.com/news/luci-baines-johnson-voting-rights.

Lewis, John. "Speech at the March on Washington." August 28, 1963. https://voicesofdemocracy.umd.edu/lewis-speech-at-the-march-on -washington-speech-text.

Pycior, Julie Leininger. "From Hope to Frustration: Mexican Americans and Lyndon Johnson in 1967." *Western Historical Quarterly* 24, no. 4 (1993): 469–494.

"Rustin, Bayard." The Martin Luther King, Jr. Research and Education Institute at Stanford University. https://kinginstitute.stanford.edu/rustin-bayard.

"Selma to Montgomery March." The Martin Luther King, Jr. Research and
 Education Institute at Stanford University. https://kinginstitute.stanford.edu
 /selma-montgomery-march.

Wingspread, Robert Goetz. "Luci Baines Johnson Relates Trials, Triumphs of
 White House Years." Joint Base San Antonio. March 3, 2008.
 https://www.jbsa.mil/News/News/Article/464261/luci-baines-johnson
 -relates-trials-triumphs-of-white-house-years.

⋆ ⋆ ⋆ EPILOGUE ⋆ ⋆ ⋆

Roosevelt, Theodore. *The Foes of Our Own Household; The Great Adventure;
 Letters to His Children.* New York: Charles Scribner's Sons, 1926.

Wagenknecht, Edward. *The Seven Worlds of Theodore Roosevelt.* Guilford, CT:
 Lyons Press, 2010.